Footsteps of Israel

*From Eden to the City of God – Spiritual Events
and Biblical Prophecies in the Holy Land*

By Samuel Greenwood

Published by Pantianos Classics

ISBN-13: 978-1-78987-278-1

First published in 1922

Contents

By faith Abraham, when he was called to go out into a place which he should after receive for an inheritance, obeyed; and he went out, not knowing whither he went.

By faith he sojourned in the land of promise, as in a strange country, dwelling in tabernacles with Isaac and Jacob, the heirs with him of the same promise:

For he looked for a city which hath foundations, whose builder and maker is God.

— Hebrews 11: 18-10.

Introduction

THE excuse for adding another volume to the world's already over-burdened bookshelf must be looked for within the volume itself, for the justification or value of a book can only be rightly determined by its influence upon the thoughts of its readers. While a book may be welcomed by one individual for its helpfulness or good cheer, it may be rejected as useless by another; so that the only fixed rule upon which all agree in the judgment of books is the viewpoint of the reader. Thus, because of the wide disparity in literary tastes, and the almost hopeless divergence of religious opinions and convictions, few books, if any, find a universal response, and the reader must elect to browse where he likes the pasture. But points of view are open to revision, and one may discover that a change of pasture turns out to be both nourishing and delightful; thus our one fixed rule vanishes, and a book is left to make its way according to what it has to give.

All books that merit consideration may, in a general way, be divided into two classes: those which entertain and those which enlighten and bless; in other words, the books which are designed to beguile the thoughts of their readers from the weight of worldly care, and thus make existence outside the walls of the Heavenly City temporarily more endurable; and the books which stimulate the reader to seek an entrance through its gates, or which aid those who are already making that endeavor. The author modestly hopes that, by some at least, this volume will be placed among the latter class.

The following pages are the outgrowth of Bible study, undertaken during late years for the special purpose of tracing the rise, development, and course of that great spiritual movement spoken of in the Scriptures under the name of Israel, and at the same time of arriving at a better understanding of the relation which undoubtedly exists between prophecy and history, particularly with reference to the present period and events. While it is true that no denomination is a unit on the question of Israel's identity in the present day, or of the facts and conditions of her restoration, or even in an interest in these things, Jesus invested the prophetic Scriptures with an importance and a value which should not now be covered with the veil of indifference, nor should the Christians of this period be called "slow of heart to believe all that the prophets have spoken."

While the author's attitude towards some of the dogmas which have come down from the time of the early Church Fathers may be challenged by some of his readers, his attitude is not, he believes, inconsistent with the fundamental truth about Deity which we find at the highest points of Scriptural revelation. The present demand, as it was in the days of the apostles, is not to cling blindly to the humanly formulated beliefs into which we may have been educated, but to "prove all things," and to "hold fast that which is good." These are days when theories and teachings which do not glorify God in His infinite nature, and which are not capable of producing the highest form of practical Christianity, will have to be "overturned" that the way of the Lord may be prepared and His name sanctified before all people.

It is naturally self-evident that the errors of human thought and life can be corrected only by a perception of and obedience to Truth; it cannot be accomplished by the worship of any personality however exalted. The covenants of Israel, from the first, have been based upon obedience, not upon an irresponsible belief in Deity, nor a dependent faith in another's goodness. It must sometime be learned that an adherence to religious doctrines, opinions, or creeds, however sincerely accepted and maintained, is absolutely powerless to bring a realization of the new birth into human experience, and without this realization there is no way by which human beings can enter the kingdom of heaven.

The reason for beginning with the story of Eden is that Israel was conceived there, although not brought forth to human view until many centuries later; and the course of that movement, in its redemptive journey through the ages, must be properly considered as having its starting-point in the experience which that story illustrates. It is certain that all that is vitally related to human welfare lies between that first glimpse of Divine law, which laid bare both the sinfulness and the deceitfulness of sin, and the final awakening of mankind to the consciousness of God as the All-in-all. The time between these points is the moral and spiritual distance between lost Eden and the New Jerusalem, and it is across this distance where the footsteps of Israel are to be found.

Israel's unique place among the nations, as the guardian of the spiritual hope of the world, gave to her history a meaning and an interest which have never faded, and we find her today more conspicuous in the thoughts of Christendom than any other race or people, although largely in the sense of an extinct rather than as an existing nation. Yet the Scriptures state, in most unmistakable terms, that Israel is to return to her place in the family of nations and carry out the mission originally assigned to her, so that according to these Scriptural statements, we should think of this people not as hopelessly buried in the grave of oblivion but as about to enact the greatest chapter of their history. The restoration of Israel is the culminating event in Old Testament prophecy, an event which was not questioned but confirmed by New Testament writers; and we today should begin to open our eyes to the imminence and significance of its fulfilment, synchronizing as it does with the second advent of the Christ. The present is a period of fulfilment more than of prophecy. The final act in human redemption, and the closing scenes of mortal history, were long since foreseen and foretold, and we should now confidently look for the presence of that "Spirit of truth" whose coming was promised by Christ Jesus, and which alone can "restore all things."

Israel is the earliest distinguishing title on record of purely spiritual significance, and that spiritual significance has not been divorced from a right use of the word, but is as closely related to the salvation of our race as at any past period, and is destined to continue thus until the consummation of the human struggle for spiritual freedom and regeneration. Ages of ignorance and superstition did not prevent the appearance of Israel when the opportunity came, and its divine nature and source precluded the possibility of its extinction in the Assyrian captivity or in the subsequent exile.

The spiritual illuminations and revelations which came to Israel in her distant yesterdays were not left behind in the human march; they have remained to light the way to higher things for all who seek to know God aright. No one has had a proprietary interest in truth which cannot be shared by every other human being, when the point is reached where it can be perceived and understood. When the angel said to Jacob, "Thy name shall henceforth be called Israel," it is apparent, by the after use of the word, that it was intended as the designation of a type or quality of thought, rather than as the name of any one man, family, or nation. The spiritual characteristics which began to appear in Shem, Abraham, Jacob, and others, indicated that the line or race which was developing from them would be distinctively representative of the seed of the woman, and would bear the light of spiritual truth to all mankind.

The fundamental teaching of the oneness of God, which Jesus embodied in Christianity, was received through the patriarchs and prophets of Israel. There has been no Gentile medium of revelation. The spiritual idea of Deity, which came to light in the consciousness of that people, and which progressed there until its fuller appearing in Christianity, was not duplicated elsewhere. The perception in Israel of the one true God was the lens or focusing-point through which all divine revelation has reached humanity. Naaman the Syrian touched the secret of the world's interest in this subject when he said,

"Now I know there is no God in all the earth but in Israel." And this God of Israel, since that long past day of Naaman's healing, has. become more and more widely acknowledged as the only God in all the earth, beside whom there is no other, defined by Christ Jesus, the Anointed of Israel, as the "one good"; and into this oneness of divinity every human being must sometime find his way, no matter what he may now call himself nationally or religiously.

Modern discoveries are inclining scientists to the conclusion that time and space are merely relative conditions, and not the fixed measurements we have hitherto supposed. This fact was declared ages ago by the Psalmist, when he said, "A thousand years in Thy sight are but as yesterday when it is past, and as a watch in the night." The long exile of Israel, running concurrently with the "times of the Gentiles," was a mental experience, and can be measured only superficially in terms of years. It was a space in which to wrestle with and overcome the temptation of false gods, and thus to prepare for the work which had been assigned to Israel before her nationhood began. This exile or captivity did not mean the end of Israel as a people any more than his sojourn in a "far country" meant the end of the prodigal son as an individual. No other nation arose to replace Israel, and we have no record or intimation of the adoption of any other people in her stead.

The "day of the Lord" neither begins nor ends, but to human sense, groping for ages amid the darkness of its materialism, it will come as the dawning of morning. We may rejoice that the distant beams of that morning are becoming dimly visible through the disturbances and the fears which mark the breaking up of the old order. To those whose faces are turned towards the "City of God," and who would spend a few hours in contemplation of the footsteps along the way, this book is offered with the cordial Godspeed of a fellow pilgrim.

Abraham rejoiced to see my day: and he saw it, and was glad.

Then said the Jews unto him, Thou art not yet fifty years old, and hast thou seen Abraham?

Jesus said unto them, Verily, verily, I say unto you, Before Abraham was, I am.

— John 8: 56-58.

"Christ's Christianity is the chain of scientific being reappearing in all ages, maintaining its obvious correspondence with the Scriptures and uniting all periods in the design of God."

— Mary Baker Eddy.

Chapter One - Paradise Lost; or the Dream of Materialism

Shall the dust praise Thee? shall it declare Thy truth? — Ps. 30:9.

Cease ye from man, whose breath is in his nostrils: for wherein is he to be accounted of? — Isa. 2:22.

THE course and destiny of that remarkable race which had its rise in Abraham, the great pioneer of monotheism, and which was later identified by the name of Israel, constitute the central feature of the history of nations, because God's revelations were given to men through that people. These revelations, attested by ample proof, and preserved in the Hebrew sacred writings, have been, and are still today, the inspiration of enlightened progress and the foundation of regenerative religion. The footsteps of Israel, therefore, are the footsteps of humanity spiritually awakening to the facts of divinity.

"Search the Scriptures," said Jesus, because "they are they which testify of me," — of "Immanuel," "the Son of the Highest," the hope and promise and glory of Israel, the light which was to lighten the Gentiles, the Saviour of the world. "The testimony of Jesus," wrote St. John the Revelator, "is the spirit of prophecy "; and the testimony of Jesus was, that he was the Son of God. The one objective of Scriptural teaching, the final goal towards which all prophecy and revelation point, is the attainment of that universal understanding of God in which Jesus' testimony will be seen to be true, not of one individual only, but of every man.

Israel has a sound of sweet melody, because it was first voiced to human ears from the lips of an angel, and has never lost its heavenly tone. It is found in that quality of human thought which, like Jacob, is seeking to know God, and which is rising, however slowly and painfully, towards the consciousness of spiritual life. Israel, in its national and spiritual aspects, was the absorbing theme of the Scriptural writers. They dwelt lovingly upon the past glories and the future greatness of the people who were to be "a peculiar treasure" unto the Lord, the while, in all honesty, they exposed their weaknesses and shortcomings. They pointed to the great destiny which lay before them as God's "witnesses" in the earth, while in humiliation they mourned over the national apostasy. They turned from the shame and sorrow of the captivity to contemplate the bright vision of the restoration. Although Israel was to be known, in a distinguishing sense, as the people of God, the patriarchs and prophets never lost sight of the fact that the seal and confirmation of that exalted relationship lay in their fidelity to His covenants.

The Biblical records naturally begin with God. The opening sentence, in its evident intent, affirms that God is the one origin or source of all things, and that there was nothing before Him. If one would grasp the full significance of that divine revelation, which extends in an arc of glory from the first to the last verses of the Bible, marking the completed course of human redemption, ever lighting the way to the kingdom of heaven, but never mingling with the shadows of earthly delusions; if one would catch the unbroken sweep of that wonderful vision, as it came to patriarch and prophet, Messiah and apostle, he must begin his mental journey at that same point of recognition, and keep that encircling bow of divinity ever in view.

Although we may not yet have learned all that is involved in the first sentence of the Bible, and in St. John's statement that "without Him was not anything made," we should know this much, that the fatal mistake of the ages has been in relinquishing that position, and in taking the stand of the materialist, that without Him many things are made. The plain teaching of the Scriptures is, that whatever does not lead human thought to know God as the one Cause, the universal Father, must somewhere in the line of progress be discovered to be false and useless; for the consciousness of enduring life and joy is not to be found outside the knowledge of God and of His Son.

Continuing our reading of the opening chapter of Genesis, we come to the most important statement concerning man which human language records, namely, that he was created in the image of God. Nothing greater could be said of man, and nothing less would be consistent with his Divine source. To lift humanity to the realization of this divine relationship is the plain purpose of the atonement, and the end of Biblical prophecy and revelation. This inspired utterance unites man to God beyond the possibility of separation. It declares the eternality of God's likeness or manifestation, since the phrase "in the beginning," in relation to God and His image, is equivalent to no beginning. In the words credited to an early Christian writer, "There certainly was not a time when God was not the Father." The creative intelligence which we name God necessarily expressed His own thoughts in man and the universe, since there was no other creative consciousness, so that what we call creation is simply the manifestation of the Creator's own being and nature, and not an aggregation of things foreign to Himself and independent of His government.

The simple record of the six days of divine unfoldment with which the Bible opens, presents the ideal universe, the new earth and heaven, and the new man, towards the perception of which human sense has been slowly moving. This first record has stood, and must so stand to the end, for that perfection of things which is to appear when time has run its full course, when the realities of being shall no longer be seen "in a glass darkly" but face to face. Thus one may see, as in prophetic vision, the coincidence of the first and last chapters of the Bible, not as the bringing in of a new or unknown state, but as the awakening to the reality of things as they have always been.

In the story of the Garden of Eden, which closely follows the first record of creation, but which is generally understood to be of different authorship, we find a second statement concerning man, a statement which is as ignoble as the first is glorious — namely, that he was formed of "the dust of the ground." In the first instance man is described as the imaging forth of Deity. His nature and character, therefore, partake of and express divinity, and could have no possible affinity with evil. This second statement, however, unequivocally represents man as evil, as that which is God's unlikeness, a creature of the earth, not of heaven, whose nature is sensual and sinful, and whose inherent depravity absolutely dissociates him from any divine origin. One cannot conceive that the likeness of God should possess an evil sense, and because it is inconceivable we should know that it is impossible.

Thus at the very outset of human history we encounter the highest and the lowest concepts of both Creator and creation. Theologians and others have presumed to declare and to teach that these contrary statements are identical, with the result that mortals have come to think of the Creator as a being of like passions as themselves, and of His image as originally but a clod of earth which later developed into a depraved mind. The very natural result of teaching the unity of these opposite descriptions of man has been to leave the first out of sight as having no present application to human salvation, and to honor the dust of the ground as the basic factor in creation. This has necessarily perpetuated a very humanized conception of Deity, and a far from helpful conception of His government as virtually subordinate to an inferior power.

"What must I do to be saved?" has been the age-long appeal of humanity. Oppressed and tormented by the bestial instincts and propensities too common to the race, mortals have been encouraged to submit to these conditions on the ground that they were derived from their primeval parents; but these evils were not inherited from the pure offspring of Deity. The great fear, which weighs so heavily and universally upon human consciousness that it has been named the "king of terrors," did not originate in the revealed truth of man's likeness to God, but in the opposite teaching, that man is material and sinful. Believing that the earth is the universal mother of men, and that the "dust of the ground" constitutes their natural condition, it is held to be inevitable that men must return to dust again. Here, then, in the generally accepted theory that man originates and exists materially, and possesses a nature and consciousness unlike the divine, lies the necessity for a Saviour and a Deliverer, so that one need not be a prophet to see along what line human redemption must come and upon what basis it must be worked out.

The problem of salvation is, therefore, as old as humanity. From the beginning of time, according to the Hebrew calendar, we find the human mind in captivity, but a captivity so subtle as to be not recognized for what it is. Long accustomed to this "durance vile," disinclined to resist its vanities and weaknesses, mortals have succumbed to the argument that materiality is man's normal and necessary state of being. From that standpoint of belief they are,

12

by their own consent, both helpless and blind, — helpless because they will not leave their groveling in the dust, and blind because they will not lift their eyes above the flesh and see God.

The perverted but too popular teaching, that the materiality of man's origin and existence, which is presented in the second chapter of Genesis, us of God, and must be accepted as true and good, a teaching which has been unlawfully imposed upon the unresisting because unenlightened human mind, is the error that binds humanity to the chariot wheels of sensualism, and that entrenches evil, in the guise of nature, in the world's centers of education. It should be obvious that this error must be reversed and the human footsteps which have been wrongly taken be retraced, before the state of being indicated in the first chapter of Genesis can be consciously attained.

Apparently, then, the redemption of mortals will not lie in their translation to some unknown and distant sphere, but in their spiritual transformation, or that process of mental correction alluded to by St. Paul, in which mortality, or the sense of life as material, is to be laid off or outgrown. In other words, it is the mental journey, going on since Adam, by which human thought has been gradually advancing towards the apprehension of the truth of being as spiritual and divine. It is apparent that the prophet Isaiah perceived these things, for instead of adopting the orthodox opinion of his day, he bravely crossed swords with the legendary theory of man's creation from dust. "Cease ye from man whose breath is in his nostrils," he said, "for wherein is he to be accounted of?" plainly implying that such is not the kind of man which God created.

Although popular theology has generally accepted the story of Adam and Eve in the garden of Eden as literal history, it is being viewed to an increasing extent in the light of an allegory, and we read that it was so regarded by some of the Jews of more modern times. St. Augustine believed the story to be historically true, but that it also embodied a spiritual meaning. It might be well to remind the reader at this point that the earlier books of the Bible, as we now have them, were compiled many centuries after the events recorded had taken place. In Genesis particularly we have the legends and traditions which had come down through many generations of the primitive Hebrews, and which were naturally more or less invested with the symbolism of a highly imaginative and poetic race.

The story of Eden would appear to be the earliest of these legends of which we have record. Its language is plainly metaphorical, but it is not improbable that, as in the case of other legends, it arose from something more tangible than human imagination. It is indeed highly probable that about this time something transpired which so deeply stirred the human consciousness and became so strongly impressed upon the primitive thought of mankind that it became accepted as the beginning of history. It has been long supposed that that event was the creation of man from "the dust of the ground," but modern discovery and research have exposed the fallacy of that supposition. It is now known that mortals inhabited the earth ages before the reputed time of Adam, although nothing has come down to us out of that practically unknown period to indicate any definite apprehension or perception of divinity, and without some clear recognition of the law of good, history could have no legitimate starting-point. From a careful study of this and subsequent Scripture, it would appear that what impressed itself upon the thought of mankind at this time was the discovery, in a degree at least, of the distinction between good and evil; in other words, there arose in human consciousness some dawning recognition of the law of God which unveiled the evil of evil.

How this came about is related in the story. In her encounter with a serpent that could talk, evidently intended to explain the appeal of evil as a subtle suggestion, the woman became aware that an acceptance of what it urged upon her would be inconsistent with her recognition of God's demands. The language implies that while she perceived something of the source and nature of the temptation into which mankind had entered, she did not discover the way out of that mental captivity. The rising up in human thought of the supposition that there is something taking place outside the realm of good, something that has substance, intelligence, and power, was plainly what the serpent represented; so that what the woman from her higher standpoint of spiritual discernment discovered was, that she, in common with other mortals before and since, had been beguiled into believing what was not true. Thus interpreted the story can be readily understood as illustrating the process of evil in the thought and experience of every human being; whereas its literal acceptance would leave one hopelessly stranded amid irreconcilable inconsistencies and absurdities.

Eve had begun to see, in a rather vague way, what St. Paul long afterwards saw clearly, that evil and the carnal mind are one. Therefore what the inhabitants of the garden were warned against was a wrong mental state; in other words, thinking falsely about God and man. From the opening sentence, "And there went up a mist," to the final expulsion from the garden, the story presents a delineation in metaphor of that spurious claim to consciousness which the Revelator describes as deceiving "the whole world," which obviously means that the whole world is under the spell of the suggestion that good is not infinite and supreme, and is not, therefore, the whole of man's life. It is perfectly certain that the world would not be deceived in accepting the testimony of the serpent if that testimony were true.

It is noteworthy that throughout this narrative the man of dust makes no claim of being godlike, nor do his speech and conduct indicate a divine origin or relationship. On the contrary, his inglorious record, right up to the present day, confirms the conclusion, beyond reasonable question, that Adam was not the man spoken of in the first chapter of Genesis as being the image of Deity. This was very clearly St. Paul's understanding when he counseled the Ephesians to "put off...the old man," for his advice would be nothing short of blasphemy if the "old man," or the Adam man, were of the same lineage as the "new man" or son of God. While ordinary theological teaching has interpreted the story of Eden as confirming the belief that God created man materially, this story is seen upon closer and unprejudiced study to point out the evil attaching to that belief.

As described in the metaphor, the "deep sleep" which came upon Adam is undoubtedly symbolic of materialism, a view which would seem to be confirmed by some later Scriptural passages, for the story makes no reference to his awakening. This would be a serious omission, after such a momentous sleep, if the story were intended to be taken literally. Scholastic theology has made the rather clumsy mistake of ignoring this point entirely, for the great lesson of the allegory will be found to hinge upon it, inasmuch as it unmistakably teaches the unsubstantial nature of a so-called existence separate from God, as well as the suffering which must attend that supposition. It is evident from the narrative that Adam was not awake to the truth of creation, in which man is the image of God, but was asleep in the dust of the ground. Even now, in this twentieth century, one has but to scan the record of events to realize that, for the great mass of mankind, that sleep has remained unbroken. Mortals are still dreaming that they are awake in the coils of the serpent of materialism, and attempting to hide their nakedness from God. For that matter we need look no further than our own mental life to discover how fast asleep we are, much of the time, to the heavenly facts of good, and how easily imposed upon by the suggestions of evil. It is very plain, therefore, that the man featured in this parable was not the expression of divinity, else materialism, with all that term includes, would be the verity of being, and the human hope of redemption an eternal mockery.

That sin, in its varying phases and degrees, is inseparable from the sensuous consciousness of mortals, is a lesson which may be gleaned from this parabolic story, and which we must learn if we would rightly understand the human problem of salvation. Because there is nothing in the spiritual sense of things which men ought not to know, or which could possibly separate them from God, or lead them into a sense of condemnation and guilt, we must naturally and necessarily turn to the fleshly or material sense to find the source of mortals' temptation and degradation. Evil is not something that exists and operates independent of the carnal mind: it is the carnal mind; and this identifies the serpent of Eden and the devil of the later Scriptures, neither as a snake nor as a man, but as that iniquitous sense which would hold men to "the dust of the ground" as the center and circumference of their being.

It is this physical sense, not the spiritual, which closes the eyes of mortals to the things of God, the unseen things which the apostle declared are eternal, the things which "eye hath not seen, nor ear heard." But if the material eye and ear do not cognize the things "which God hath prepared for them that love Him," it naturally follows that these senses do not and cannot cognize the man and universe which He created, or made manifest. The only logical inference is, that what appears to physical sense, not being the "things which God hath prepared," must be the phantasmagoria of a false and sinful sense, or the objectified thoughts of the so-called carnal mind, and not a divine creation at all. By what process of reason or fancy can one intelligently conceive of the grandeur and glory of the Infinite as appropriately expressed in a man made of dust, and a woman fashioned from a piece of his bone? Such grotesque figures may have a fitting place in the fairyland of Oz, where scarecrows talk and tin men go about, but to call them the work of God is to caricature His handiwork. Shakespeare caught a glimpse of the illusory nature of material things when he wrote,

> We are such stuff
> As dreams are made on.

The story of Eden does not set a seal of degradation or of condemnation upon the man whom God created, as has been wrongly taught, but points to the mistake and the folly of giving evil a place in consciousness. It shows also that mortal and sensuous existence, as set forth in the creation, temptation, and demoralization of the man of dust, is of the false nature of a dream, a dream, however, of years and centuries and millenniums, and which still waits to be dispelled at the full appearing of the Christ. The psalmist of Israel who sang, "I shall be satisfied when I awake, with Thy likeness," evidently did not look upon materiality as the truth of his being.

There are a number of appeals in the Scriptures to awaken. "Sleeper, awake, arise from the dead, and the Christ shall give thee light," urged the apostle. (Eph. 5: 14, Twentieth Century New Testament.) But why the call to awake, if one's mundane experiences represent the reality of his being! And why the call to arise from the dead if life inheres in matter! Nothing can be more obvious or certain than this, that if a material sense of persons and things expresses the reality of God's creation, then men are not asleep in that sense but awake, and man's immortality would consequently and necessarily be a myth.

Returning to the story, we find the woman and the man falling victims to the argument that evil was something they were privileged to know, and that to know it would enlarge their understanding and increase their prestige. The serpent insinuated that God had deceived them in limiting their consciousness to good alone. The bitter experience that followed apparently opened their eyes to the error into which they had been led. The fruit of this false knowledge was found to be fear and shame and suffering; and they heard, as it seemed to them, the voice of God pronouncing a curse upon the participants in this great tragedy. Henceforward, in sorrow and trouble, mortals were to struggle with their material thoughts of life, until the seed of the woman should ultimately destroy all sense of materiality.

The point of this parable is plainly not limited to ancient times. Notwithstanding the sorrows of human experience, the mistake of Adam and Eve is being repeated by mortals today. If the inhabitants of the garden had the prerogative to maintain their sense of good intact, without entering into a knowledge of evil, men and women have still the same prerogative. It is dishonest, therefore, to condemn Adam and Eve for being enticed by the serpent's suggestions, when we are doing precisely the same thing. If evil in the year one, or at the beginning of recorded time, was the delusive belief that man's life and intelligence are not God, Spirit, but something else, liable to change to imbecility and death, it is the same lie still, and it will continue to be so, and to impose its delusions upon men, until they acknowledge and obey only the Mind which was in Christ Jesus.

"The fruit of that forbidden tree" which, in the words of Milton, "brought death into the world and all our woe," was not an apple, or any other form of earthly fruit, but a mental experience. It was the human partaking of or entering into a sense of being that was entirely foreign to God and His creation. St. Paul properly classified this delusive sense of things as the fleshly mind, or the mind that finds its consciousness in matter. "The carnal mind," the apostle writes, "is enmity against God," thus identifying materiality with the loss of paradise, and with all human error. His preceding statement, "to be spiritually minded is life and peace," full of profound and glorious significance, reveals the all-important fact, which Christendom has largely overlooked, that paradise can be regained only as men turn from material-mindedness to spiritual-mindedness. We should maintain the classification of consciousness given in the Scripture just quoted, and no longer affirm that evil is properly any legitimate part of human knowledge.

The Bible from cover to cover is a condemnation of the carnal mind. Nowhere within its pages is the dust of the ground likened to the being of Deity or to His likeness. At no point do the sacred records endow the flesh with the qualities and substance of divinity. The influence of materiality in human experience has never disclosed the faintest trace of the heavenly, but on the contrary it has ever proved the means and the medium of evil. The serpent's nefarious machinations in beguiling the hearts of men in this year of our Lord in nowise differ from its nefarious machinations in the garden of Eden. Submission to materialism still shuts human consciousness out of paradise, and the earth accordingly brings forth its thorns and thistles, while mortals continue to earn their bread by the sweat of their brows.

"Except a man be born again," said Jesus, "he cannot see the kingdom of God," clearly teaching that the man of dust is not the man which came forth from God, else a second birth would not be required of him. We read also in Isaiah, "Behold, I create new heavens and a new earth: and the former shall not be remembered, nor come into mind," — but wherefore should they not be remembered if God created them? and why the necessity for new heavens and earth if what materially appears is the truth about them? "What God doeth, it shall stand for ever," says the Scripture. Of a surety, the human sense of materiality, with its perpetual round of sorrow and trouble, can be nothing more substantial than the "deep sleep" of Adam, from which Christianity, understood and made practical, is the awakening.

Chapter Two - The Woman and the Serpent

And the Lord God said unto the serpent,...I will put enmity between thee and the woman, and between thy seed and her seed. — Gen. 3: 14, 15.

And the dragon was wroth with the woman, and went to make war with the remnant of her seed, which keep the commandments of God, and have the testimony of Jesus Christ. — Rev. 12: 17.

A FACT which cannot safely be overlooked in taking up the study of Israel in its broader aspects, and one that cannot logically be separated from the prophecies relating to the latter days, is that the movement of the human consciousness towards its ultimate freedom from evil began with woman. It was the woman in the story, not the man, who recognized the character of evil and its method of attack; therefore it was the woman, not the man, towards whom the enmity of the serpent was directed. "I will put enmity between thee and the woman, and between thy seed and her seed," and then follows that first great prophecy of Scripture, which includes in itself all subsequent prophecy, that the seed of the woman should bruise the serpent's head, or, in other words, destroy the carnal mind.

In this announcement woman's destiny, as the channel through which a redemptive knowledge of the truth is to reach mankind, is set forth in unmistakable terms. This should be kept well in mind for it is the key to the ultimate fulfilment of the prophetic Word. In the story the man apparently had not awakened to any feeling of enmity towards the serpent, and would, seem to symbolize that purely physical sense of being which is fully at home in the body. He represented that state of mortal thought which is too much in sympathy with materiality to discern its evil nature, or to make any sustained protest against its influence. On the other hand, the fact that woman first expressed that higher quality of thought which called forth the enmity of evil should not only establish her advanced moral and spiritual status, but her logical leadership in moral and spiritual reform.

One has but to read the history of nations, from the standpoint of their treatment of woman, to have this view confirmed. It will be found that the most spiritually enlightened nations are those which accord to woman the freest opportunity to express her rightful place in the universe. In the proportion that woman's equality in all ways with man has been acknowledged and given unobstructed scope, the moral tone of the national life has invariably improved. On the other hand, other things being equal, the most benighted and spiritually unprogressive peoples are those who treat their women as inferiors. Woman's right to fulfil her high mission has been opposed at every turn by the sensual egotism of the mortal man, expressing its evil will in despotism and slavery. Unquestionably, the only possible true democracy must include the acknowledgment of woman's equality with man, not as a favor, but as an inherent right.

That which has stood and still stands in the way of the moral betterment of the race is the sensual apathy of the man who is "of the earth, earthy"; and after six thousand years following the Edenic prophecy, it is highly significant that the enmity of evil is still directed against the woman and her seed, against her high place in prophetic fulfilment, and her spiritual leadership in the work of bruising the serpent's head.

It is apparent upon the face of the narrative that "the woman" and her seed meant something far greater than the person of Eve, or her natural offspring, and that was the awakening discernment of spiritual being which uncovered the truth about her tempter, and the increase of that spiritual discernment in human consciousness. The logical inference from the story is, that woman stands highest in the order of creation, and is therefore more susceptible to spiritual impressions or intuitions, so that it was perfectly natural she should be the first to recognize the claims of the carnal sense as something which ought not to be admitted. Eve's discovery, that she was lured into a state of error through a mesmeric subtlety, otherwise spoken of as the serpent, could only have come about through some recognition, however faint, of the purity of God's creation, and this germ of spiritual awakening was to increase until it would finally displace a sense of evil in human consciousness. The true idea, thus dimly perceived, was, undoubtedly, the seed of the woman, and it grew and unfolded and increased until it reached its full blossom in Christianity, finally to express its perfect fruition at the coming of the Comforter.

This exposure of the nature of evil brought with it its condemnation, and the prediction of its final destruction. It is full of meaning that evil is neither named nor implied in the Elohistic account of creation, while in the story which follows, it appears only as a condition of mental deception, in which the opposite of good takes on a semblance of intelligence and life; and this error or delusion is to run its course in human belief until its fraudulence shall be fully unmasked. Popular religious teaching obscures the full glory of this prophecy, because it maintains that this opposite of God, instead of being entirely erroneous, is itself a self-conscious entity, possessing eternality of power and being. The most that this teaching can be said to offer is that eventually a minority of mankind will escape from the grasp of this evil, while the other and larger portion of the race will be held forever under its control. Were this the finality of truth, it would annihilate hope for the majority of mankind, and brand as a mockery what men have come to regard as divine revelation. In contrast to this view, the inspired prophecies of the Scriptures point unmistakably to a time when the devil and his works shall be totally and eternally destroyed; and the Biblical evidence of evil's self - destructive nature, when confronted with the demonstration of God's omnipotence, reassures us that this doom will be literally fulfilled.

In the metaphor of the garden the material conception of life, represented by Adam and Eve, virtually condemned itself to toil and suffering and mortality; but the woman's discovery, that this sense of life was not of God, and that its only sponsor was a lying serpent, an embodiment in symbolism of the

19

supposition that the nature and reign of Spirit is finite, was the starting-point at which humanity began its long and painful pilgrimage to the Heavenly City, so wonderfully described at the close of the Hebrew Scriptures. The history of this pilgrimage out of a sense of evil is the history of the awakening spiritual thought of humanity, first seen and articulated in Israel, and later in Christianity. Hence the unfailing interest possessed by the subject of Israel, and the vital import of the yet unfulfilled, or partially unfulfilled, prophecies relating to her restoration in the latter days.

Commencing with the expulsion from Eden, the human record, on its material side, is mainly but a succession or procession of so many Adams and Eves, or the continuous repetition of the temptation and shame of the garden, with the continuous but futile effort of mortals to hide their errors from God. But there went out at the head of that procession, and ever accompanying it, the angelic assurance that the seed of the woman would finally reverse the lie of evil concerning man, and swing open the gates of paradise. This was the mission openly committed to woman at the very beginning of human history, and this because she had glimpsed enough of the truth of creation to detect evil's disguise, and to call forth that great prophecy which runs throughout the inspired record, a prophecy which imparted a glory to true womanhood that was never fully obscured, and which in this age is shining with the splendor of dawning achievement.

It is quite freely admitted that Adam and Eve seriously erred in yielding to the sophistry of the serpent, which plainly means that they should have refused to accept the allegation that there was anything besides good to be known. No church in Christendom could afford to teach otherwise. Yet this position once taken establishes it as the duty of mortals today to reject the same allegation. It is plain that the seductive suggestion of evil, from that day to this, neither originates with God nor involves anything which is included in the divine consciousness, otherwise evil would be necessarily inseparable from good. It is logically inconceivable that God should warn the inhabitants of Eden against knowing what was true, but rather against being deceived into believing what was not true. It would be grossly irreverent, on the face of it, to assume that God Himself entertained a knowledge of that which the truth of His infinitude forbade man to know; or that infinite wisdom and intelligence believed what Adam and Eve were punished for believing. This is implied in the question, "Who told thee that thou wast naked?" In her confession Eve absolved God of any participation in her temptation, and explained her misconduct as due to the beguilement of the serpent. That this view is not more generally accepted simply proves how tenaciously the spell of the serpent has held the human mind, until its false testimony has come to be accredited as truth.

One thing, however, is certain: that if divine power and wisdom admitted evil to the garden, the tempter's arguments were valid, and it would not have been sinful on the part of Adam and Eve to become acquainted with it; but the language of the story, in voicing God's condemnation of the whole transaction, leaves but one possible interpretation, namely, that evil had neither the Divine sanction nor permission. All this, of course, can have but one logical meaning and application: that the knowledge of evil, as put forward and defended so persistently by the serpent, and by all false teachers since, is but the knowledge of a lie, or the knowing of things that are not. When this is understood, when evil is universally regarded as but the contradiction of good, and mortals no longer believe and obey it, the kingdom of God will, of a surety, be nigh at hand.

If this story were being related by a modern writer it would probably be said that Adam and Eve were hypnotized by the serpent, and in that condition of abnormal belief, as everyone knows, they would see what was suggested to them as the normal reality. Although the woman perceived something of this, she was unable to break the spell; but a beginning had been made, and the time was to come when woman's clearer spiritual vision would fully expose the hypnotic nature of evil, and point the way to mortals' disillusionment.

In direct accord with this view is the statement of St. John the Revelator: "And the great dragon was cast out, that old serpent, called the devil, and Satan, which deceiveth the whole world." Here in a single passage we have four terms used as synonyms of evil as the deceiver or hypnotizer of mankind. Prior to this, Jesus had designated this evil or devil as "a liar, and the father of it," and as having "no truth in him," so that one may safely conclude from his analysis that that which in the beginning deceived the thoughts of mortals, and outlined that deception in the human experience of sin and death, had neither part nor place in God's universe, but was an entirely abnormal and mistaken sense of things. And an utter mistake it has surely proved itself to be throughout human history, and a mistake it is proving itself to be today. The nature of a lie is ever the same, in that it is always untrue, and the work of a lie has always been to deceive those who believe it. "And the woman said. The serpent beguiled me "; and it was this same evil suggestion that tempted Jesus in the wilderness, that St. John speaks of in the Apocalypse as persecuting the woman and her seed, and that persecutes the woman and her seed in the present hour.

The enmity of the serpent against the woman, specifically mentioned in the first and last books of the Bible, does not imply any radical discrimination between mortals as men and women, but illustrates the antagonism of the carnal mind towards spirituality. There is an inherent and irreconcilable conflict, as the apostle intimates, between the flesh and Spirit, or between the sensual and spiritual elements in human consciousness; in other words, between the truth and the error of human experience.

The Eden allegory teaches the antithetical and contradictory natures of good and evil, and the folly of attempting to believe both of them. On the side of the serpent are the debasing influences which impel the race towards moral and physical corruption, while the woman, on the other hand, prefigures the coming of the Christ. She stands as the type of spiritual overcoming,

21

the subjugation and elimination of the animal instincts of mortals, and this type is preserved throughout subsequent Scripture. On her side is found every uplifting and regenerating influence which touches the human consciousness. It is through this spiritual ascendancy only that humanity can find deliverance from the subtleties of the serpent, and reach the actual consciousness that man is the son of God.

Those who are inclined, for reasons of their own, to belittle the sphere of woman, or to discriminate against her capacities, should remember that the highest endowments are not measured by intellectual qualities or worldly attainments. The chief factor in appraising the value of either men or women is not the dust of the ground, nor anything that springs therefrom, but their possession of genuine spirituality. Human standards are too imperfect and unstable to replace the judgment of divine truth and equity, in which goodness takes precedence over cleverness, and where virtue outlasts and outweighs all that the human senses can bestow. The cause of woman has never been popular because the great mass of mankind have followed the serpent's lead, and opposed everything of a really spiritualizing nature; but the time is rapidly approaching when woman's part in the world's awakening will be fully recognized. Then will come the woman's hour, when it will be seen that it was her spiritual insight which pierced evil's boastful assumption of authority, and the age-prolonged subtleties and delusions of the carnal mind will finally be exposed.

In a word, the seed of the woman, in its general application to humanity, may be defined as spiritual-mindedness, in opposition to the carnal-mindedness represented by the serpent, an analysis which places every mortal on one side or the other. They should not fear to fight under the woman's banner who would escape from the oppressions of materialism. Because her seed is spiritual its increase is inevitable; and, however slow its growth, it spells the certain doom of the groveling serpent. The footsteps of Israel must be found in the spiritual line indicated by the woman, for there can be no heavenly vision in the service of material sense, or by whatever other name the serpent may be disguised.

Although the woman referred to in this first prophecy is not identical with the human species, it is generally admitted that even the human sense of woman represents a more ethereal type of consciousness than the human sense of man, and that, all things considered, she is more spiritually perceptive and receptive. However this may be, the higher spiritual quality of thought, first expressed by woman, has been the medium by which every message from God has reached mankind; and the outgrowth or development of that gleam of divine light, in the early morning hours of that first day of human awakening, must eventually lead to that seventh and better day, wherein the truth of being shall be fully understood, and the serpent, the spirit of evil, known under many aliases, be "cast into the lake of fire," the consuming truth of God's infinitude.

Woman's place in prophecy, and in its historic fulfilment, is something which must be seen and understood before one can read prophecy and history aright Prophecy began with woman, and until "the woman" accomplishes her divinely appointed mission, prophecy will not be wholly fulfilled. When the world shall come to perceive and acknowledge these things, the day of Israel's restoration will be at hand, her Identity and destiny will be revealed, and the "throne of David," the reign of the Christ, be established among all nations.

Chapter Three - The Early Morning of History

The kingdom of heaven is like unto leaven, which a woman took, and hid in three measures of meal, till the whole was leavened. — Matt. 13:33.

WITH the expulsion of "the man" from Eden, the curtain falls upon the first act of this allegorical story. The use of this term without naming Adam and Eve, who, it has been supposed, were the only inhabitants of the garden, is consistent with the metaphorical nature of the whole narrative, and evidently signifies type or kind instead of particular individuals. It is expressly stated that the man was cast out because of his knowledge of evil, which shows unmistakably that such knowledge is impossible to God, and necessarily excludes its possessor from the deific presence. This kind of man was clearly not the ideal of the son of God, and could not, therefore, be acknowledged by the Father. The sequel of the story would imply that the man whom it featured was a sham and an impostor.

The woman's recognition that evil, masked in the story as a serpent, was a beguiler or enchanter, was naturally followed by the self -exposure of sin's inanity and the realization that no ungodly mode of thought or its embodiment had any possible place in paradise. It was plainly the uncovering of the evil nature of this kind of man which banished it from the garden, and doomed it to self -punishment and death, evidently implying that good and evil, Spirit and flesh, are the true and the false, which have nothing in common and cannot dwell together.

The next great act staged in the drama of mortal man, an act which followed the events of the garden in logical sequence, is presented in the story of the Deluge. To what extent its description is historically accurate may not be determined, but its general correctness would seem to be corroborated by the traditions of other races. To the conscience of the early Hebrews it was accepted unquestioningly as the divine punishment for human wickedness, but the utter futility of attempting to purify the earth by drowning its inhabitants was so impressed upon Noah, that the assurance that this experience would not be repeated was later recorded as a covenant from God. The clearer vision of the prophets saw that the evil in human thought would have to be burned out with the fire of Truth.

In this story, the Creator is represented as thoroughly disappointed and displeased with His own work. The man of the earth had turned out so badly as to be unfit to live, and so we read that the great flood came and destroyed "all in whose nostrils was the breath of life," with the exception of the family of Noah. The whole story, in its metaphysical aspect, bespeaks God's utter repudiation of materialism, for it undoubtedly teaches that the man formed "of the dust of the ground" is not the man in whom He delights. Beyond all question, the material concept of being had utterly failed to show forth the glory of God, and this failure revealed its absolute unlikeness to Deity. Speaking to this type of man, which was cast out of Eden, Jesus said, "Ye are of your father the devil, and the lusts of your father ye will do," a pronouncement which should prove conclusively that God was not its author.

The outstanding feature of the story of the Flood is not that the world was deluged because of its wickedness, but that one man was found good enough to preserve himself and his family from the general destruction. The incident of the ark is the first recorded instance of the protective power of a knowledge of God in the presence of physical danger. We learn from the narrative that Noah's preservation was due to his righteousness, or rightmindedness, and not that God singled him out for the purpose of prolonging the human race. This fact is far-reaching in its significance and application, and its evidence will be seen to increase as we trace the journey of the human consciousness towards its perception of the Christ. It should be well understood that the salvation of Noah and his family was not the work of chance, or a piece of mere good fortune, but was due to the operation of a law which transcends material conditions, and which was brought to bear upon the present need through Noah's nearness to God in his own consciousness. Had there been others of the same class, they would undoubtedly have been included in the same salvation.

We have heard from childhood the story of Enoch's exemption from death, and of Noah's deliverance from the Flood, but we have been wrongly taught to read into the sacred records the inference that these were special favors from God, which should not be expected under similar circumstances by other human beings. This inference is the thinly veiled philosophy of the carnal mind, which ever seeks to deprive man of his divine rights. It was plainly Enoch's close acquaintance with the divine life of man, which lifted him above the reach of mortality, and not that God had more respect for him than for others who might reach the same degree of spiritual consciousness.

The Bible came into being that the way to "overcome the wicked one" might be revealed to men. If the possibility of escape from moral and physical evils, through an apprehension of divine power, did not exist, the Scriptures would, in consequence, have no practical value for oppressed humanity. Confined by its own theories to matter, human sense would be without any appreciable evidence of the existence of Spirit, or of the applicability of spiritual law to human need, except as material evils were overcome by supermaterial means. When it is remembered that the serpent is but a figure in metaphor to represent the deceptive nature of evil knowledge, it can be seen that as men begin to emerge from the delusions of that false knowledge, and to know that God is the only power or law in the universe, they would naturally begin to have dominion over the traditional fears engendered by a physical sense of being. From this standpoint one may readily understand the incidents recorded in the Scriptures which have seemed miraculous to the human mind.

The recurrence of these signs or proofs of divine power over so-called earthly forces, which we find throughout the history of Israel, would indicate that they are an inseparable characteristic of a genuine knowledge of God. As human consciousness becomes spiritually illumined, the darkness of materialism must, to that extent, lose its apparent substance and power, and cease to obscure a realization of God's omnipotence. The human sense, groping among the shadows of materiality, has been struggling towards what St. Paul called "the light of the knowledge of the glory of God," and it is this human struggle to find the truth about God which is recorded throughout the sacred writings of the Hebrews.

The conflict between the flesh and Spirit, between the seed of the woman and the seed of the serpent, foreshadowed in the Edenic prophecy, is what human history in reality consists of, for all true civilization implies some degree of evil grappled with and overcome. A nation or a people which possessed no moral fiber, whose ideals were not founded upon righteousness, or which felt no quickening desire to be a blessing in the earth, would have no history worth recording, or any memories fit to survive. We may confidently look forward to the time when whatever had its rise in evil will be expunged from human records, and good will be recognized as the only rightful sphere of man's consciousness and activity.

Conflict, however, naturally involves more than one, hence the belief in a plurality of minds provides the only possible basis for strife and division. Without a belief in the opposite of divinity, there could be no conflict of interests, and no evil to strive with; but the acceptance of both good and evil as power and intelligence has ever involved humanity in perpetual discord. A mutual hostility necessarily exists between the right and the wrong of things, whether in individual mentalities or in the ideals of nations, and peace cannot be experienced between these opposite states. This enmity must continue until human consciousness shall be so illumined with the consciousness of the infinitude of good that evil will disappear as the moral darkness that it is.

After the Flood we find the human race branching out into three streams, flowing from the sons of Noah, and representing types or gradations of human thought. In Noah's prophetic declaration regarding his sons, the chief blessing and the chief place are bestowed upon Shem. The benediction, "Blessed be the Lord God of Shem," was not repeated of the other two sons, neither was the promise that God would dwell in their tents. This passage evidently implies that Shem possessed the highest concept of Deity, and that, in all probability, his descendants would maintain the same distinction. It is not to be assumed, however, that Shem was chosen before his brothers to be the progenitor of Israel for any other reason than that he possessed above them the quality of thought through which God could best become known to men.

It will be observed that the ancestry of Israel did not include all the sons of Shem, for but one of them was named to carry on the elect line, and this process of selection went on from, generation to generation, taking but one from each family, until we come to the twelve sons of Jacob. The "tents of Shem," therefore, cannot be interpreted as meaning all of his family descendants, but evidently referred to that chosen or selected race which afterwards came to be known as the people of God. This selective process was not always confined to the first-born son, so that a higher influence than family considerations was plainly at work in forming what the apostle called, "a chosen generation."

We gather from the records that the interval after the passing of Noah presented little evidence of any general improvement. As it was with mankind before the Flood, so it was after the Flood. We look in vain for any sign of moral betterment on account of that experience, its impression being soon forgotten or erased. The second trial of the man of dust proved as discreditable and disappointing as the first. In the midst of this spiritual stagnation, about ten generations after Noah, we read that Abram heard the voice of the Lord, saying:

"Get thee out of thy country, and from thy kindred, and from thy father's house, unto a land that I will shew thee:

And I will make of thee a great nation, and I will bless thee, and make thy name great; and thou shalt be a blessing:

And I will bless them that bless thee, and curse him that curseth thee: and in thee shall all families of the earth be blessed."

Abram obeyed without questioning. He had apparently reached out for and had found a higher mental and spiritual plane of consciousness than others of his people, else he would not have heard and understood the divine message. In the words of the writer of the book of Hebrews, he went out to look "for a city," that is, a consciousness of life, "whose builder and maker is God." His maturing conception of the real nature of God pointed to the wisdom of seeking another home and country where he might find the freedom to express his better sense of Deity. His recognition of the necessity for this complete separation impressed him as the divine call, "and he went out, not knowing whither he went."

What it really meant was, that the glimmering dawn of Israel was beginning to break. "The Spirit of God" was moving "upon the face of the waters," the heterogeneous human mass, and was preparing the formation of a nation whose recognition of the one infinite and only God was to be its distinguishing feature. It was necessary, in the very nature of things, that a racial distinction would sometime arise between those who had some definite knowledge of God, and the residue of mankind. Ever since the enmity between good and evil had been uncovered to human consciousness, it was logically inevitable that the mental qualities nearest to the right conception of God, as they became more defined and coherent, would sooner or later find their family and national expression.

It was no doubt the unconscious stirring of these things that impelled Abram to leave the idolatry of his father's house, and that took form in his thought as a covenant or assurance from God. He beheld himself — not in the sense of personality, but as the representative of the true idea of God — becoming the founder, not only of a great nation, but of a great spiritual movement that, in the fulness of time, would cover the earth with its blessing, and gather all mankind into its fold. This great destiny, which was unfolded to Abram as the legacy of his race, cannot be rightly viewed as an arbitrary predestination by a personal Deity, but as the obligation naturally resting upon the most spiritually enlightened people. It was Abram's preeminent fitness that alone selected him for this work, as it has been with every great leader and reformer.

About twenty-five years later, when Abram was ninety-nine years old and there seemed little prospect of its fulfilment, the heavenly covenant was reaffirmed to him, with the assurance that the son who was to carry on his line would be born of Sarai. But the carnal mind argued that this could not be, because his wife had passed the time of motherhood allotted by so-called physical law. The enmity of the serpent arrayed the plea of matter against the continuation of her seed, but, although human faith staggered at the material argument, it was proved to be without power or authority. The law of Spirit prevailed, and in the process, the natures of Abram and Sarai were so deeply touched by a higher sense of life than matter, that they were henceforth to be known by new names.

It was obviously in accord with the necessity for spiritual progress that the faith of Abraham and his wife should triumph over the so-called laws of the flesh, for only as they overcame evil could their experience bless "all the families of the earth." Abraham had long since left his father's house, with its worship of materiality, and was here struggling with the ungodly claim that man is a creature of the dust, dependent for his life upon material conditions, instead of upon God. Were these material conditions to overrule the divine promise and prevent its fulfilment? It could not be. Abraham's higher thought of God, which had inspired him to seek "a better country," and which had not failed him during the intervening years, emerged triumphant. The son of promise was born.

And thus at the close of the first long lap of the human journey, it was demonstrated that a diviner law than physical sense governs the creation of man, and this experience lifted human thought to a distinctly higher plane of preparation for its final freedom from evil, the goal towards which all right

27

human endeavor is directed.

Chapter Four - The Rise of Israel

But thou, Israel, art My servant, Jacob whom I have chosen, the seed of Abraham My friend. — Isa. 41: 8.

And I will make thee exceeding fruitful, and I will make nations of thee, and kings shall come out of thee.

And I will establish My covenant between Me and thee and thy seed after thee in their generations for an everlasting covenant, to be a God unto thee, and to thy seed after thee. — Gen. 17: 6, 7.

Therefore sprang there even of one, and him as good as dead, so many as the stars of the sky in multitude, and as the sand which is by the sea shore innumerable. — Heb. 11: 12.

ABRAHAM is our father," argued the Jews with Jesus in their attempted self-justification, but the Master pointed out with incisive directness that to be Abraham's descendants meant something more than racial affinity. "If ye were Abraham's children," he said, "ye would do the works of Abraham." And so while we follow with interest the course of Israel in the flesh among the races of the earth, we must not forget that the promises primarily belong to the Israel of Spirit.

Abraham is a notably outstanding figure in the history of human development, not because of personal prestige, but because of his spiritual accomplishments. He had the remarkable distinction of being called "the friend of God." While his contemporaries were absorbed with the worship of idols, he was making the close acquaintance of the invisible Principle or cause of being which mortals name Deity, not through the medium of any physical sense, but through mental obedience to his highest understanding of good. Abraham's fidelity to the demands of God, so far as he apprehended them, brought him eventually to the point where he must choose between the human and the divine idea of fatherhood. Did he as a mortal glory over Isaac as his own son? — then he must surrender this human claim, this concept of man's earthly origin, that Spirit might be to him the only Father, and His image and likeness the only Son.

Whether this may or may not have come to him, in the crude fashion of his times, as a call for the literal sacrifice of his son's life, is of minor importance. The record indicates that he was prepared to go to even that extremity if he felt that God required it, but that would have been the interpretation of the carnal mind, and its logical ultimate would have required Abraham to offer up his own life also. What progress was impelling him to learn was that Isaac, as the divinely provided means for continuing the chosen seed, belonged not to him but to God. It was a rebuke to the material sense of fatherhood which later found its perfect antitype in the spiritual conception of Jesus.

Reviewing this incident, it would seem that Abraham was here awakening to the recognition that man has no life other than God, and, consequently, that there was no" life in Isaac's body which God required him to destroy.. This naturally led him to see that what God did require him, as well as other mortals, to sacrifice was the sense of life as material, a sense of life which God neither creates nor destroys. The patriarch's enlarged perception of the spiritual nature of man which came to him in this experience, and his unreserved response to the demand to lay his earthly treasure upon the altar, made him the virtual starting-point of the line of the Messiah, and destined Israel to be the bearer of spiritual light to humanity.

The process of selection, referred to in the preceding chapter, is again seen in the declaration to Abraham, "In Isaac shall thy seed be called," or named. The sons of Abraham by his other wives were thus not classed with the "seed," which would indicate that, in its truer meaning, this word was intended to apply only to the offspring or outgrowth of his spiritual sense of being. In his epistle to the Galatians St. Paul makes this distinction clear when he distinguishes between the son of Hagar and the son of Sarah, as between one born after the flesh and one born after the Spirit. In other words, he implies in his metaphysical analysis that the lesson of Isaac's birth, as the one designated beforehand to carry on the line of Israel, is the distinction which it makes between the spiritual and material sense of being.

"For it is written that Abraham had two sons, the one by a bondmaid, the other by a freewoman. But he who was of the bondwoman was born after the flesh; but he of the freewoman was of promise." The apostle then goes on to explain the allegorical meaning of this story, as indicating the bondage of material sense on one hand, and the freedom of spiritual sense on the other. "But as then he that was born after the flesh persecuted him that was born after the Spirit, even so it is now." In this verse Paul illustrates the enmity of materialism towards the seed of the woman, and confirms the conclusion, if it needs confirmation, that *the seed of the woman is Israel.*

"Now we, brethren, as Isaac was, are the children of promise...So then, brethren, we are not children of the bondwoman, but of the free." Hence the natural conclusion that the people who should be named after the name of Isaac would be the children of freedom, the lovers and defenders of liberty, but a people, it must be remembered, whose freedom would be achieved and maintained by reason of spiritual enlightenment rather than by material force. By this freedom is meant the "liberty of the sons of God," — than which there is rightly no other, — first rather dimly seen in the acknowledgment of individual rights, then in liberty of conscience, and finally, as the ideal of Christianity is fully lifted up in human consciousness, in freedom from the domination of the carnal mind.

"In thy seed shall all the nations of the earth be blessed," said the angel of the Lord to Abraham for the second time, *"because thou hast obeyed My voice."* In this last clause lay the only secret of Abraham's greatness, and of Israel's prosperity and Influence as a nation; while the withholding of this obedience was, on the other hand, the source of Israel's failures and eventual downfall. On this basis there was and is absolutely no respect of persons. The view frequently adopted by writers on these topics, that God arbitrarily selected one nation above all others to be His own particular people, irrespective of their spiritual qualifications, is manifestly incompatible with the Divine nature, and would in effect place God upon the plane of human caprice.

As a matter of fact, the choice in this case rested entirely with the Israelites. They were rightly called God's chosen people only in the sense that they alone out of the nations recognized and acknowledged Deity as One and supreme. This of itself, in an age of idolatry, would constitute them a "peculiar people." It is true that the primitive Hebrews, in their simple and almost superstitious way, regarded themselves as especially set apart by Jehovah from the rest of humanity, and recorded this impression in their sacred writings, but this does not affect the perfectly logical position that the distinction between the Israelites and their neighbors was one of consciousness and not of person. Their only advantage or superiority consisted of their better knowledge of God. It was not, therefore, because the seed of Abraham, according to the flesh, were literally to multiply into many nations, or because they were to possess the gates of their enemies, that the world was to be blessed, but because of their obedience to God. This applies itself equally to the Israelites of today. It should be recognized that obedience to good, in all times and circumstances, is the unexceptional condition of blessing, and the only real covenant of God with man. "Obey My voice, and I will be your God, and ye shall be My people" (Jer. 7: 23), declares God's lasting covenant, and when this obedience is lacking, the covenant is not in force. This point should not be permitted to get into the background, for without obedience to God the word Israel would have no spiritual application or value.

We find that emphasis is again placed upon this point in the assurance to Isaac that in his seed also the nations of the earth should be blessed, *"because that Abraham obeyed My voice, and kept My charge, My commandments, My statutes, and My laws."* We cannot assume that the nations of the earth, nor even Israel herself, would continue to be blessed on account of Abraham's personal obedience, but that Abraham was preparing the way whereby his seed, the seed of the woman, should in due time make known the way of salvation to all men. As before intimated, the word "seed" did not always mean the natural descendants of Abraham, or of Isaac or Jacob as the case may be, but was also used to signify the type or quality of thought which especially characterized these founders of the line of Israel and made them what they were. The word is thus used in a distinctively spiritual sense, in which case it was sometimes applied in the singular, and without doubt referred to the one perfect Truth, or the Christ, which was being dimly foreshadowed in the lives of the patriarchs. That Jesus clearly recognized this is indicated in his statement, "Abraham rejoiced to see my day."

The prophecy in Genesis 22:17, "Thy seed shall possess the gate of his enemies," is generally interpreted in a purely national or military sense, or as relating to the seed which was to become "as the sand which is upon the sea-shore," that is, to a large multitude of human beings; whereas the use of the singular pronoun "his" in the phrase "the gate of his enemies," would indicate that the word was here intended to mean one and not many, even that one of whom Isaiah said, "the government shall be upon his shoulders." This is without question the one who, in the fulness of time, is to "possess the gate of his enemies," which naturally means, as the word is evidently used in a fig-urative sense, that the spiritual seed of the woman is to dispossess the carnal mind of its strongholds. Whatever reference this and similar passages may have to the Israelites as a nation, — and they have without doubt a legitimate use in that connection — it is secondary and subordinate to their spiritual meaning and application, which invariably point to the real and permanent issue in every case, as we shall discover all along the way.

Isaac was the connecting link in the great patriarchal triad of Israel, and is remembered more as Abraham's son of promise, pre-appointed to carry on the line of the seed of blessing, than for anything which particularly distin-guished his own career. Contrary to his own preference and design, he saw his elder and favorite son supplanted in the succession by the younger, not recognizing the divine influence that was plainly at work, an influence which has never yet been overruled by the shortsighted indifference or opposition of men. Before the birth of her twin sons, when she inquired of the Lord con-cerning them, Rebekah was told that "the elder shall serve the younger.

In the *Book of Jubilees,* a Jewish work of the second century B.C. dealing with the events recorded in Genesis and referred to by some of the early Christian authors, we find the following interesting passages: "Abraham saw the deeds of Esau, and he knew that his name and seed should be called for him in Jacob, and he called Rebekah and commanded her concerning Jacob, for he saw that she too loved Jacob more than Esau. And he said to her: My daughter, watch my son Jacob, for he shall be in my stead upon the earth as a blessing among the sons of men...and I know that the Lord has chosen him for himself...add yet to do something good for him and let thine eyes be over him as the beloved, for he shall be to me a blessing over the earth.'" (Page 60)

Before we pass judgment upon the method by which Rebekah secured Isaac's blessing for her younger son, or the means by which Jacob had be-come possessed of the birthright, we should remember that this primitive people cannot justly be condemned by the moral code of a more enlightened age. Acts which would offend our moral sense were looked upon, under cer-tain circumstances, as pardonable or even legitimate. We are too often con-fronted by a choice of evils in our own more progressive times to dwell too harshly upon the conduct of Jacob and his mother. It is difficult at this date adequately to estimate the importance which the people of that day attached to the birthright and to the father's blessing, therefore we cannot fully realize the tremendous influence which the possession of these would have upon the consciousness and the destiny of Jacob, especially when coupled with the conviction that he was the divine choice in the line of succession.

31

Jacob, however, did not go entirely unpunished. His fear of Esau drove him from his father's house and country, and he served twenty years as an hireling with his uncle Laban. It is not likely that he understood, at the time, the real value or significance of either the birthright or the blessing. He probably saw a vision of flocks and herds, and the exercise of power attached to the headship of his people, and the vision proved too much for his worldly thoughts. He had not then grown to see that the prosperity of Abraham and Isaac was the result of their fidelity to their understanding of spiritual good, and that the real substance and meaning of the family heritage was not material riches and power, but a knowledge of the one true God.

Thus the carrying on of the line of Israel, as Jacob was afterwards to learn, meant vastly more than to be the heir of his father. It meant that he was to maintain the spiritual ideal of Deity which had separated Abraham and Isaac from the idolatry of their times, and through which salvation and blessing were to come to all the races of the earth. The first recorded instance of his awakening to these things occurred as he fled from the vengeance of Esau. It came as a vision of the night, when the affairs of the world were less obtrusive. He saw as it were a ladder that reached from earth to heaven, by which angels ascended and descended; "and, behold, the Lord stood above It, and said, I am the Lord God of Abraham thy father, and the God of Isaac: the land whereon thou liest, to thee will I give it, and to thy seed; ...and in thee and in thy seed shall all the families of the earth be blessed."

This vision made a wonderful impression upon the fugitive. He felt that he had come very close to the presence of God. We find throughout the Scriptural record that dreams or visions of the night were frequently the channel by which men became aware of God's messages, and it is only the belief that physical means or modes are necessary to convey thought, that makes these things seem supernatural or mysterious. In reality it is no more mysterious to receive impressions from God, divine Mind, in what are called one's night dreams, if he is prepared to receive them, than to be thus inspired at other times, since all divine impartations are necessarily mental, whenever or however they may touch human consciousness.

"Surely the Lord is in this place," said Jacob, "and I knew it not." He was beginning to learn, what we are all too apt to blindly ignore, that God is present with men whether human sense is ready to perceive it or not. The influence of this experience was so spiritually uplifting that he set up his stone pillow for a memorial, as it afterwards proved, to all subsequent ages, and consecrated it as a visible token of the unseen Divine presence. "This stone," Jacob said, "shall be God's house," and he there dedicated the first church. The idea behind this solitary memorial later expanded into the tabernacle, and the great temple of Solomon. It is behind every Christian church and every Jewish synagogue where that idea is truly perceived, pointing men to the privilege and opportunity of communion with their Creator.

In view of all this it is not difficult to believe that this particular stone, so instinct with sacred memory, and so inseparable from an important stage of their spiritual history, would become an object of reverence to the Israelites. Some writers are of the opinion that it was this stone to which Jacob later referred, in his memorable prophetic blessing on the house of Joseph, as "the stone of Israel," or "Israel's guardian stone," as it is rendered in Ferrar Fenton's translation. It is not to be inferred that Jacob attached this high significance to a mere piece of rock, or because it was his pillow the night of his heavenly vision at Bethel, but for what it represented to him and to his people. It not only commemorated his first real acquaintance with God, at the beginning of his long exile, but the assurance of the Divine presence and protection which he there received, an assurance which reached out beyond his personal career and has rested upon the people whom he afterwards came to represent. "Behold, I am with thee, and will keep thee in all places whither thou goest, and will bring thee again unto this land: for I will not leave thee, until I have done that which I have spoken to thee of." (Gen. 28: 15.)

It must be remembered that these were very primitive times, the earliest dawn of Israelitish history, when there was no written literature such as we have today, and oral tradition took the place of books. From what has come down to us, we know that in those days there were literally "sermons in stones," and this "pillow-pillar" of Jacob's undoubtedly helped to preserve a vital message for this nation that was yet only in its birth-throes. Even in our own more cultured and enlightened twentieth century, there is more store set by signs and symbols than most of us are willing to acknowledge. That this stone would be treasured and preserved by the Israelites may be accepted without question, and that it is still with them as a memorial of promise and prophecy is not beyond belief. Such things as these do not pass away "until all be fulfilled."

In the "ladder set up on the earth," whose top reached to heaven, Jacob got a glimpse of the fact that mortals must lift their thoughts above the earthly or material sense of things if they would understand and worship God aright. This is evidently the true meaning of Bethel, the "house of God." His receptivity to the divine unfoldment was fitting Jacob to carry on the line of the covenant made with his fathers, and to complete that threefold declaration of Deity to Moses, "I am the God of Abraham, the God of Isaac, and the God of Jacob." To bring the true idea of God to human beings, and thus to give them a consciousness of heaven while yet on earth, is the great mission committed to the house of God, the true Church, typified in that age by a solitary stone set up at Luz, but a stone which was to become a token of God's everlasting care and protection over His people.

The sequel to his vision at Bethel came to Jacob as he was about to meet his brother Esau. The call had come to return to his own country, but as he came near he found himself confronted by the same fear which had driven him forth. On the eve of this dreaded meeting, after having cared for his family, "Jacob was left alone; and there wrestled a man with him until the breaking of the day"; and then follows a brief account of the transforming experience which set the divine seal upon the destiny of the line of Israel. This account is plainly metaphorical rather than literal. Jacob was not wrestling with another man like himself, for the record distinctly states that he was alone. The conflict described was apparently taking place in his own consciousness, rather than to his external senses. Jacob had reached a crisis in his mental life. He had come to the place where the evil which tormented him had to be squarely faced and the issue fought out. "There wrestled a man with him," and what other man was this but his own better self, his angel, the Jacob which was not of the earth earthy, but which was the son of God. His selfish, sensual sense was struggling with the divinity of his real being, and the godlike in his consciousness "prevailed."

Jacob's conquest over the "old man," the man who had wronged his brother and was afraid to meet the consequences, won for him the new name of Israel. This word literally means "prince of God," or as it is sometimes rendered, "son of God." The Scriptures teach that this "son of God" is the real man, or the "new man" referred to by the apostle, and the struggle in Jacob's thought, as it must be in the thought of every human being, was between this true idea, and the evil sense of man, as sensual and mortal. Jacob could flee from the vengeance of his brother, but he could not escape from the evil which he had made part of his consciousness; and until he had striven with this evil and recognized its unlawful nature, he was not ready to carry on the line of the woman. The patriarch's experience and its result establish the conquest over sin as one of the chief foundation stones of Israel. If this part of the foundation is removed, the human superstructure, however imposing, will not stand.

"And Jacob called the name of the place Peniel: for I have seen God face to face"; which calls to mind that profound saying of Jesus, the Son of God, "He that hath seen me hath seen the Father." Jacob had caught a glimpse of God as made manifest in His son, that is, he had caught a glimpse of the truth that man is created in God's image, and this vision gave a meaning to Israel that transcends the human distinction of nationality or race, and that will remain until all mankind catch the same vision, and prevail in the same conflict.

The seed of the woman was surely treading upon the serpent's head. The day of Israel, the human recognition of the reign of Spirit, had begun.

Chapter Five - The Meaning of "Israel"

And Jacob called the name of the place Peniel: for I have seen God face to face. — Gen. 32: 30.

He that overcometh shall inherit all things; and I will be his God, and he shall be My son. — Rev. 21:7.

AND he said, Thy name shall be called no more Jacob, but Israel: for as a prince hast thou power with God and with men, and hast prevailed." The name Israel, encountered here for the first time, was given to Jacob in recognition of his change of character. Originally bestowed to commemorate this patriarch's apprehension of man's spiritual nature, its meaning and influence in time extended beyond his person and generation, beyond the nation which adopted it as its name, outlasting the long oblivion into which that nation disappeared, and is today one of the most pregnant words in the English language.

It will be noticed throughout the subsequent narrative that Jacob is still largely spoken of by his former name, which would indicate that the word Israel was regarded chiefly as defining his spiritual status, and the spiritual status and destiny of the nation which flowed from him. Even at the present day the personality of this patriarch is identified by the name of Jacob rather than Israel, showing that the latter appellation has a larger and higher meaning than the name of a man or of a nation. The only proper basis upon which the Hebrew race could adopt the distinctive name of Israel would be that they accepted the burden of proof that the God with whom Abraham communed, and whom Jacob saw "face to face" at Peniel, was the only God in all the earth.

Although the meaning of Israel is, strictly speaking, confined to its spiritual significance, it necessarily has its correlative application as designating that chosen people in whose consciousness God's supremacy was acknowledged, and by whom all mankind were to be eventually evangelized. This word, therefore, while originally signifying that which transcends the human personality, has come to have a dual application. The Israelites stood in the same relation to the spiritual truth behind the word Israel, that Christians do to the truths of Christianity; but Christians are not synonymous with Christianity, neither were the Israelites synonymous with Israel. If we keep this distinction in mind, we can use the word Israel as designating the Hebrew nation, without divorcing the word from its spiritual significance.

It may be well here to consider more fully the real meaning of Israel, not only because that meaning is so vitally important to the redemption of humanity, but because the signs indicate that we are now in what the Scriptures call the "latter days," wherein we may rightly expect the beginning of that great event of prophecy known as the Restoration of Israel. But unless we know what Israel means, and the nature of what was involved in its loss, we shall not be prepared to recognize the fulfilment of the prophets' vision when it comes.

As already noted, Israel was much more than a person. The disappearance of a person, however prominent or esteemed, would not affect the individual status of those who remained. By the same token Israel is also much more than a nation, since a nation is but the continuous aggregation of persons united by a common type of thought. Thus the disappearance or reappearance of national Israel, although possessing great human interest, would not of itself be momentous to human destiny. We have seen that Jacob was awarded the title of Israel because he had, in some measure above the ordinary, prevailed over the suggestions of the serpent, and the nation which came from him could rightly merit the same name only as it did the same thing.

When it is said, however, that Israel is more than a nation, it does not mean that the word does not involve a national use. The greater must necessarily include the less. The larger spiritual meaning of Israel must necessarily hold within it some application to a nation, for the simple reason that the Israelitish people were to have existence as a nation for the very purpose of giving that meaning concrete expression and activity. The evident mistake is in limiting the word to its national application. The selection that went on from Adam to Jacob was clearly mental, and betokened the development of a people whose quality of thought would be particularly susceptible to spiritual influence. Unless this development of a "peculiar people" was taking place, that is, unless there was actually in process in human consciousness a definite improvement over the man of dust, and a growing recognition of spiritual being, there could be no final salvation in prospect for the human race.

While it is a mistake to lose sight of the spiritual identity of Israel in the doings or misdoings of the Hebrews, it is, on the other hand, as great a mistake to assume that Israel has today no national representation, or that she will never again resume her leading place among the nations. The former position led to the error of thinking that the less includes the greater, while the latter position would obscure the greater by denying the less. The human sense of things will naturally continue in evidence until this sensual or material sense is outgrown, and a state of wholly spiritual consciousness is attained.

The Hebrews were called Israelites for the sole reason that a knowledge of the true God was found among them; but this does not imply that every individual Hebrew possessed that knowledge. The national consciousness of the Hebrews presented the least resistance to divine revelation, therefore God was revealed through that nation, beginning with Abraham and continuing at intervals to the present age. Thus Israel as a nation meant the national acknowledgment of one God, as distinguished from the idolatry of Gentile nations, so that in time "the God of Israel" came to be synonymous with the Supreme Being, the God who is "above all gods." The use of the word Israel related primarily to the spiritual side of the nation's life and character, and inseparable from this meaning is the prophetic statement that all the earth is to be blessed in Israel, that is, in the spiritual truth which was being revealed through it.

It is true that many of the Israelites, and at times almost the entire nation, were wicked and idolatrous, but that is equally true of the so-called Christian nations today, and only proves that without the spiritual inspiration which transfigures consciousness, words and names have little value. The spiritual element alone is the real heart of a nation, and the salt of the earth. This may be seen in the selective process which singled out Noah, Abraham, Jacob, Moses, etc., as special avenues or instruments of Divine truth, a process which has gone on more or less conspicuously down to our own time. It will be re-membered that Elijah once believed himself to be the only loyal Israelite in the nation, but he was assured of the Lord that there were still seven thou-sand who had not bowed the knee to Baal. These were, beyond argument, the only true representatives of Israel in the nation. And so it has always been, and is today. The restoration of spiritual Israel is what the world has looked and waited for, and is what the prophets foresaw as the reappearing of the Messianic Truth, first presented to mankind by Christ Jesus; and this final reappearing of the promised Deliverer was to be followed by the bringing to life, or the resurrecting from its oblivion, of Israel after the flesh, or in other words national Israel. There must always be the two witnesses. The letter and the Spirit must coincide in prophetic fulfilment, If the Scriptures are not to be broken, and It was plainly so seen In the visions of the prophets. It is Idle at this date to attempt their separation, for while men are gathered Into nations, there must always be the one that stands nearest to God, and that nation will necessarily be the one which understands Him best.

The conclusion of any rational human being, based upon experience and personal observation, as well as upon the testimony of history, must be that what separates him, together with the rest of humanity, from the realization of perfection and immortality, is the sense or consciousness which we call material. This sense of things includes all that is held to be mortal and unde-sirable. From it arise all the dread and the fear that terrorize humanity, from creeping infancy to stalwart manhood and weary age. All that is included in the word sin, its motives, means, or objects, its vicious appetites and pas-sions; all that is meant by the word suffering, the miseries, torments, and desolation that oppress humanity; all that makes existence discordant, that embitters the human cup, that covers earth with a mantle of sorrow, all that is outside the kingdom of heaven, arise from and pertain to a physical or cor-poreal conception of life and consciousness. "For I know," said Paul, "that in me (that is, in my flesh,) dwelleth no good thing."

It is quite apparent that the Deliverer of humanity must come from an op-posite mental direction to that of its oppressor. No good thing, as the apostle frankly states, can come out of the carnal mind; hence mortals have no alter-native but to look for their Saviour in the direction of the divine Mind, or what St. Paul called "the mind of Christ." That the "fruit," the outcome, of hav-ing this Mind is "love, joy, peace," establishes the fact that the kingdom of heaven must lie in that direction. Thus whatever actual progress the race has made, or that remains to be achieved, must necessarily be in the direction indicated by a more spiritual consciousness of being.

Without an abiding perception of these things we shall miss the true mean-ing of Israel, as well as the lessons of the history of the nation which bore that name. The word, as originally defined, meant having power with God, or that enlightened spiritual sense through which His power became available to men. It means the recognition that man is the son of God, and implies that exalted mental state by which men may become conscious of God's presence, and of His sovereignty in human affairs. The so-called physical man is not capable of this. Neither the human eye nor ear nor hand has ever become cognizant of the presence of Spirit or of man as His offspring. The Scriptures clearly imply that, while human thought is at home in corporeal sense, it is "absent from the Lord"; so that there is absolutely nothing in a corporeal or physical sense of being that can connect man with his Creator; and whatever is incapable of doing this must naturally express the nature of evil, of that which, to human belief, separates men from God.

In his experience at Peniel Jacob struggled all through the night to lay hold of the spiritual nature of man, and his success ineffaceably stamped itself upon human consciousness. It was the birth of Israel. A birth, however, is not the appearance of a full-grown man; and that which came to light in the consciousness of Jacob, as he wrestled with his angel visitor, was but the infantile promise of the glory which was to come. This infant would take centuries and millenniums in place of years in reaching maturity. What was it, then, that broke in on Jacob's vision as the morning ended his long vigil? What did he see face to face? Was it not a glimpse of the same Truth that blinded Saul with its glory on his way to persecute the Christians at Damascus, and which transformed his nature also?

Stated in the simplest possible terms, "Israel" means the spiritual sense or understanding of being, which can alone reveal God and the perfect man. That which prevailed and had power with God was entirely separate and apart from Jacob's materiality. This is naturally very obvious, but it is important that we recognize its bearing upon the whole subject of Israel, and the whole subject of Scriptural interpretation and human redemption. That which wrestled and prevailed in that memorable experience at Peniel, is what must wrestle and prevail in the consciousness of every human being, a fact which brings these distant occurrences very close to the present time, and invests the whole story of Israel with intense personal interest. If we have not already learned them, the lessons of the past will have to be repeated, for we must all take our place somewhere along the line of Israel's uncompleted journey.

Since it is self-evident that the sensuous human mind can provide no salvation from its ills and evils, that is from itself, a time would necessarily have to come when men would begin to think less materially. If evil was ever to be overcome, as we know it must, human consciousness would have to reach the point where some glimmer of spiritual light could penetrate and illumine its material darkness. These points of spiritual illumination mark the progress of Israel throughout the Biblical records, and they still serve as beacons of promise in keeping aglow the hope of humanity. These were revelations of divinity, of the glory which is not of earth or sea or sky, the glory which Christ Jesus had with the Father *"before the world was."* For those who have eyes to see, they light the way out of the flesh into the realm of Spirit. Without this divine unfolding, and the spiritual teachings which grew therefrom, the Scriptures would be as helpless to lead mortals out of their errors as would a treatise on astronomy.

The spiritual movement known as Israel, which grew out of Jacob's illumination at Peniel, was a distinct and lasting challenge to the carnal mind. It stood first and last for the bruising of the serpent. Admitting, as in honesty we must, that what so deeply influenced the patriarch and his descendants was an impartation from the divine Spirit, we should be frankly ready to acknowledge that the word Israel, which Jacob accepted as confirming the nature of his experience, was wholly spiritual in its import. The use of the word in designating the Hebrew race is a courtesy as well as a convenience of speech. Had the Hebrews as a people been wholly devoid of the spiritual characteristics indicated in the name of Israel, they would have been on the same level with other races, so far as exerting any decisive influence in the shaping of human destiny.

Naaman the Syrian, as before pointed out, touched the key to the whole situation, both literally and spiritually, when he said, "Now I know that there is no God in all the earth, but in Israel." He knew this for the very simple reason that he had been healed of his leprosy in proof thereof, for none of the gods of the Gentiles could do this thing. There naturally could not be more than one true God. A false god is a self-condemned lie, whether formulated in human doctrines, or objectified by man's device. Naaman's conclusion must hold true to the end of time, for there is and can be only the God who was revealed to the patriarchs and prophets of Israel as a doer of wondrous things, as a Saviour, Protector, Deliverer. That was the distinguishing mark of Israel when it was being established among the nations, and it must be her distinguishing mark when the time comes for that nation to be restored.

The danger attending any great spiritual movement is the tendency to lose sight of its real inspiration and purpose in the multitude of its externals; in other words, the danger of regarding persons and things as the means rather than the medium of its accomplishment. For this reason there is danger of giving too much attention to the purely national aspect of Israel's present and future status. "Righteousness," a great Israelite said, "exalteth a nation," and nothing else can, no matter what a nation's lineage may be. But righteousness is not begotten of the carnal mind, nor is it natural to the carnal sense, so that it is clearly evident that a nation can be exalted or blessed, or be a blessing, only as it forsakes its material concepts and motives for spiritual ideals, and approximates these ideals in its character and life.

The word "Israel," like the word "Christian," has been subject to some misuse, in applying the name as if it betokened the life, whether or not the nature accompanied it. "He is not a Jew which is one outwardly," said Paul, "but he is a Jew which is one inwardly." Likewise a real Israelite is one who knows in himself that he is a son of God, and if this inward assurance is lacking, his national designation has no higher meaning to him than that of a Hottentot. We also rob the word Israelite of its proper signification if we use it as if it belonged only to a particular race, and could never have a broader application. It would be quite as logical to use the word Christian as belonging only to the Jews because its Founder was a Jew. Being universal in its nature, the word Israel belongs to the world, and in its new name will sometime be applicable to all humanity.

The descendants of Abraham, through Isaac and Jacob, were the first among mankind to acknowledge themselves as Israelites, that is, as children of God. The nations about them, while no more mortal than themselves, were without a knowledge of the one Deity, and served idols, or "strange gods." The best, therefore, among the Israelites always marked the highest human advance towards the apprehension of being as spiritual, and this alone is why Israel was named upon them as a nation. This national embodiment is what is sometimes called "literal Israel," in contradistinction to "spiritual Israel," or the application of the word in its purely spiritual meaning.

At the same time, however, it should be remembered that, without literal Israel, that is, without some visible human medium or instrument, spiritual Israel would have lacked the opportunity to become humanly known, just as it would have been impossible for Christianity to have obtained recognition and establishment, without some personal representatives through whom its nature and value might be expressed. It required the personal Jesus to make the Christ known to human sense, and for a similar reason, it has required the great body of his personal followers to continue that work.

The truth about God and man has always been present, but until it was perceived by the Hebrew patriarchs it remained out of touch with human need. Thus it was through the personal experience of Abraham, Isaac, and Jacob, that the Israel of Spirit, the revelation of the oneness of God and the divine sonship of man, began to be humanly apprehended; and while human sense lasts, the Word will continue to be made flesh and to dwell among us — in other words, be humanly apprehended and expressed. Until human thought is wholly regenerated, the letter and the Spirit must bear witness together; for without the letter, the literal or outward manifestation, the Spirit could not reach humanity; and without the Spirit, as the apostle writes, the letter would be dead.

Consequently, when Israel as a nation relinquished her hold of spirituality, she lost the mainspring of her nationhood, and became dead, to herself and to the world. But her history is not to end there. When the time of her oppressor runs its full course, when the Israelites return to the worship of the God of their fathers, their national existence is to be revived. The one could not take place without the other, any more than Jesus could have brought Lazarus from the dead without giving back to him his quickened body, in order that he might be known to his friends and resume his place among them.

Therefore, while this book is mainly concerned with the spiritual side of Israel's restoration, it will not lose sight of the physical or national side, for Israel redivivus must have its body through which to act. We must, however, avoid the mistake of putting the first last and the last first. When the Israel of Spirit is brought to light, Israel after the flesh will also be revealed; but to restore the latter and not the former would profit mankind nothing. When Shiloh comes, to him shall be "the gathering of the people," or the gathering of national Israel, but this gathering will not take place before. Israel the nation will bear its testimony at the right time, if the prophets saw their vision truly, but let us not forget that this national reappearance is secondary and dependent. Humanity is waiting to awaken to the presence of spiritual Israel, its purpose and meaning, and when this is realized "all nations shall flow unto it."

Chapter Six - Joseph and Judah

For Judah prevailed above his brethren, and of him came the chief ruler; but the birthright was Joseph's. — I Chron. 5: 2.

Gilead is Mine, and Manasseh is Mine; Ephraim also is the strength of Mine head; Judah is My lawgiver. — Ps. 60:7.

Give ear, O Shepherd of Israel, Thou that leadest Joseph like a flock. — Ps. 80: 1.

THE process of Divine selection, referred to in previous chapters, by which one was taken and the other left, and in which the order of human precedence was entirely ignored, is again seen in the choice of Joseph.

In his dream of the stars Joseph perceived that, although the second youngest son, he was to be given the highest place in his father's family, that is, in Israel, and that in time his race was to become the dominant factor in the world's affairs. And why? Evidently because of the unchanging law of the fitness of things, and not because of personal preference. Joseph's subsequent history demonstrated that he of all his brethren best embodied the idea of Israel, and this of itself would naturally point to him as chief among his brethren, and to his tribe as the logical head of the nation.

Joseph's star, to speak after the fashion of his dream, could only have been in the ascendancy, because he came next in the spiritual line of "the woman." The Scripture indicates that he was born in answer to Rachel's prayer. Material sense, in one of its many vagaries, had again attempted to prevent the continuance of Israel, inasmuch as Rachel, not Leah, was the wife of Jacob's choice, having been supplanted by Leah through her father's deception. It is well to remember, in reading these Hebrew narratives, that they deal primarily with conditions of thought, and not simply with material persons or passing events. "Things which are seen," said the writer of the book of Hebrews, "were not made of things which do appear." Neither is human destiny put together out of the driftwood of chance circumstances, but continually follows the upward movement of human thought.

From what the Scriptures reveal of the divine plan, it can be seen that God has never been influenced by the opinions of men, nor has He paid the slightest respect to the claims of human personality. Because of the omnipresence

41

of God, we know there is a law of good spiritually active in human affairs, a law of righteousness and goodness and truth. No one has ever ascended the hill of the Lord who had not clean hands and a pure heart. And so we shall find that the progress of Israel through human history has always been the progress of a higher sense of being than is found in the beliefs of materialism. Although these early pioneers of Christianity were men of like passions as other mortals, they undoubtedly had some genuine perception of the absolute nature of God, and were as loyal to that perception as the conditions of the age permitted. Their work was to prepare the way of the Lord, not to force conclusions which neither they nor the state of human thought were ready to adopt.

Betrayed by his own kindred, Joseph was taken into Egypt as a slave and sold to an officer of Pharaoh's court. The serpent sought to destroy him through the enmity of his brethren, after the manner of Cain, but failing in this it struck at him again, with more subtle and insidious intent, in the house of Potiphar, and he succeeded in retaining his moral liberty only at the price of a prison cell. Every reader of the Bible remembers his dramatic transit from that cell to the position of second ruler in the kingdom. In the interpretation of the king's dream it was given to Joseph to foresee the impending famine, and the means of preserving the people from destruction. We are all familiar with the beautiful story of the disclosure of his identity to his brethren, who had sold him into Egypt many years before and who had now come to buy corn; also the joy of his old father at learning that his favorite son was still alive and in such great power. Thus we find Jacob and his family, the embryonic nation of Israel, settling in Egypt under royal favor and taking root there.

When Joseph believed that his father's days were drawing to a close, he brought his two sons, Manasseh and Ephraim, born of his Egyptian wife, to receive the parental blessing. The high value attached to this act in the patriarchal age may be seen in the anguish of Esau when he discovered that he had been deprived of the blessing which was due him as the first-born. It was believed that the father spoke with the authority of God, and that his declarations would surely come to pass. Jacob accordingly blessed Joseph and his two sons, and formally adopted the latter into his own family. "And let my name be named on them, and the name of my fathers Abraham and Isaac." And what was Jacob's name to be thus conferred upon these boys, and what was the name of his fathers, used here in the singular as applying to both of these patriarchs, but the name of Israel? Names were frequently used by the Hebrews to denote the character of the person, and especially so when it was afterwards changed, as in the case of Jacob to Israel. This word was also used to imply authority, as in the phrase, "in the name of the Lord."

Jacob here used the word in both senses. Manasseh and Ephraim were to be endowed with the characteristics of the three great patriarchs, and were to bear their name, that is, continue in their race the authority and power over evil implied in the word Israel. They were jointly to take up the line of succession as inheritors of the promise made to Abraham, Isaac, and Jacob. In calling his name over them, Jacob was thinking of something greater than the personality of himself or of his fathers. He was evidently referring to their close acquaintance with Him who had called the universe into being, an acquaintance so well founded and confirmed that to describe Him as the "God of Israel" was sufficient assurance of correct designation. In here calling the name of Israel on the sons of Joseph, he was doing more than merely admitting them into his family, more than placing them upon an equal footing with his sons: he was making them the joint guardians and defenders of the covenant. Theirs it would be, in a special sense, to make the God of Israel known in all the earth.

"The Angel which redeemed me from all evil, bless the lads." What had protected Jacob from evil? It was very evidently not a person, but what he believed and knew of God. In his dream at Bethel the Lord said to him, "Behold, I am with thee, and will keep thee in all places whither thou goest," and it was this realization of the presence of God which gave him the assurance of divine protection. According to the manner of his time, he called this transcendent consciousness of good an angel, that is, a messenger of God, which in reality it was. In this passage Jacob intimates that these boys were to be blessed by the same knowledge of God which had formed the basis of the covenant with himself and his fathers, and which was and is and ever will be the spiritual life of Israel.

In placing his right hand upon the head of Ephraim the younger son, as a sign that he was to have the chief place in Joseph's family and in the nation, Jacob was guided by spiritual insight and not personal caprice. The transfer of the birthright from Reuben to Joseph, because of the former's moral unfitness, need not be enlarged upon here, except to note the fact that moral and spiritual qualities, and not the order of birth, was the one consideration or influence in laying the foundation of the line of Israel. Jacob had seen enough of the Divine impartiality to know that the human law of primogeniture was entirely secondary and inconsequential in relation to His purposes. This ancient custom was a purely human institution, and carried with it no spiritual blessing or privilege above the rest of the family. There was, therefore, no added blessing due to Ephraim because he was chosen before his elder brother as successor to the birthright, nor, for the same reason, was Manasseh deprived of any real good in being given second place. It is well to note here also that, although Ephraim was to have the headship of the nation, there was no intimation of any servitude on the one side or of domination on the other. The two were to remain united as the house of Joseph, and thus united, they were to fulfil the destiny of Israel among the nations.

This is brought out more fully as we read further: "And he blessed them that day, saying, In thee shall Israel bless." In "thee," — in Ephraim and Manasseh as one, — "shall Israel bless," or give out blessing. If Jacob had intended to discriminate between the two in this spiritual blessing, he would not have thus spoken of them as one. All that is implied in the name Israel was to be their special charge, — not as two, but as one. Their real blessing was that they should be a blessing, and should bring all nations to a knowledge of the Lord.

In view of the place they were to fill in the world, the equality of the blessing pronounced upon the sons of Joseph is highly significant, and its importance should not be passed over. Although Ephraim was to have the precedence, and it was to be the ten thousands of Ephraim and the thousands of Manasseh, the blessing spiritually was the same for each. As the standard-bearers of the covenant they were to be one, — one in aims, ideals, efforts, and success. "In thee [the house of Joseph] shall all Israel bless, saying, God make thee as Ephraim and as Manasseh," thus placing them upon a distinctly equal footing, save for priority. The mere birthright, for that matter, never did mean anything more than material inheritance and responsibility. Manasseh possessed no spiritual superiority over Ephraim on account of being the first-born, nor did the placing of Ephraim at the head of the family give him any spiritual advantage over his elder brother. It is well to remember that any importance attaching to the birthright was purely human, and had nothing to do with the spiritual line of Israel. We have already learned that God makes His selections according to worth, not according to birth. And so in the case of Ephraim and Manasseh, we can rightly think of them only as being unitedly the representative and executive of Israel. It is true the enmity of the serpent, always intent on promoting strife among brethren, might bring about a season of estrangement, but the unity of their destiny as the keepers of the covenant, and as the instruments of the accomplishment of Israel's mission in the earth, is stronger than evil and all its machinations.

Next in the record we have the classification of Jacob's twelve sons according to their individual characteristics, as given in the picturesque and figurative language of that time. Jacob was briefly describing what should befall them "in the last days." From this phrase it is evident that he was not speaking of them as individuals, but as branches of Israel. It was in his consciousness that Israel was born, and Jacob is now looking across the intervening years to the fulfilment of God's promise concerning his line. Great things had been spoken of his seed as had been of his fathers before him. Up to this time the stream had been flowing in one channel, but now it was to branch out into twelve. What was to be their course, and their relative influence and importance?

From Jacob's analysis of the character and quality of these human branches, it would appear that not all of them would contribute to the moral and spiritual strength of the nation. While admitted into the human family of Israel as the sons of Jacob, they were not all of the selected seed. To paraphrase a well-known passage in the New Testament, They are not all of spiritual Israel who are of national Israel. As Paul wrote to Timothy, "In a great house there are not only vessels of gold and of silver, but also of wood and of earth; and some to honor and some to dishonor." And so in the human side of Israel, that is, among the personal units making up the nation, there would be

44

the gold and the silver, the wood and the earth, some to honor and some to dishonor.

In his long and intimate association with his sons, during which he had doubtless instructed them in all that he had learned of God, he would naturally observe the quality and tendency of their thoughts, having in mind the time when they would enlarge into a nation, and become "as the sand which is upon the sea shore" for multitude. How had they received his instructions? or to what extent had they responded to the truth which he had imparted to them? What would be the blossom and the fruit to be borne by these vines, or types of thought? The old patriarch had probably pondered deeply and often over these things which were so near his heart, but he never lost the faith of his vision, and felt assured that Israel would in the end accomplish her high purpose.

It will be noticed that in these final prophetic words of Jacob, the most attention and the greatest prominence are given to Joseph and Judah. We have already seen the high place which the family of Joseph held in his thoughts, and here the old man's words glow with loving pride as he pictures the great destiny of his best beloved son. But it was not alone the effusion of a fond father, it was rather the joy of knowing that these blessings from God would come to the house of Joseph because it was the most worthy to receive them. The chief family among his sons in his own time, and the chief family of the nation that was yet to be, Joseph would become the object of envy and hatred. "The archers have sorely grieved him, and shot at him, and hated him: but his bow abode in strength, and the arms of his hands were made strong by the hands of the mighty God of Jacob: (from thence is the shepherd, the stone of Israel)." This "guardian stone," as Ferrar Fenton translates it, this symbol of God's presence with Jacob, was thus to be with Joseph "in the last days." He was to be strengthened by "the mighty God of Jacob," because, with the doubly-blessed families of Ephraim and Manasseh, would be found the vision of Jacob at Bethel, and the victory of Israel at Peniel.

The special distinction of Judah was that from him would come the kingly line. "The sceptre shall not depart from Judah, nor a lawgiver from between his feet, until Shiloh come." The records give scant information of this member of Jacob's family so far as possessing any particular fitness for this distinguished position such as we find in the case of Joseph. But Jacob was not depending upon records or human judgment. He was reading the future, somewhat dimly to be sure, in the light of revelation. His family as yet were but a handful, and centuries were to elapse before they would become a nation, or be under kingly government; but Jacob foresaw a royal line emerging from the family of Judah, and he foresaw that it would continue unbroken until such time as a greater than earthly rulers should appear in Israel and take over the government, first of this nation, and eventually of the whole world.

This remarkable pronouncement regarding his sons would naturally be treasured in their traditions, and its substance was probably put later into the poetic form in which we now have it. While it is presented in figures of speech which are not readily understood or interpreted by the modern reader, the important points that stand out with sufficient clearness to be not easily mistaken are these: that his statements referred to a period which would not begin for centuries after they were spoken, and which would continue until merely human government would be outgrown — that is, when divine law would be sufficiently perceived and loved to supersede it; that during that period Israel the nation would be divided into two main branches, that of Joseph and Judah; that the line of Joseph was to be the guardian, protector, and preserver of what Israel stood for, both literally and spiritually; that the line of Judah was the line of royalty, and from it would proceed the dynasty which would reign until people and nations learned to be governed by their obedience to good, rather than by human persons.

While these utterances of Jacob are valuable as confirming, in the light of subsequent events, the substantial accuracy of the early Scriptural records, it would be the crudest superstition to suppose that the future status of Joseph and Judah, or their relative positions in the family of Israel or in the world, were in any sense at his disposal. It would be equally superstitious to suppose that he was uttering the arbitrary decrees of a personal deity, of like changeableness and of like belief in good and evil as are the thoughts of mortals. Jacob was one of the parties to the Abrahamic covenant of blessing, and the one in whose experience Israel first appeared by name. "By faith" he saw the fulfilment of these promises "afar off" (Heb. 11:13), and he saw them being fulfilled in Joseph and Judah, and in a lesser degree in some of his other sons. From that mental elevation he perceived, in a rather general way, what would be the outcome of the seed implanted in human consciousness by himself and his fathers. Jesus referred to this exalted vision when he said to the Jews, "Your father Abraham rejoiced to see my day."

The chief function of Joseph, in being thus placed at the head of the nation, was not merely to supply the multiplicity of seed mentioned in the covenant with Abraham. This was the least vital part of the covenant. The supply of a large population to Israel is entirely inadequate as a reason for Joseph's preeminence. It is obvious that a multiplicity of seed would not of itself bless either Israel or the race generally. It would signify absolutely nothing to human welfare for the house of Joseph to become as the sand upon the seashore for multitude, unless this multitude also possessed the spiritual qualities through which good might reach and uplift mankind. We read that the angel said to Hagar, the Egyptian, "I will multiply thy seed exceedingly, that it shall not be numbered for multitude," but that does not place Ishmael on a level with Joseph. For that matter, the Chinese outnumber the Anglo-Saxons, but that does not mean they are more important to progress and civilization. As has been pointed out, the difference between the Israelites and the rest of the human race was not material but mental; it was a difference of consciousness, not of person or of numbers. The only advantage of a multiplicity of the seed of Israel after the flesh would be a correspondingly multiplicity of the seed of Israel after the Spirit, to be a leaven among the nations, which would mean that Joseph's high place in Israel and in the world implied something more valuable than numbers or material prestige. The promise to Abraham of a numerous posterity was contingent for its blessing upon his spirituality, and the spirituality of his seed, for otherwise they would be no greater blessing to the earth than a like number of other mortals.

It is true the kingly line was to come from Judah, but that does not necessarily imply spiritual superiority. The average king has not proved himself to be better, or more valuable to his race, than the average commoner. That kings should be born of Abraham was not the cardinal point of the covenant. Kings were born of Gentiles also. The foundation of the covenant with Abraham was not a question of kingship, but of his knowledge of and faithfulness to God. This oft-repeated covenant is summed up in the promise, "And thou shalt be a blessing," or more comprehensively stated, "In thee shall all families of the earth be blessed." It was wholly a covenant of blessing, and its nature was therefore essentially spiritual. The other and lesser features were incidental, and while they will not be lacking, their importance should not be unduly emphasized. The man who had left his father's house and his kindred, and who had proved his willingness to sacrifice his own son, if necessary, "for the kingdom of heaven's sake," would not be without his earthly reward. The good things of the human were to be his also, — lands, possessions, kindred, dominion, but the identifying sign of the rediscovery of Israel will not consist of these secondary things. It will not be found in a multitude of seed or of nations, nor will it be wealth or dominion. Israel in the latter days must be found blessing all the nations of the earth, and that will be the real test.

The history of the house of Judah up to the present time, that is to say, the history of the Jews as distinguished from the house of Joseph, and as dispersed among the nations, gives no indication of the fulfilment of the terms of the covenant. The Jews have not proved themselves to be the guardians and preservers of the true idea of Israel, or to be a blessing to all the families of the earth. Although the Messiah came through Judah, in the line of David, the Jews as a class absolutely repudiated him, and have since continued to do so. When the light for which Israel had waited and watched so long eventually came, as the prophets of Israel had foretold, Judah would have snuffed it out as a candle. The Jews were so blinded by the thought of earthly kingship that they could not recognize their heavenly King when he appeared, much less do him honor. "He came unto his own," his own family in Israel, the family of the kings, "and his own received him not."

Thus we turn to Joseph, the chosen representative of Israel, for the fulfilment of the covenant, not the covenant relating to a multitude of seed, or of material prosperity, or of political dominion, although these are necessarily included, but the covenant of spiritual blessing. It remains to be seen if Ephraim and Manasseh, the two in one of the house of Joseph, are found in their place in these latter days, the guardian of God's covenants, and a blessing to the human race.

47

Chapter Seven - From Horeb to the Red Sea

And God said unto Moses, I AM THAT I AM: and He said, Thus shalt thou say unto the children of Israel, I AM hath sent me unto you.

And God said moreover unto Moses, Thus shalt thou say unto the children of Israel, The Lord God of your fathers, the God of Abraham, the God of Isaac, and the God of Jacob, hath sent me unto you: this is My name for ever, and this is My memorial unto all generations. — Ex. 3: 14, 15.

And what one nation in the earth is like thy people, even like Israel, whom God went to redeem for a people to Himself, and to make Him a name, and to do for you great things and terrible, for thy land, before thy people, which thou redeemest to thee from Egypt, from the nations and their gods? — II Sam. 7: 23.

For He remembered His holy promise, and Abraham His servant.

And He brought forth His people with joy, and His chosen with gladness. — Ps. 105: 42, 43.

SOMETIME after the passing of Joseph a new dynasty arose in Egypt which looked upon the Hebrews with disfavor, ostensibly because of their rapid increase, and means were sought to prevent their becoming a menace to the Egyptians. A system of industrial oppression was deliberately planned and executed in order to lessen their numbers, but failed of its purpose. Finally according to tradition, the king, becoming frightened because of a prophecy that a Hebrew would be born who would overthrow his kingdom, decreed the destruction of all the male infants of the Israelites.

With the birth and remarkable preservation of Moses the line of the woman again swings into view. The enmity of the serpent, becoming instinctively aroused at the approach of the next step, forward in the spiritual march of Israel, would have wiped out the whole Hebrew race to prevent it. The carnal mind's resistance to everything spiritual would have frustrated the deliverance of Israel by destroying the human instrument chosen for this work, an attempt that was repeated some thirteen centuries later at the time of the birth of Jesus; but the means by which God has been made known to humanity has never been left unprotected, for it is not in the power of evil to deflect a single ray of Truth on its way to earth.

God's impartial choice of an instrument for His purpose is again seen in the selection of Moses. He was at this time to be made known to Israel, not as to a solitai-y individual, or to a family, but to a people; and the most receptive thought for this work was found neither in Joseph nor in Judah, but in Levi. It might be of interest to note here that, according to the Jewish Talmud, the men of this tribe had refused to enter the service of Pharaoh, for which wages were at first paid, and that they were not therefore pressed into the unpaid servitude later imposed upon the Hebrews. This would imply that the Levites were more alert than their brethren in detecting the snare which had been laid for them. Whether this may be true or not, it was again evident that

God is not influenced by the claims of human birthright or of family distinction, but is best known at the point in human consciousness where there is least resistance.

As an inmate of the royal household, Moses was necessarily dissociated from his own kindred, but with! all his Egyptian education and environment he remained at heart an Israelite. Eventually fleeing from Egypt, in consequence of his impetuous attempt to avenge a fellow countryman, we next find him in Midian employed as a shepherd by his father-in-law. In his quiet pastoral life, which appears to have continued during the forty years of his exile, he naturally thought much of the history of his race, of God's covenant with Abraham, Isaac, and Jacob, and of the desperate plight of his brethren in Egypt. There is no doubt that his communion with God, in the secret of his own thoughts, and his mental appeal for the deliverance of his people, prepared him in large measure for his unique mission.

On a day memorable in the history of Israel, Moses had taken his flocks to the slopes of Mount Horeb, when he was attracted by the appearance of a flaming bush, which burned without being consumed. Whether what he saw and heard that day was but the objectification of his own thoughts is immaterial. When it comes to that, nothing that we see or hear is external to our own mental consciousness. One thing, however, is certain: Moses there came face to face with a higher revelation of the nature and being of Deity than had yet been m.ade known. He became aware, not through the eye or ear, or any material sense, that he was in the very presence of the God of his fathers; and he felt that what was there present to his spiritual sense was not for the human eye to see, for we read that he "hid his face."

Moses was undoubtedly conscious of God's voice speaking to him, whether audibly or only mentally matters not. His subsequent history abundantly demonstrated that his instructions and his commission came from a divine source. We need have no doubt whatever, if we believe in God at all, that on this occasion Moses actually communed with the Infinite, and that he became aware, with the distinctness of a spoken command, that he was divinely commissioned to undertake the deliverance of his people. His natural reflections upon his humanly obvious infirmity, and his timorous lack of confidence, were met by the same divine assurance that came to Jacob at Bethel, "Certainly I will be with thee."

Moses' request for a definite name by which he could speak of God to the Israelites indicates the vague conception of Deity which apparently obtained among them. The result of his appeal was an unfoldment of the eternal nature of God. It became clear to him that what he and his fathers had worshipped was self-existent and unchanging Being. "And God said unto Moses, I AM THAT I AM"; in other words, I am now what I always was and always will be. Out on the quiet mountain side, far from the oppressor and the oppressed, the highest revelation of God up to that time was becoming articulate to human consciousness; and this divine revelation was to accompany Moses and enable him to be the deliverer of the children of Israel. He was to say that the I AM had sent him, and to assure them that this supreme, self-existent Being was the same God whom their fathers Abraham, Isaac, and Jacob had known; and that this was to be His name, His changeless character and identity, forever. Here was a clear affirmation of the oneness of Deity, whose nature, and whose relation to man, are necessarily incapable of change.

Moses, however, persisted in the belief that the people would not believe him nor credit his mission. How could he convince the Israelites that lie came to them from God? What token of authority could he show them that they would accept? And he was there given three signs, to prove to his people that God was with him, and would bring to pass all that he promised in His name. To the outward sense of things these "signs" might seem little better than juggler's tricks, wholly inconsistent with the dignity of the Almighty, so that it is necessary to get their metaphysical sense in order properly to appraise their value, or to understand their human and divine relation.

The first sign plainly signified the overcoming of the serpent. What could this sign mean except that the subtlety of evil had no power to harm when handled by a knowledge of the omnipotence of God? Many centuries later the great Master said, "Behold, I give you power to tread on serpents"; which obviously means far more than treading unharmed upon poisonous reptiles, and that is, overcoming the enmity of the carnal mind. This was exemplified throughout Moses' encounters with Pharaoh, when God gave him power to meet and defeat the hatred of evil towards the spiritual purpose of Israel.

The second sign distinctly implied the power to heal disease. The actual presence of God had been spiritually unveiled to Moses, and in that glorious light his fear of the disease most dreaded by the Hebrews was visibly uncovered to him and destroyed. To the unchanging perfection of the infinite I AM, disease could have no presence, and in this experience it was proved unmistakably that leprosy, with all other forms of disease, was but a falsity of human sense. This exhibition of divine healing was to be a sign to Israel of the authority of God's messenger. God declared Himself in Horeb, as He did afterwards in the wilderness of Shur, as "the Lord that healeth thee." This sign of healing, it will be remembered, also sealed the authority of the Messiah, and it must, consistently, be a sign also of the coming of "Shiloh," at the end of "the times of the Gentiles."

The third sign, that of the changing of water into blood, which was to be the most convincing of them all, would seem on the surface to be merely an act of magic, without the faintest relation to Moses' God-ordained ministry. But it may be recalled, in this connection, that, according to St. John, the first sign of Jesus' ministry was the changing of water into wine. The apparent metaphysical meaning of this third sign was, that an understanding of God gives men dominion over so-called material laws. This was to be a sign, not only to Moses but to Israel, and in this particular instance was to furnish the final proof of his divine authority. The evident design was to show that matter had neither law nor inherent substance wherewith to oppose man's spiritual dominion. It is undeniable that the intelligence or power which lay back of these signs, when thus metaphysically understood, was the Mind which we call God; and their logical purpose, when this is considered, was to show the unreliability of the evidence put forward by the mind which we call evil or material, otherwise designated as the carnal mind. Anything short of this would be purely human in its origin and purpose, and therefore incapable alike of blessing the human or of proving the divine. Moses was going forward on his mission to deliver his people by means of the truth that good and not evil is power, and the perception and expression of that truth has been and must continue to be the foundation of Israel in all ages.

It need not be supposed that the signs here delivered to Moses were for his day only, to be used merely for the purpose of convincing the doubting Thomases in the land of Goshen. They were to prove to the Israelites that the God of their fathers was not a myth but a reality, and that in His name they were to be redeemed; but these signs were, naturally, to remain until the "restitution of all things" is accomplished. These proofs of authority must, consequently, be presented by spiritual Israel today and tomorrow as well as yesterday. The Israelites of the twentieth century, held in the oppressive grasp of materialism, are not more likely to accept the divine Word without the proofs of its verity, than were the Israelites who were groaning under the oppression of Egypt. In the confusion of these latter days, when evil seems to be "going to and fro in the earth," there is danger of forgetting that "I AM THAT I AM" is God's name forever; and that His reign and authority must be understood and made visible "till He hath put all enemies under His feet."

While the Israelites were convinced that Moses was sent of God, Pharaoh was obdurate in refusing their appeal for liberty, and there followed that wonderful series of retributive experiences known as the plagues of Egypt. The carnal mind, insane with its sense of power over the bodies of men, and deaf to the demands of justice, blindly entered into a conflict with God. Pharaoh increased the oppression and multiplied the hardships of the Israelites, of those to whom God had said, "I will take you to Me for a people, and I will be to you a God." Pharaoh's challenge to the Almighty was like the beating of the sea against a rocky cliff, the only effect of which was to send the waves recoiling upon themselves. The sensual element in human thought would have destroyed Israel for its own gratification, but its hatred and fury only returned in torment upon itself.

It was not necessary for Moses, standing before Pharaoh as God's representative, to do more than to let the carnal mind experience the lash and the sting of its own evil thoughts, for it is certain that these evils or plagues could have no origin or source outside the carnal mind itself. Although the superstitious and unenlightened may believe otherwise, we should know in this day that it is morally and literally impossible for evil of any sort to come forth from God, or to be made use of by Him, since in His very nature He is essentially all good. Human consciousness is frightened and tormented by the images created by its own baleful thoughts, and by the exposure of its

51

own sinfulness, but never by the Love which is God.

Threatened finally with the fear of extinction, Pharaoh released his stranglehold upon the Israelites, and they began their momentous journey to the land which had been promised to Abraham, and to his descendants through Isaac and Jacob. The impressive prelude to this journey was the institution of the Passover, designed to commemorate Israel's deliverance from Egypt, and which remains in the language as a type of human redemption. More particularly, it may be said to typify the human journey from a material to a spiritual consciousness of existence. This ordinance was to be observed by the Israelites until the advent of the Messiah should make it unnecessary, but while the form and the symbols are no longer needed, the idea remains, and must continue inseparable from the real nature of Israel.

The morrow was to bring the Israelites freedom from industrial slavery, the right to national existence, and ultimately the possession of a national home. This liberty had been won, not through warfare or political influence, but through the demonstration of the sovereignty of Spirit over the asserted despotism of the carnal mind, although to the great mass of the Hebrews at that time it meant little more than release from intolerable hardship. The conflict between Moses and Pharaoh foreshadowed the greater and more lasting conflict between spiritual understanding and material belief, a conflict which must continue until evil is finally extinguished for lack of evidence. "We be Abraham's seed, and were never in bondage to any man," said the Jews to Jesus; but the Master, thinking of higher things than human posterity, replied, "If the Son...shall make you free, ye shall be free indeed." At Peniel Jacob had gained his spiritual victory as a "prince" or son of God. Moses was here doing the same, not for himself alone but for the nation. This idea of freedom was inherent in Israel from the beginning, and was finely expressed by St. Paul as "the glorious liberty of the children of God." Wherever Israel is today, she will have to prove her position by establishing freedom within her borders, in its industrial, political, medical, religious and other aspects, for the true seed of Abraham, those who rejoice to see the day of the Christ, cannot be held in bondage. As it was in Egypt, so it will be in America and England, and in the world: spiritual Israel will bring freedom to literal Israel, and eventually to all mankind.

And so we find the young nation setting out on its pilgrimage to the land promised long before to Abraham and his seed; but what they apparently did not understand was, that their journey was in reality mental, and that the real promised land was to be reached through dominion over their evil thoughts. Had they' recognized this, they might have been spared their long and needlessly devious wanderings. Because of its natural perversity and disinclination to reform, the human mind makes for itself a long road through the wilderness, along which it must learn its needed lessons.

It is true the Israelites had come "out of great tribulation," but they were withal a rebellious and stubborn people. They railed at Moses while he was working for their freedom, and when Pharaoh came in pursuit they reproached him for taking them out of Egypt. But with all that, other things being equal, the average Israelite of that time, standing fearfully before the Red Sea, and thinking of the comparative safety of his slave pen in Egypt, was not inferior to the average Christian of today if faced with as great danger.

The great distinction between the people of Israel and the nations around them was, that in Israel God was being proved to be a demonstrable reality, and not a mythical personality, as the prophet Elijah so convincingly proved in later years.

This, without question, must be regarded as an important point in the consideration of Israel restored, for the God of Israel must be proved by His people today as fully as He was in the early morning of our history; and this experience will be as indispensable in restoring Israel to her rightful place, literally and spiritually, as it was in bringing her out of Egyptian servitude. It were better that we seal our lips and lay aside our pens on the subject of Israel's restoration, unless we can show that the signs of Moses are being revived, and that our God is able to deliver from the Pharaoh of the twentieth century.

In a narrow pass, with the Red Sea across their path and the pursuing Egyptians close behind, the Israelites seemed indeed to be in their last extremity. From a materialistic standpoint there was no possible avenue of escape unless they could defeat the Egyptians, which seemed too unlikely to consider. What could God do for them in such a plight? Why had Moses led them there to die so miserably? Yet the command came for the children of Israel to go forward. "Certainly I will be with thee," God had said to Moses; and during their journey His presence was palpable to the human sense of the people as "a pillar of cloud," and at night as "a pillar of fire." "And the angel of God, which went before the camp of Israel, removed and went behind them; and the pillar of the cloud went from before their face, and stood behind them." Here was a wall of protection which no earthly power could break through. We read that this visible token of divine presence, which was a guide and a light to the Israelites, appeared as darkness to the Egyptians; and so it must ever seem to the carnal mind. In the light of this incident the story of the "angels of Mons," protecting the rear of the retreating British, does not seem such a remote possibility.

The Lord, Moses announced, was to fight for them that day, — not against the persons of the Egyptians in their rear, but against that which frightened them in the way forward, and that was their belief that matter could destroy their life. The human decree of material power, which threatened the Israelites with death if they obeyed the command to continue their march, was clearly shown to be without divine sanction. It was a self-destructive edict of the carnal mind, whose enmity spiritual Israel was to confound that day and save the nation alive. Moses was about to give them again, in an even larger meaning, his third sign, the proof of man's spiritual dominion over matter. Many centuries later Jesus gave the same proof by walking on the sea.

It is a matter of regret that writers on the Restoration period, as a general

53

rule, pay little or no attention to these tremendously vital points, inasmuch as the mental and moral enemies of Israel have been the same in all ages, and the means for their defeat must of necessity remain the same. The Scriptural record indicates that, as these enemies were overcome, the external enemies of the nation were easily vanquished. If it is true that Israel exists among the nations of the world today, she must stand for the same thing she stood for in the beginning, and that was the bruising of the head of the serpent, or the conquest of the carnal mind, the source of all evil. If this were not the purpose of Israel's existence, it must, naturally, be the opposite; that is to say, it would exist for the perpetuation of materialism. There is no choice but to acknowledge one of these positions. Israel restored would mean, without question, either the defeat or the enthronement of materialism, with all that is necessarily included in that term. One would have to read history with blind eyes not to know that the latter outcome would belie every revelation of God which came through Israel, and every announcement of her mission to be found within the covers of the Scriptures. Joshua made it unequivocably plain that Israel stood for the service of the Lord, not of Baal; of divine Mind, not of the carnal mind; and this fact must be recognized if one would not lose the keynote of this whole subject. Without her spiritual vision, Israel would be an empty sound, meaning nothing and imparting nothing to human welfare.

The children of Israel, encouraged by the undismayed faith of Moses, went forward, and the sea made way for their safe passage; but the pursuing Egyptians, urged onward in the mad effort to thwart the will of God, had no defense against those walls of water. To the immature thought of the Hebrews, their enemies met destruction at the hands of God, and even Moses appears to have gloried in that belief, but to the best thought of the present age such a view is harsh and repellent. It is to be remembered, however, that those were pre-Christian times, and although there had come the perception that God was all-powerful and eternal, apparently there was not the faintest glimpse of God as Love, of being Himself the life of all His creation.

Their remarkable deliverance naturally made a deep impression upon the thought of the Israelites, but there began to creep in at the same time the belief that the Almighty personally favored them above the rest of mankind, and that He looked upon their enemies as His enemies. Thus we find Moses and the people celebrating their escape from the Egyptians in a song that breathed the spirit of an Indian warrior gloating over his fallen enemies. "The Lord is a man of war," sang Moses; "Thy right hand, O Lord, hath dashed in pieces the enemy." It is true that this is poetry, and many extravagant expressions may be covered by poetic license, but this sentiment appeared to be the genuine conviction of the Israelites, and the crude conception of Deity therein set forth was no doubt responsible for the inhuman deeds which stained much of their later history. The unregenerate human mind is cruelty in itself, because its sole concern is for itself; and when this socalled mind claims Deity to be its particular champion and defender, it is capable of the utmost barbarity, as human records darkly testify.

Without doubt, it was Moses' absolute reliance upon God which preserved the Israelites at this critical time, but the Egyptians were plainly drawn to their destruction by their own evil impulses. God was no more the instrument of death to those thousands of mortals than He is to a new-born infant. It is sinful human thought that involves individuals and nations in trouble and disaster, and unless we recognize this fact of evil's self-punishment, we are not prepared to fully understand God's impartial attitude towards all mankind, and to discriminate between the utterances of divine inspiration and the human misinterpretation of God's relation to Israel which we sometimes find in the Old Testament narratives.

"And God spake unto Moses, and said unto him, I am the Lord; and I appeared unto Abraham, unto Isaac, and unto Jacob, by the name of God Almighty, but by My name JEHOVAH was I not known to them." The word which has been rendered thus into English has been given various meanings. According to one translator it meant literally a chief or chieftain, as the lord of a tribe or clan, and from this may have arisen the Hebrew concept of God as Jehovah, that is, as their own national and exclusive Deity. This idea was expressed in the song of Moses, and appears to have been readily accepted by the people. That God was to be their own Lord, the great chieftain or head of their group of families or tribes, afterwards to be known as the nation of Israel, naturally appealed to the thoughts of this primitive race, but it developed a narrow conception of Deity that was not helpful to themselves, either spiritually or nationally. It fostered the belief that they were a specially sacred people, of more consequence to God than the nations about them, the effect of which was to close their eyes to the nature of God as infinite good, and therefore as being in reality the same to all.

This limited or imperfect apprehension of divinity contained the seeds of future idolatry, but, notwithstanding this misconception of the Supreme Being, which was probably due in large measure to their association with the Egyptians, what was then known of the true God was to be found among the Israelites; and this knowledge, inseparable as it was from their national identity, precluded the possibility of their national extinction.

Chapter Eight - The Covenants in the Wilderness

He sent His word, and healed them, and delivered them from their destructions. — Ps. 107: 20.

If iniquity be in thine hand, put it far away, and let not wickedness dwell in thy tabernacles. — Job 11: 14.

THE Israelites were now well on their way to the redemption of God's promise to Abraham regarding their possession of the land of Canaan, but a long way it was destined to prove, and few of this large host were privileged to enter it. It was truly no light thing in that day nor is it in this, to acknowledge oneself to be an Israelite, for the inner meaning of that name implies dominion over evil. Because Jacob prevailed over his earthly weakness, up to the point of being divinely blessed, he was given the name or title of Israel; and the same subjugation of evil tendencies pertains to that name wherever it is rightly used. If we keep this well in view we shall find that we are not dealing with ordinary human history, but with the gradual unfolding to human consciousness of spiritual truth, as it was coming through this people.

Israel, so far as its meaning was rightly understood, constituted a challenge to the legitimacy of a dual nature in man. It took up the issue with evil on the ground of God's supremacy, that He alone is represented in creation, and, although the conflict was more or less fitful, the Israelites alone represented this issue in the world, and for that reason they were marking a course through history distinctly different from that of any other race or nation. It is sometimes difficult from this distance to fairly appreciate the peculiar position of this people, or how much they were accomplishing for the future of the human family. Notwithstanding their primitive and uncultured state, we must gratefully admit that they filled a most essential and vital place in the spiritual development of mankind, the logical outcome of which was the coming of Christianity.

The prolonged sojourn of the Israelites in the wilderness was but the expression of their mental unreadiness to be governed by God alone. The innate reluctance of human sense to yield to the divine, that is, to abandon the sensual for the spiritual, necessarily subjects it to disciplinary experiences. The Hebrews were willing enough to be Abraham's seed so far as inheriting a land "flowing with milk and honey," but it was quite another consideration to be the children of Israel in the true sense of overcoming their sinful tendencies. The thought of freedom in a land of plenty was certainly more attractive than making bricks in Egypt for a mere subsistence, but the larger meaning of liberty as the freedom to obey God, for which their father Abraham left his home and kindred, was not, it would seem, very clearly understood or esteemed by them.

The Israelites are frequently referred to as the people of the "covenant," meaning usually by that term the well-known covenant with Abraham, as if there were but one. There were two other covenants, however, up to this time of sufficient distinction to be named, and these were the covenants of Eden and Noah. Spiritual Israel began with the first, and may properly be called "the line of the woman," meaning by that phrase the spiritual subjugation of the carnal mind, as distinguished from the too unresisting submission to its suggestions by the majority of mankind.

The idea of national Israel began with the Abrahamic covenant, wherein, among other things, is the assurance of an innumerable posterity, which was to become divided into a "multitude of nations." This covenant was afterward confirmed with Isaac, and again with Jacob, which thus confined the constitution of national Israel to the latter's descendants. We read that God made this covenant with Abraham because he had obeyed His voice in preference to the impulses of human nature. This condition of obedience constituted its paramount factor on the human side, and its observance must necessarily be inseparable from Israel's destiny, both spiritually and as a nation.

In the course of time other covenants were added which amplified the meaning and mission of Israel in the world. The first of these was announced after the incident of the healing of the waters at Marah, and may be called the Covenant of Health. Possibly a more fitting name would be the Forgotten Covenant, since it appears to have completely escaped the notice of writers on this subject, although it will be found that nothing pertains more intimately to the function of the true Israelite, or to the interest and well-being of the human race. The phraseology is significantly clear and final: "If thou wilt diligently hearken to the voice of the Lord thy God, and wilt do that which is right in His sight, and wilt give ear to His commandments, and keep all His statutes, I will put none of these diseases upon thee, which I have brought upon the Egyptians: for I am the Lord that healeth thee." In Isaac Leeser's translation the last clause reads, "for I the Lord am thy physician," a most momentous statement surely, in view of the universal need of humanity for better health.

This covenant is a definite undertaking, under prescribed conditions, to maintain the health of Israel. The language and the meaning are unmistakable. Here it is given on Scriptural authority that the basis of health is righteousness, alias right thinking; while, conversely, it necessarily implies that the source of disease is unrighteousness, alias wrong thinking. This covenant also shows that health and healing lie directly in the line of spiritual Israel, while the processes of disease are to be found only in the carnal mind. Moses was teaching the children of Israel that only as they conformed to God's requirements could they receive protection from the troubles of the Egyptians, a term which to them meant the people who knew not God.

To emphasize this covenant it was repeated at Sinai: "And ye shall serve the Lord your God, and He shall bless thy bread and thy water; and I will take sickness away from the midst of thee." There is still another repetition in Deuteronomy 7:15. Why all these repetitions if this covenant was not intended to be operative, and if it did not involve in its operation the real life and prosperity of the Israelites? This oft-repeated covenant is precise and emphatic in its provision for the health of the people, without a modifying reference to or allowance for a human substitute. The statement, that God is the Physician of His people, is too absolute for exception, precisely as it is in other matters wherein He is named as their Saviour and Deliverer.

It is recorded in the book of Hebrews that Moses was "educated in all the wisdom of the Egyptians"; he must, accordingly, have been conversant with the modes of healing practised in that country. Therefore, in announcing this covenant of the Lord with reference to the health of the Israelites, and the divine means of healing disease, he could not have been ignorant of the fact that physicians and material medicines existed among the other nations. But he was also well aware that Israel was not to be patterned after these other nations. It had been declared that God would take them to Him for a people, and that He would be their God. The fact that no other nation acknowledged the God of Abraham, Isaac, and Jacob, was sufficient reason for the radical differences that might exist between Israel and her neighbors, in this as well as in other matters. God had brought them out from Egypt with "a mighty hand." He had taken them in safety through the Red Sea, and was surely equal to the redemption of their bodies from disease, provided they obeyed His voice. Had they not seen the sign of healing which Moses brought to them in Egypt, direct from his communion with God?

There appears to have been no murmuring or complaining on the part of the Israelites on account of this covenant. There was to them nothing illogical in the announcement that their health was to be contingent upon moral rather than physical conditions. It is apparent from this that they had progressed farther than the nations around them, inasmuch as they were ready to learn that disease was a product of evil thought. That this covenant was accepted literally by Moses and the people is seen from the fact that, in the elaborate code of laws and regulations which he later provided for them, there was no provision for the medical treatment of disease. There is no authentic record that the practice of medicine was ever taught in the Hebrew schools, or that there were any native physicians among them.

In a standard Bible Encyclopedia, these things are deplored as implying an inferiority on the part of the Israelites, totally unmindful of the fact that the practice of material medicine originated with idolatrous nations, not with the worshippers of the one God. To assume, therefore, that the healing efficacy of a right apprehension of Deity, supported by obedience to His commandments, is inferior to a pagan device, or to a chemical or herbal product, is to exalt the material above the spiritual, and to subordinate God in human esteem. When the Creator of all things became known to Israel as "the Lord that healeth thee," is it to be implied that He would be less skilful or successful than the physicians of Egypt? Or does this age impugn the wisdom of Moses and of the Israelites in accepting this covenant as providing the best means for maintaining or restoring their health? When David, long afterward, recognized God as One who "healeth all thy diseases," are we to assume that those who thus relied upon Him were placing their lives in jeopardy? or that He was less capable of exerting healing power than the physicians of the Gentiles? Is it possible that the standard of healing among the Israelites was below that of their image-worshipping neighbors, because they accepted this divine covenant of health?

We must remember that Israel was "a peculiar people" among the nations, not because her people were physically different, nor because they did not share with others the common feelings and failings of humanity, but because they acknowledged and worshipped God as One, and not as many. This, however, did not make them inferior to these other nations, but quite the contrary. They were certainly not to be condemned for refusing to conform to the ways of their idolatrous neighbors, since this is precisely what they were enjoined to do. We find that their troubles arose when they went after the "strange gods" of these same neighbors, and ceased to "hearken diligently" to the God of their fathers. It should not be thought strange that the Israelites adopted a mode of caring for their sick that was in conformity with their better ideal of Deity, but rather that that method should ever have been abandoned.

We are following the course of Israel for the simple and sole reason that the highest spiritual thought of the age was always found in her, and because of this, Israel has ever been the medium of divine revelation. God, being Spirit, plainly reveals Himself through spiritual sense, not through the material; why, then, should not the omnipotence of good be more readily apprehended and applied through spiritual than through material means? When Naaman the Syrian came to a prophet of Israel to be healed, it was not because there were no physicians in his own country. And when the healing was accomplished he did not say, "Now I know there are better physicians here than in my own land"; but "Now I know there is no God in all the earth, but in Israel." His experience unquestionably proved that there was a healing power in Israel that far surpassed the medical art of the Gentiles, no matter how much the materialistic commentator may deplore the inferiority of the Hebrews in that respect.

The great point of interest for students of the Scriptures, looking eagerly towards Israel's approaching restoration, is this: when she emerges from her long oblivion to take her place among! the nations, and to be the same spiritual force as of old, where will she stand in relation to these early covenants, which were given when God was to her a living and tangible reality? Will she, for instance, accept or repudiate this covenant of health, which was given to the Israelites after their wonderful deliverance from Egypt? Will she gladly acknowledge her former covenant, or will she say substantially. We are too material in this stage of our history to depend upon God for our health? Would this be Israel, the spiritual line of the woman, God's peculiar people through whom all the families of the earth are to be blessed? Will this be her position after the opportunities of thousands of years to progress beyond the knowledge of Moses and the people of that early period? If this be so, one might well ask in what direction our faces are turned?

Disappointing as it might seem, it is nevertheless true, that if Israel is today too absorbed in materialism to occupy the position she had reached thus early in her course, she is not ready to inherit the promise given to Abraham concerning his seed; for the essence of this promise is wholly spiritual, and its central purpose is to bless the nations. It is certain that if Israel is too spiritually impoverished to observe her covenants, then the "times of the Gentiles" are not yet ended, all statements to the contrary notwithstanding. What it really amounts to is simply this: if there is not sufficient spiritual light in

Israel to enable her to see that the Lord, as of old, is the real source of health to man, she has not reached the position of being blessed "above all people," for the conditions attached to all of the covenants were practically the same. It is very obvious that the restoration of Israel, if it means anything at all, must include the restoration of her former relationship to God in all that it meant in her early history, so that it could be said to her again, "I am the Lord that healeth thee."

The second covenant in the wilderness was announced at Sinai, and may be called the Covenant of Morals. "And Moses went up unto God, and the Lord called unto him out of the mountain, saying...Ye have seen what I did unto the Egyptians, and how I bare you on eagles' wings, and brought you unto Myself. Now therefore if ye will obey My voice indeed, and keep My covenant, then ye shall be a peculiar treasure unto Me above all people: ...And all the people answered together, and said, All that the Lord hath spoken we will do." In what is known as the Ten Commandments, the Israelites were shown specifically what the divine law demanded in its application to human life. In addition to this, the record contains a mass of detailed regulations, covering almost every conceivable misconduct in the relations of human beings, and which is usually referred to as the Mosaic law. These regulations, however, are not included in the Decalogue, which is a summary in ten definite statements of what men are not to do in order to maintain a right moral standard.

The moral law, as interpreted and annunciated by Moses, was probably as far as that age was prepared to go in its recognition of God's requirements. As it was, to the superstitious and terrified sense of the Israelites, this law was declared amid thunder and lightning, and accompanied by earthquake, fire and smoke. That this commotion symbolized the fears of the carnal mind, not the majesty of Jehovah, may be read in the clearer light of the New Testament. The writer of the Book of Hebrews contrasts the crude beliefs of that primitive period with the more enlightened and metaphysical ideals of the Christian era, albeit the relation of divinity to humanity remained unchanged. "For ye are not come unto the mount that might be touched, and that burned with fire, nor unto blackness, and darkness, and tempest, ...But ye are come unto mount Sion, and unto the city of the living God, the heavenly Jerusalem, and to an Innumerable company of angels." (12:18, 22.)

It is notable that this covenant of morals is the recognized basis of civil and criminal law in all English-speaking countries. The first mandatory clause, "Thou shalt have no other gods before Me," states the most profound truth of the inspired. Scriptures, namely, that God is One and All. To what extent this truth is understood and accepted in the countries referred to, as the substance of all real law, it is difficult to say; but that this understanding and acceptance must come, and be the chief agency in individual and national progress and salvation, should need no argument in its support.

While the highest apprehension of God's requirements in the Mosaic age was expressed in the Decalogue, their true import was well-nigh buried in their material interpretation and application. Although these laws were not perfect, they have been indispensable in the transitional journey of humanity towards the more spiritual meaning of divine law which is found in the teachings of Christ Jesus. In the harsher view of the earlier Israelites, it was believed that God was angry over mortals' transgressions of these laws, and that His anger could be placated only by punishment and sacrifice, a belief which is not yet entirely outgrown.

This belief, that vengeance upon the wrongdoer is pleasing to God, was terribly exemplified on the occasion of Moses' descent from the mountain with the tables of the law, to find the Israelites worshipping a golden calf. Apparently feeling himself called upon to vindicate the divine vengeance, he commanded the Levites to go among the people and slay without discrimination. This act seems to have been accepted without protest as quite consistent with the nature of Deity. Such an occurrence in a Christian land today would be Inconceivable, not because God Is not the same as then, but because human thought has Improved. This fact Illustrates the progressive nature of divine revelation. It has been found that human experience largely corresponds to the thoughts which are entertained of God. To the untutored thought of these Hebrews, Deity possessed many of the qualities which they found In themselves. They thought of Him as a "man of war," moved to anger and revenge as they were, and dealing pitilessly with the offender; but later in their history, thought had arisen to see Him as the "altogether lovely," as one who pitieth as a father and comforteth as a mother.

This concept of God as the punisher of sinners fell short of the ideal presented by the Messiah, in which good destroys evil, not the evildoer; but it met the need of the cruder thought of that time, and helped to clear the way for a more rational and redemptive view of the Almighty. The covenant of the law was at that time the next step forward, but being imperfect it would sometime have to be superseded, a fact which Jesus indicated when he summed up the whole law as love for God and man. The lesser light of the law is naturally included in the larger light of the Gospel, therefore the Ten Commandments are still taught in Christian lands. The true Christian obeys the moral law because of his love of goodness, and has, therefore, outgrown its condemnation; but Christianity, as a controlling spiritual force, has not yet taken its proper place, even in the countries of Christendom. Thus while the law of Sinai is superseded by the letter of Christianity, it still remains a very essential factor in the life of the world.

Although Moses was naturally influenced by the superstitious thought of his time, he towered above it like a mountain peak. One cannot read the record without being impressed with the fact that he possessed a very real and demonstrable knowledge of divine power, and with his steadfastness in fulfilling the great mission entrusted to him in the face of seemingly insurmountable difficulties. It is true that we find him, at one time, singing of God as a warrior chieftain triumphing in battle, but it was probably because he desired to contrast His almightiness with the impotence of the evil forces that opposed Him, and to do this in figures which the people could readily understand. And while he seems to have taken personal vengeance upon the people for their idolatry, it was doubtless prompted by jealousy for his God. There is no question that, far as his ideal may have been from that of Christianity, his knowledge of God was everything to him; and because of this, because he was loyal and obedient to what he perceived of the God of Israel, he was able to prove His supremacy even to material sense.

The covenants which were delivered to Israel in the wilderness journey, like the covenant which had been given to the fathers of the nation, were, without exception, conditioned upon obedience to God. No covenant would be worth anything to humanity that rested on anything less. The very name Israel, applied to a people, naturally meant, in its original sense, the children of God, or the people to whom the true God was becoming known. This does not mean that God, at any time, revealed Himself personally to every individual in the nation, but that the nation represented a knowledge of God that was available to every person in it. Those who were faithful to the recognition of God's oneness were true Israelites, but those who failed to do this were not, for that very reason, identified with the real Israel, although they may have been, in a racial sense, classed as members of the nation.

Thus we find that every covenant recorded in the Scriptures, which relates to man's relationship with God, is wholly conditional upon human thought and conduct, a fact which becomes self-evident when one realizes the unchanging nature of Deity. God could present no other side to humanity at any time but His infinite goodness. As the writer of the book of Job pointed out, it can make no difference to God whether men do well or ill, although it makes every difference to men themselves. The man who makes good predominant in his thoughts will have a vastly better experience than the man who allows evil to be predominant therein, let God stands in the same relation to both. It was the same with Israel and her covenants. They were operative when the human conditions were fulfilled, but without this they were as dead letters.

In announcing the covenant at Marah, Moses was giving utterance to a truth that applied not alone to the Hebrews in the wilderness, but to all humanity, and for all time: a truth as old as the multiplication table, and as simple and certain in its operation. Those who may have doubted the reliability of this compact were those who were not prepared to meet its requirements. As sure as God is God, and as sure as He is the same in all ages, no human ingenuity can devise a lasting or effective substitute for this divine source of health, any more than it can find a substitute for the multiplication table. In every age mortals have striven for means to evade the conditions of this covenant, but with only an apparent and transient success. The vanity of mortals, finding satisfaction in the flesh, seeks an alternative for goodness, but there is none to be found. If there were a real substitute for the health that results from obedience to God, then His government and protection are proved unnecessary.

In the covenant of Sinai, the first provision includes every condition divinely imposed upon man. The human transgression of this command has been illegitimately confined to the worship of heathen deities, such as prevailed at that time in the surrounding nations, and this may have been its immediate intent; but its more comprehensive significance, understood as men have learned more of the nature of divinity, involves the conclusion that this one God, the "one good," is the All of true being, the sum total of reality. "Do not I fill heaven and earth, saith the Lord?"

It does not seem likely, however, that this larger view of Deity was perceived by the Israelites of that period, but it is certain that the consciousness of the patriarchs and prophets was lighted by flashes of this truth, and that these flashes of spiritual light came to them as revelations from God; else they would not have caught their wonderful visions of the final destruction of evil, and the coming of the undisputed reign of good upon the earth. Human consciousness was very slowly journeying towards the "light" which St. John declares is God; but it was then only the very early hours of the morning, and there was a long way yet to be traversed. The end of the human journey will be the full realization of the infinitude of divinity, the all-inclusiveness of God and His creation, a realization which Jesus possessed, and which constitutes the transfiguring power of Christianity.

Chapter Nine - Proving the Word of the Lord

Your fathers tempted Me, proved Me, and saw My works forty years. - Heb. 3: 9.

When thou passest through the waters, I will be with thee; and through the rivers, they shall not overflow thee; when thou walkest through the fire, thou shalt not be burned; neither shall the flame kindle upon thee.

For I am the Lord thy God, the Holy One of Israel, thy Saviour. — Isa. 43: 2, 3.

THE forty years consumed by the Israelites in their passage from Egypt to Canaan covers one of the most eventful periods in human history, not because of the magnitude of the undertaking in transporting this large host with all their belongings across a difficult country, but because of the many palpable evidences of divine protection which accompanied them. It is a very simple matter for an individual or a nation to acknowledge belief in God, to establish forms of worship, to build temples for religious uses, to conform to an elaborate ritual; but it is a long step from an outward and superficial expression of religious belief, to a practical reliance upon divine power in time of need. The average religionist of today, for example, would be startled at the demand for a humanly tangible proof of the verity of the God of his creed, and of His protective and redemptive power.

And yet Moses did this, day in and day out, during forty years, for two or three million people, and in forms that the sceptic could not set aside as being incidental to the ordinary course of things. The spiritual mission of Israel, the necessity, in fact, for her existence, was to subdue and eventually destroy the carnal mind, and this would naturally involve experiences which might seem miraculous to that so-called mind, in that they would set aside its fixed beliefs of law and order. It should be self-evident on the face of things that a human being could not maintain a definite and prolonged spiritual activity without meeting opposition from the fleshly sense, and the necessity in every such case would be either to conquer that opposition or submit to its claims. This fact, which is confirmed in individual experience, accounts for the many backslidings of the Israelites.

As the leader of the children of Israel, taking them upon what may have seemed a venturesome enterprise, unaccustomed as they were to moral discipline, Moses was faced with the constant necessity of giving them definite evidence of the presence of their God to guide and deliver. It would have been not only useless, it would have been suicidal on more than one occasion, for Moses to have urged them to be satisfied with a prescribed religious belief, or with prayers to an unknown and distant Deity. It was at times a question of preserving their lives. When they came to Marah they found the water undrinkable, and that must needs be remedied. In the wilderness of Sin they found no means of subsistence, and the situation again seemed desperate. With the people clamoring for food, and with no visible supply at hand, what indeed, was Moses to do? The carnal mind argued that they would surely perish in that barren place, but, instead of despairing, Moses took the matter up with God. Was not the Lord the creator of the earth and the fulness thereof, and could He not sustain the Israelites where they were?

And where no food seemed to be, it was not only provided in abundance, but the supply was maintained, so that they suffered not from hunger during their prolonged wanderings. And where no water was, it was given them, more than once, from the rock. Thus signs were furnished them in plenty that the God of Israel was not a myth, or a far-off, inaccessible mystery, but a provable and present reality. And why not, since "the earth is full of the goodness of the Lord," and the goodness of the Lord is not made manifest in famine of bread or of water or of any needful thing? Moses rose in spiritual thought to see that, because the sustenance of life was spiritual, it was unlimited, as did Elisha and Jesus in after years; and his perception of this truth was sensibly manifested to the people in the supply of their need. If it is true that God is omnipresent, it must be possible at all times for mortals to realize His presence both humanly and divinely, that is to their physical as well as to their spiritual sense. These experiences in the wilderness should assure us that wherever the real Israel is today, there must be the proofs of God's presence as the Saviour of those who trust in Him. To discover Israel thus in these latter days is infinitely more important to humanity than the discovery of her national identity alone could possibly be.

When Israel left her bondage in Egypt and began her journey to the land of Canaan, it was to prove the word of the Lord as it came, first to Abraham, and lastly to Moses. Her beginning as a separate people rested on the same foundation, and this purpose of her national life was never withdrawn, though it was lost sight of for long periods; but whenever she came to know herself aright, it was always as God's instrument for making Himself known to men. Practically all of the books that have been written on the identity of modern Israel, although chiefly confined to the national or material phases of the question, are attempts to prove that the word of the Lord concerning her has worked out true. It is not logically possible, therefore, to separate Israel's career at any point from this specific and essential aspect of her existence, a fact which imparts a particular prominence to the existing force and effect of the covenants which have been given to her from time to time, and which cover and include all the essentials of a nation's welfare and success.

From her earliest history, when we must rely largely upon tradition for our information, to the time of her disappearance, it was a case of, "And the Lord said," or, "Thus saith the Lord"; and all through their experiences, the Israelites knew that that word had never failed them. It was always verified in good to them when they themselves were true. Therefore when Moses announced in what manner their food would be supplied while they were in the barren country, or how their water would be forthcoming where the country was dry, it did not seem unduly strange, or inconsistent with their thought of Deity, that He should care for them in this eminently practical way. It had been proved to them, over and over, that the word of the Lord was certain and conclusive, and when the need arose, its potency was found to be more effective than any possible human agency. This, of course, may not have expressed the attitude of every individual Israelite, but it certainly did express the loyal thought of the nation, and the remembrance of these things will simplify one's study of the history of this remarkable people, and will especially aid in determining the marks of her identity today as well as in days to come.

To be sure, it has always been the aim and endeavor of the carnal mind to discount or discredit everything in the Scriptures that suggests the miraculous, or that has arisen of a like nature in subsequent human experience. It has consistently, and often ingeniously, striven to account for the proofs of divine power in human affairs on the basis of what it calls natural means, and has eagerly seized upon every circumstance that might lend color to a possible coincidence or accidence in explanation of God's care and protection over His people. It has diligently worked out an explanation of some of the plagues as having resulted from purely natural occurrences, and of which Moses cleverly took advantage to deceive the Egyptians. In the same way, it has found that Naaman recovered from his leprosy by bathing in the river Jordan, and that Jesus healed the blind man with a bit of mud.

Confronted by the dread prospect of famine, the carnal mind asked in derisive terror, "Can God furnish a table in the wilderness?" The material thought of the Israelites taunted them with having left their Egyptian flesh-pots to perish of starvation, for how could they obtain food for their families in that desolate place? "And the Lord said, Behold I will rain bread from heaven for you," and He did so. What then became of the taunts of the carnal mind? On its own evidence it had been proved a false prophet and an unreliable witness. And the story would be told long afterwards to their children, and passed on through the generations, of how this large host were fed from day to day, as it were by the very hand of God, when there were no visible means from which to draw. It was thus proved that there was in very deed a God in Israel.

In this case also attempts have been made to show the absence of any superhuman agency, but, while it is claimed that a substance similar to the manna is found by the Arabs at a certain season of the year and under certain conditions, it is acknowledged that its continuous and abundant supply to the Israelites, and its absence on the Sabbath, must be attributed to divine power. It is not to be expected that the carnal element in human thought would willingly acknowledge the verity of spiritual facts, or the supremacy of divine law, for this acknowledgment would be fatal to its dominion over mankind; but it is plainly this very element of sensualism which the advancing perception of spirituality must destroy before paradise can be regained.

It is the recognition of such things as these which imparts a universal interest to the story of Israel, and links up the struggles of this early people with present-day problems and experiences, for to be positively assured of the verity of the divine Word is as vitally important now as then. The failure to realize that the goodness of God is ever at hand seems as apparent today as at any time in the past of our race. We cannot be said to have progressed so very far spiritually in advance of the Israelites in the wilderness, when "the cares of this world, the deceitfulness of riches, and the lust of other things" continue to prevent the Word from expressing its living reality in our midst. Surely the long expected restoration of Israel must mean vastly more than a political event, occurring in fulfilment of prophecy; more than the recognition by a great people of its ancient ancestry. To be complete, it must be the resurrection to spiritual-mindedness, and a return to the days when it was considered the natural thing to prove the words of the Lord, not as implying doubt, but as the expression and confirmation of faith in time of need. At the risk of undue repetition let it be said again, that it was only because there was proof in Israel that their God was above all the gods of the Gentiles, omnipotent in power to redeem from evil, that this people held God's covenant of blessing above the Canaanites or the Egyptians.

It will appear more fully as we proceed that a discussion of the subject of Israel cannot rightly be separated from its spiritual aspect. Throughout the Old Testament records we find that this nation prospered or failed according to its fidelity or infidelity to its highest concept of good, irrespective of external or so-called natural conditions. We know in all honesty that changes of time and circumstance do not exempt mortals from the demands of God. Although the outward face of things may change, and improved customs may replace the old, the connection between cause and effect, the nature of good and evil, and the commands of God, remain unaffected. The point in considering these things is this: before Israel can recover her lost position and identity, she will have to prove herself to be better than in former days, for the simple reason that the times of the Gentiles will not come to an end because of any arbitrary decree or the order of chronology, but because the thoughts of her people are returning to God.

The proving of the word of the Lord, however, was not always a pleasant experience for the Israelites. God's word was verified as surely in their failures as in their successes, in their defeats as well as in their triumphs, since the condition necessary to their prosperity had been plainly stated as obedience to His laws. This may be noted in connection with the covenant of health. Moses had announced the conditions under which their health would be maintained, but they repeatedly rebelled against the observance of those conditions, and suffered in consequence of their moral defection. Through their disobedience and rebellion they were slowly learning the absolute unchangeableness of the word of the Lord, and the consequent impossibility of ignoring it and remaining immune from suffering. The pestilence that befell the Israelites on more than one occasion did not disprove the covenant, but quite the reverse, since it was thereby shown that God's laws cannot be disregarded with impunity. Our boards and councils of health could learn from this an invaluable lesson, and instead of inspiring people with fear of disease, and with the belief that health can be maintained without respect to moral conditions, should arouse them to the necessity of bettering their moral and spiritual status. It is the unqualified teaching of the Scriptures that health is inseparable from holiness, that is, purity of thought and conduct, and it is unfortunate that our modern health authorities are conspicuously silent upon this supremely essential point.

The reason for touching on the relation of Israel to the question of health is that the Scriptures thus relate them, and that very intimately, so that the inner history of the Israelites and their prospective restoration cannot be reviewed without considering this aspect of their religious faith, and their recognition that God's help was available in all that entered into their human experience. Many works on the subject of Israel appear to largely if not entirely ignore this phase of her relation to God, and thus unwittingly confirm the arguments of the carnal mind. This silence would be unaccountable were it not that the general thought, even of Christendom, is still held In the grasp of materialism, to the evil of which it has not yet fully awakened. In the covenant of health the relative positions of Israel and Egypt, alias the Gentiles, are clearly set forth on this particular subject, and it would be but a partial view of the situation that left untouched a point so intimately related to both spiritual and literal Israel, not only in that age, but in every age, until human salvation shall finally be accomplished.

Israel, with its wealth of meaning, was not the outcome or the expression of a human theory, doctrine, or speculation. It did not rest upon the blind acceptance of any unproved proposition, or upon faith in an unknown or unknowable Deity. It grew out of something more tangible than the vagaries of human belief and superstition, and that was upon logical and actual evidence, too conclusive to be smothered in a theory, and too satisfying to be put aside as problematical. It was a degree of personal knowledge that assured Enoch, Noah, and Abraham of their relation to God and of His nearness to man. Faith they had, but it was born of communion, not of doctrine or education. They were too simple-hearted and open-minded, those old patriarchs, to be troubled over creedal definitions and sectarian differences. They lived nearer to the heart of things then. Artificiality in sentiment and superficiality in religious feeling were not the mental states that brought forth Israel, nor will Israel be brought back by any emotional makeshifts for spirituality. It is impossible to compress the world-wide scope and purpose of Israel's existence within the limits of a self -centered nationalism, or to confine the liberating spirit of this divinely inspired movement within the deadening folds of materialism, either in religion or medicine. The word *Israel* means to *rule with God,* a meaning which is quite the antithesis of subjugating oneself to the dictates of the carnal mind, and accepting its decree that spiritual truth has no dominion over the physical or animal sense.

Even Moses could not be induced to take a message of deliverance to the Hebrews in Egypt without some convincing token that he was telling them the truth. They must, naturally, have had some knowledge of the history of their beginning as a people, and of the extraordinary intimacy which had existed between their fathers and the God of Israel; and Moses was well aware that they would demand some proof that his communication was authentic, and that his promise of deliverance was well founded and dependable. It does seem somewhat remarkable that, in that supposedly credulous and superstitious age, they were more particular about demonstration than are the religionists of this more enlightened period, when the most amazingly contradictory theories about God are accepted without question. When the prophet Elijah restored her son to life, the widow of Zarephath said, "Now by this I know that thou art a man of God, and that the word of the Lord in thy mouth is truth." It should not be doubted that there will have to be a return to that primitive order of things before redemption will draw nigh to Israel, so that we also can say, Now I know, rather than. Now I believe.

In our thought of Israel's restoration, there is need to guard against repeating the fatal mistake of the Jews who, in their mad desire to set up a worldly kingdom, missed the vision of the Messiah. Many estimable and able men have devoted much of their lives to the solution of the identity of Israel in the present age, and there seems to be a danger among those who are following up their work to allow the material and temporal side of this question to overshadow the spiritual. In the fulfilment of the prophecies concerning Israel, the chief end is not the possession of a great kingdom, nor the attainment of political power and material prosperity, but that the Christ shall come to light again through her, that is, come again to human recognition, not to be rejected, but to establish God's government in the earth.

There was certainly no greater need for the Israelites, in their passage from Egypt to Canaan, from the land of bondage to the land of promise, to prove the truth of God's word, than there is for the Israel of today, confronted by different phases of the same enemy, in her emergence from an age-long captivity and obscurity to the re-possession of a new promised land, and her rebirth as the chosen of the Lord. As we look about us, what are we expecting to see as the real signs of her return? Unless there is a faithful attempt to prove the word of the Lord, in the latter days as in the former days, how may Israel know that her God today is the God of Abraham and Isaac and Jacob?

The other side of this question was, of course, the proving of the Israelites themselves. The part set before them was to obey the voice of the Lord, and to walk in His statutes. While their attitude to God was that He should bless them with His presence and protection, they were not always as willing in return to render Him their entire allegiance. There are always two parties, at least, to a covenant, and it is naturally binding upon all alike, according to their position. Although the Israelites were but human beings, and far from being the children of God in the full meaning, there was a degree to which they could go in fulfilling the law of righteousness, and to that possible degree they were not exempt from God's demands. The proving of the Israelites, however, was not an ordeal set for special occasions, or for a special people, but was the demand which rests upon all men to express the best they know. This demand seemed to apply more especially to them only because they knew more of the nature of Deity. The apostle teaches that a man is judged by what he has, not by what he has not. Thus the law of morality, which seemed to be as high as human thought could go at that time in the way of understanding and obeying God, is the standard by which we must judge them, rather than by the enlightenment and experience of later years.

The culminating test of the Israelites came when they approached the land which had been promised to them. One man from each tribe was chosen to spy out the country and report as to its condition and the obstacles to be encountered in its invasion. Two only of these representatives reported favorably, namely, Joshua of the tribe of Ephraim, the personal servant of Moses, and Caleb of the tribe of Judah. The others gave such an evil report that the people then and there abandoned all thought of attempting the invasion. They mourned and wept for disappointment, and complained against the Lord for having brought them into such a plight. Joshua and Caleb pled with them in vain. They became so mentally paralyzed with fear that they forgot what God had done for them since Moses came to their rescue in Egypt, and they were now as anxious to return to their wretched bondage as they had been to be freed from it.

But Moses knew that the word of the Lord could not be broken or set at naught by this rebellious people, notwithstanding that his labor and sacrifice appeared to have been in vain.

At God's direction he took them back into the wilderness, there to prepare another generation to carry out this enterprise. After about thirty-nine years we find Moses, with this new body of Israelites, again approaching the land of Canaan; but this time it was he who was not permitted to enter it. According to the record, he had transgressed in smiting the rock the second time to provide water for the people. His instructions were to "speak" unto the rock, but in his vexation over the rebellion of the Israelites he allowed his human selfhood to becloud his duty to God. In other words, he had exalted himself instead of giving God the glory, and in his remorse he felt that he had lost his own right to enter the land.

This incident cannot, of course, be regarded as implying that Moses was less worthy than the people under him. He naturally judged himself on the ground of his past knowledge and experience, and his self-condemnation was so complete that he doubted not it was the divine decree that he should not lead Israel into Canaan. So loyal was Moses to this conviction that, although in perfect health and vigor, he meekly accepted what he believed to be his just punishment, and retired unto the mountain to end his days.

The writer of the closing chapter of Deuteronomy thus speaks of one whose influence was deep and lasting upon the history of his race: "And there arose not a prophet since in Israel like unto Moses, whom the Lord knew face to face." The character of his thought is seen in his appeal that God might be with him in his leadership of Israel: "If Thy presence go not with me, carry us not up hence. For wherein shall it be known here that I and Thy people have found grace in Thy sight? is it not in that Thou goest with us? so shall we be separated, I and Thy people, from all the people that are upon the face of the earth." It was also written of him, and nothing could better describe his high qualities and attainment: "The Lord spake unto Moses face to face, as a man speaketh unto his friend."

Moses knew that Israel would mean nothing, and be nothing, without the presence of God, for only that realization could separate her from evil. The answer to his appeal was that glorious promise, "My presence shall go with thee," a promise that must remain while Israel shall endure. If this great patriarch recognized, so early in the day, that their consciousness of the presence of the Lord could alone distinguish this people, how much more should we realize this as that day is drawing to a close, and seek to identify Israel, not by material signs alone, but by the satisfying manifestation of the presence of God.

Chapter Ten - The Nation in the Making

In the same day the Lord made a covenant with Abram, saying, Unto thy seed have I given this land, from the river of Egypt unto the great river, the river Euphrates.

And I will give unto thee, and to thy seed after thee, the land wherein thou art a stranger, all the land of Canaan, for an everlasting possession; and I will be their God. — Gen. 15: 18; 17: 8.

Open ye the gates, that the righteous nation which keepeth the truth may enter in. — Isa. 26:2.

ANYONE who has carefully followed the history of the Hebrews, up to the time of their last captivity, such as is furnished by their own imperfect chronicles, must be impressed with the discouraging prospect that they would ever become, in very reality, the people of the Lord. It is natural to feel a sense of disappointment that a race which began so auspiciously, which produced so many shining lights, and bequeathed such a wealth of inspiring literature to the world, should apparently end its career so ignominiously. The answer to that, of course, as anticipated and recorded by themselves, is that their career is by no means ended, and that the greatness and glory of Israel is yet to be made manifest. Upon the fulfilment of that expectation rests the veracity and value of much of the Old Testament writings, and therein also lies the interest which many feel in the relation of Scriptural prophecy to the present age.

At the time of her sojourn in the wilderness, the nation of Israel was but an unformed, rude mass, waiting to be burned and hammered into shape by the terrible experiences through which she was to pass. When Moses took this people out of Egypt and led them safely to the borders of Canaan, he was no doubt persuaded of their readiness and ability, under God's direction, to take possession of the land; but their utter failure even to make the attempt led him to see that a long time must elapse before the nation would be spiritually ready to receive the blessings which God had promised to the seed of Abraham. This appears to have been impressed upon him still more during their protracted wandering in the wilderness, in view of his many warnings and exhortations, and his expressed fears concerning their future.

It becomes more evident as we proceed that we cannot judge this people altogether by the ordinary standing of nations, either of their time or ours, for from the beginning they constituted a class by themselves. There was something about this race which preserved it from sinking wholly to the moral level of the surrounding nations, and which is destined to bring them into their proper place and recognition, and that is, that through it runs the line of "the woman"; although a very thin line it has seemed to be as we follow its course, at times disappearing altogether, but always reappearing. And like the famous "thin red line" of the British armies, it has withstood all the efforts of the enemy to break through and destroy Israel. The selection of the descendants of Abraham, through Isaac and Jacob, to become a separate nation, was undoubtedly to provide a refuge for the spiritual seed of the woman, and the opportunity for its development and increase, so that through it all mankind might eventually be redeemed.

Thus the real significance of Israel, used as a title rather than a name, is found to be the spiritual conquest of the carnal mind, a conquest that must necessarily be fought out on the recognition that man is in reality the son of God, and not a creature of the earth, earthy. A practical knowledge of this original and unchanging truth of creation is all that can effectually bruise the head of the serpent, and unfold the fact of their real divinity to the spiritual consciousness of men. But to ascribe divine qualities to the human race of Israel, or to assume that they were as mortals the children of God, is not warranted in the Scriptures, and subjects the human to a demand it is obviously unable to meet. The Israelites in the flesh were the same as all other mortals. It was the higher thought of Abraham, his spiritual perception of being, spoken of in the Scriptures as the seed of the woman, that made Israel Israel; and it was this spiritual sense of God and man that constituted her peculiarity in contrast with other races, and her only means of blessing herself and others. When the Israel of Spirit was in the ascendancy, when the nation recognized God for what He is and was faithful thereto, she was invariably prosperous and safe; when she did not do this, she was overcome by her enemies, and evil invaded her land. This shows precisely the relation to each other of spiritual and national Israel.

It is certain that nothing can result but disappointment if we look to the Hebrews, as a group of mortals, to find the good things which are spoken of Israel; for the good which human thought is spiritually capable of perceiving is not within but outside of itself. What Abraham and others gained such glorious glimpses of, was not derived from the human consciousness, but from the Divine. Therefore whatever of the truth about God which was perceived in Israel, through the exalted thought of her patriarchs and prophets, was not her private possession, and strengthened and enriched her national existence only as this truth governed their thoughts and lives. The human side of Israel was like the glass which admits light but is not the light. When there ceased to be any transparency through which it could appear, the divine glory was obscured to human sense, and at these times Israel felt that the Lord had forsaken her. When their sense of God's presence was thus beclouded, through their wickedness and idolatry, the Israelites were in the same spiritual darkness as their neighbors, and could claim no protection on account of being in the flesh the children of Abraham. The Ishmaelites and the Edomites, when it comes to that, were also in the flesh the children of Abraham. When the Hebrews gave themselves over to the worship of strange gods, they quickly discovered that the God of Israel made no discrimination between the person of an Israelite and the person of a Gentile.

The fidelity to God which was characteristic of Abraham does not come to a people by inheritance. It was not to be reasonably expected that the nation of Israel would be made up of Abrahams, Isaacs, and Jacobs, or that it would comprise a body of men of the type of Moses.

While the great Lawgiver had gone so close to God in consciousness that the divine glory shone wondrously upon the nation, it is apparent that the sensual element was dominant in the great mass of the people, and that it was vain to look for their immediate transformation. One has but to consider how painfully slow has been the evangelization of the so-called Christian nations, in order to understand the spiritual inertia of national Israel and the sluggishness of her upward movement.

It is a mistake, therefore, to demand great things of the Israelites at this time. Taking into account the average lifetime of nations, this people were but in their infancy. We have seen how Moses had to coax and coddle them like children, and correct them for their waywardness, ever since he brought them out of Egypt. They had increased in a strange land until they were a numerous people, but they had no national home, no national government or laws to whose restraint they might have grown accustomed from childhood; and upon the top of all this came the crushing weight of their serfdom to the Egyptians. Apart from the fact of a common lineage, all that seemed to bind them together were their religious traditions, in which was preserved the prophecy made to Abraham that his seed would be in bondage in a strange land, and that "afterward shall they come out with great substance." This no doubt kept alive their hope, and prepared them to some extent for the mission of Moses; but it does not appear from the record that they had developed to any appreciable degree the qualities which had distinguished the fathers of their race.

Out of this unformed mass Moses patiently evolved some definite form of organic unity, in which God was acknowledged to be the chief Head and supreme Judge. He worked out for them a well-defined order of government and a code of civil and religious laws by which their affairs were to be regulated, not only as they applied to their nomadic life in the wilderness, but when they were to be finally settled in Canaan. Every contingency in family and public life, in social and business relations, was provided for, with the details of enforcement, the agrarian laws being particularly wise in forestalling the possibility of the country becoming absorbed by large landholders. It was a confederation of twelve separate states or republics, held together by a community of religion rather than of race or worldly interest.

While the Israelites were awaiting the proper time for the invasion of Canaan, Moses diligently impressed upon them the imperative necessity of obeying God's laws. He set before them in plain and graphic language the blessings which would be theirs if they remained faithful to the service of God: prosperity, health, and safety would attend them wherever they might be. In even more forceful and vivid language he pictured the reversal of these blessings if they disobeyed the word of God: disease, misfortune, famine, defeat, were to be their lot. It was not because of chance or accident that these evils were to come upon them, but as the direct result of serving more than one God.

The remarkable series of lessons, appeals, and admonitions which are recorded in the book of Deuteronomy give evidence of the nature of the material Moses had to work with in his efforts to mould a nation for the service of God. If Jesus so many centuries later could call the Jews a wicked and adulterous generation, one can readily appreciate the disappointments and difficulties which beset the great Lawgiver. The making of the Israelites into a nation fitted for God's purposes involved a greater task than delivering them from Egypt. The salvation of this nation, who were called to be God's people, meant something far more than the conquest of a small country or the setting up of a model commonwealth. It meant the conquest of more stubborn enemies than any to be found within the borders of Canaan, and these enemies were their own evil thoughts.

It was the essential destiny of Israel to belong to God alone: no other king and no other god were to be found there. "Thou shalt have no other gods before me" was to be the keynote of her religion and the foundation of her national existence. This truth alone contained the secret that was to make Israel a "peculiar treasure" above all people. It signified that the true Israelite was not to share his thoughts with evil, nor bow down to the lusts of the flesh. To him there could be but one God, one good, while evil, in all its seductiveness, was not something to be obeyed but unbelieved: that is, the claims of whatever would seek to usurp God's place were to be utterly repudiated. History records the continuous failure of the Israelites to be even approximately true to this divine command, nor does the history of the Christian nations, with all their accrued privilege, add greatly to the page. But the fact necessarily remains, struggle as mortals may to evade it, that the only road to the Heavenly City lies through the truth expressed in this First Commandment, announced to Israel at Sinai and later confirmed by the great Teacher of Christianity.

Moses' straightforward appeal to Israel to be loyal to her God has lost none of its force in the hundred or more generations which have since followed. His fine analysis of human perversity is equally pertinent to our own age, so slow has been the transforming process in human consciousness. The long road that stretched from Eden to Sinai, and that there widened out in its onward course, is not yet within sight of the end. All the hammering and burning endured by the sons of Jacob in their times of sore travail has not cleared their vision to behold the son of God; and until this is accomplished, until Israel is purified of her earthliness, these refining fires will not be extinguished. The God who said to Abraham, "Walk before Me, and be thou perfect," could never acknowledge less than His own likeness as the model for His people. It is the carnal mind which complains of this demand, which attempts to evade the First Commandment, and claims the right to enter heaven without self-sacrifice. We must think of Israel, therefore, in our own day also, as still in the making, and cease looking to sensual mortals for the impress of the divine idea.

In pronouncing his farewell blessing upon the children of Israel (Deut. 33), Moses, like Jacob, was thinking of far distant days rather than of the immediate future. His language is somewhat less mystical than Jacob's and he dwells with more kindliness on the qualities of some of the tribes. On this occasion, also, Joseph received the highest honor. It is particularly noteworthy that instead of blessing Ephraim and Manasseh as separate tribes, he, like Jacob, unites them in the house of Joseph, distinguishing between them only in point of numbers. As he saw it, they were to share the same blessing and work out a common destiny.

"His glory," he said of Joseph, "is like the firstling of his bullock"; in other words, the most excellent among the bullocks. The writers of the Old Testament, true to the Oriental mind, delighted in symbols and metaphors which are not always clear to the modern reader. In this passage the bull is symbolic of great strength and power; literally it meant the "strong one." This phrase would seem to refer mainly to the political power and financial strength of Joseph as the representative nation of Israel, and naturally indicated a time when the Israelites would be out of Canaan and fill a larger place in the world's affairs than they could possibly do in that small country.

"And his Horns are like the horns of unicorns: with them he shall push the people together to the ends of the earth." In the line of Symbolism this would seem to refer to the spiritual standing of Joseph among the nations. It is claimed that the translation here is faulty, there being no such animal as a unicorn except in ancient mythology. In the Revised Version this word is rendered "wild ox," but this does not improve such a passage as Psalms 92: 10, which reads, in that version, "My horn hast Thou exalted like the horn of the wild-ox," since there is no such animal as a one-horned wild-ox, and such a rendering entirely robs this fine passage of its meaning. Notwithstanding the opinion of scholars it seems very probable that the Hebrew writers had the unicorn in mind, mythical though it may have been, and that it conveyed a distinct meaning to them.

In the Old Testament the word horn is a symbol of power, conquest, dominion, kingdom, etc., according to the connection in which it is used. Here it seems to combine all of these meanings, and points to the far-reaching spiritual influence of the house of Joseph. In Harold Bayley's *Lost Language of Symbolism* it is said that the unicorn was the ancient crest of the kings of Israel, and that its horn typifies "the sword or Word of God." He also quotes an ancient Chinese tradition, probably derived from the Hebrews, in which the unicorn represents "the Alone, the powerful One, or the one God." These facts immediately invest the use of this word with a significance which anyone can apply for himself. All this, of course, happened before exception was taken to the use of this word, before the translation itself existed, so that we may well suppose the translators of the King James Version had sufficient reason for thus rendering these passages. Unfortunately the scholar and the higher critic are sometimes so absorbed with externals as to entirely miss the inner meaning.

If the house of Joseph is ever to fulfil the vision of Jacob and of Moses, it will surely have to be by her fidelity to the word of God. "The Alone, the powerful One, or the one God" certainly points to the opening command of the Decalogue, and the basic truth of the entire Scriptures. What else could make the house of Joseph great, and give her the chief place of honor among the nations, but her faithful recognition of the one God? What could exalt her horn, her power and dominion over evil, except her use, her demonstration, of the divine Word? What clearer interpretation of the ultimate spiritual triumph of Israel is there than this: "Not by might, nor by power, but by My spirit, saith the Lord"? Not by material might or political power shall Israel reach her high destiny, but by her spiritual understanding of the Word of God.

This is what St. Paul calls "the sword of the Spirit," and it is with this spiritual weapon, not with bayonets and guns, that Israel is to "push the people together to the ends of the earth." This clearly does not mean extermination, but their conquest through the blessing promised in the covenant with Abraham. The Gentile nations, those who are spiritually outside of Israel, are to be pushed to the end of their idolatry, to the end of their materialism, by the power of the Word demonstrated. That is, in the end they will become Israelites, and fulfil the prophecy of Isaiah that all nations will come to worship the Lord in Zion. May it not be more than a coincidence that the greatest power among the nations today, namely Great Britain, and no other, has the unicorn on her crest or coat of arms? and that the two great branches of the English-speaking race have literally scattered the Bible to the ends of the earth and among all nations? The next step will naturally be to follow this up with the proof of its spiritual power, that is, to carry the "signs" to the people in Egypt.

To quote again from Mr. Bayley's work: "In early Christian and pre-Christian times, the symbol of purity was the Unicorn," and as such we are told, it was frequently used as a trade mark by paper makers. "Among the Puritan paper makers and printers of the Middle Ages," says this writer, "the unicorn served obviously as an emblem, not of material, but of moral purity." This most effectually disposes of the opinion of the scholarly critics that the word unicorn was not a proper translation. What truly satisfying; meaning could one get from the statement that Joseph would "push the people" with "the horns of the wild-ox," or "wild-antelope" as some prefer? Surely the translators of the King James Version proved their wisdom, for they have given us a rendering of deepest meaning and exquisite beauty, and considered in the light of its symbolic significance, it is the only rendering that could properly fit the case. Moral purity is a surer mark of greatness than is political prestige, and not only Israel but all the nations must sometime take this to heart if they would learn the lesson of past ages and avoid their toll of suffering.

Thus the symbol of the unicorn, as the representation of moral purity, has a basic meaning and importance that continue along the whole line of Israel. This figure plainly stands for oneness. It means that good is unity and not mixture. It brings us again to Jesus' teaching that there is but one good, and this good, being spiritual, includes no materiality. The attempted mixture in man of the material and the spiritual, or of both good and evil, is not purity but adulteration. The making of Israel means the purifying of Israel, the clearing out of those adulterous qualities that were ever going after strange gods, strange men, and strange women, that is after the ungodlike. This was the adultery of Eden, that claimed to blend evil with good, the sensual with the spiritual, and to call it the God-created man; and it is the same subtle falsity that runs through all the idolatry of past and present.

The one God of the law accepted by Israel must be the foundation of her whole national life, if that nation is to endure and take her appointed place in God's plan. And this accepted law of oneness means, and can only mean, purity in all things, or unadulterated goodness. The one power indicated by the horn of the unicorn stands for the government of good alone, the kingdom of righteousness, in which evil is neither acknowledged nor obeyed. It stands for freedom from foreign elements, that is, freedom from what is meant by Gentile dominion. The house of Joseph, the representative of Israel in the latter days, must recognize this, and let it control her councils, impel her development, and inspire her administration. For what nation, fearing God, worshipping Him as the "all-powerful One," could aspire to the possession of an authority or an influence that is not wholly good!

The presence of the unicorn on the coat of arms of Great Britain today is a perpetual and prophetic challenge to that nation to lay hold of its ancient significance, and examine her attitude to the God of her fathers and to the covenants long since made with His people. The hands on the dial of destiny have moved so far forward that it is not too early to do this, and to take an inventory of things as they are, and have been, and of what they must be.

Chapter Eleven - The Covenant of Possession

Every place that the sole of your foot shall tread upon, that have I given unto you, as I said unto Moses. — Josh, 1: 3.

For if ye thoroughly amend your ways and your doings; if ye thoroughly execute judgment between a man and his neighbour;

If ye oppress not the stranger, the fatherless, and the widow, and shed not innocent blood in this place, neither walk after other gods to your hurt:

Then will I cause you to dwell in this place, in the land that I gave to your fathers, for ever and ever, — Jer. 7: 5-7.

IT is recorded that when Abraham left his father's house and came into Canaan the Lord said unto him, "Unto thy seed will I give this land." After his separation from Lot the promise was repeated: "Lift up now thine eyes, and look from the place where thou art northward, and southward, and eastward, and westward: for all the land which thou seest, to thee will I give it, and to thy seed for ever." It thus came to be known as the Promised Land, sacred to Israel as her God-provided heritage, and because of the promises which still cluster around it. Now that this land has been freed from the grasp of Turkey (Edom), the eyes of both Jewry and Christendom are centered upon it. Jesus said, "Jerusalem shall be trodden down of the Gentiles, until the times of the Gentiles be fulfilled," and men are asking each other if that time has not come. Are the promises, repeated again and again to the patriarchs and prophets of Israel, about to be redeemed? Will Israel and Judah, as long foretold, again become one nation and together acknowledge the government of God?

Abraham received this promise at a time when he was without home or country which he could call his own. when he had come out from his own kindred "unto a land that I will shew thee," and he was naturally expecting some direction as to his new abode. The inspired conviction that all the land where he then was would be the inheritance of his family came to his thought as a covenant from God, and he accepted it without question. To leave his ancestral home to become a waif and a wanderer was not God's reward for his unquestioning obedience, and we need feel no doubt that wisdom led him to regard this land as God's gift to himself and to his race.

At the time of the great famine, Jacob and his family left Canaan and became domiciled in Egypt, whence his descendants were taken by Moses about four hundred years later; and they were now about to claim possession of the land which had been promised to Abraham, and which they had doubtless continued to regard as the rightful home of Israel. Since "the earth is the Lord's," one portion can be no more sacred than another, but to the human sense of the Israelites the right to possess and occupy this particular country was practically incorporated in their religion. That God desired this people to inhabit the land of Canaan was as certain to Moses as that God had directed him to deliver them from their bondage and lead them hither.

Moses had rehearsed in detail the part which the Israelites were to play when they entered the land of Canaan. He made no attempt to minimize the difficulties they would encounter, nor the fierce nature of the people with whom they would have to contend. He did not encourage them to believe that God would do their work for them. Moses had declared, it is true, that God would cause their enemies to flee before them, but that was only in the event of their being obedient to His commands. The substance of their instructions, in addition to expelling the present inhabitants, was to destroy all traces of idolatry throughout the whole land, that their recognition of the true God be not turned aside or defiled, all of which is plainly metaphysical in its inner meaning and application. "An idol," Paul said to the Corinthians, "is nothing in the world." The altars, groves and images were but so much mindless matter, and in themselves were neither good nor bad; so that the command chiefly concerned the thoughts of the Israelites themselves. The ascent or improvement of human consciousness necessarily involved the casting out of evil, the overthrowing of the altars upon which it had sacrificed to its own passions, the breaking down of the mental images which inverted the divine qualities in man, and exalted evil in the name of good. In short, what was required of them in proof of their honesty was to put all unrighteousness out of themselves and obey good alone, which must naturally be the consummation of all true religion.

The chief object in providing a national home for the Israelites implied something more important than material ease and plenty, and that plainly was that they might there develop unhindered the pure worship of the one

God, which could not be so easily accomplished in a land of mixed races and ideals. This would seem to be the only logical reason for driving out the inhabitants of Canaan, and removing everything which might suggest false gods. That the failure fully to carry out the prescribed conditions of conquest would eventually lead to a compromise with the carnal mind, and so defeat the very purpose of possessing the land at all, is apparent at a glance, and confirms the wisdom, if not the means, of obtaining complete and undisputed occupancy.

Moses, however, appeared to have little confidence that the Israelites would follow his counsel, and made no attempt to conceal his belief that in the end they would become morally recreant and give themselves over to evil practices. While he does not exclude the possibility that they may be faithful and obedient, the plain inference is that they will join themselves to the wickedness of their enemies, and be lured into the depths of national perdition. The wisdom of thus impressing his forebodings upon the thought of the Israelites is decidedly open to question, since the anticipation of evil certainly has the tendency to bring it to pass. Having the forecast of their wrong doings handed down in their traditions and entered in their records, keeping it before the thought of themselves and their children, would bid fair to weaken their moral resistance and aid in bringing about their downfall.

It was the superstitious belief in those days, as it still is to some extent, that God dispenses evil as well as good to men, and Moses may have felt that the proper thing was to acquaint the Israelites with the evils which he believed were to come upon them, and to do this in the name of the Lord; but in the clearer light of Christianity, God is seen to be alike incapable of imparting evil or of acknowledging a power besides good. Predictions of evil, therefore, are not divinely inspired, except as they relate to its self-destruction as the necessary corollary of human progress. Notwithstanding the proclamation at Sinai of the First Commandment, Israel had not yet awakened to see that, as the acknowledgment of evil was the acknowledgment of a power besides God, it was identical with idolatry.

Because of their idolatrous materialism, the Israelites were to be eventually expelled from their own land, regardless of the promise to Abraham, and be dispersed among the nations of the earth; but the silver lining to Moses' gloomy forebodings is found in the covenant delivered to the Israelites while they were in the plains of Moab, and which related to their occupancy and possession of Canaan. Even though the nation of Israel should depart from the true God, the promise was that she would certainly return to her allegiance, and fill the place which had been assigned to her.

Israel's future is here touched upon only in general terms. The chief points in this covenant are: (1) Israel would not retain the possession of this land unless she fully executed her part of the covenant. She could not expect her lapses of disobedience to be passed over, or her periods of forgetfulness to be condoned. The result of playing fast and loose with the Almighty would be certain banishment from Canaan to endure her punishment among the Gentiles. (2) In this period of her second exile, she would awaken to her position and return to the service of God. (3) When she recovered the consciousness of her true relation to God she would be released from her captivity, restored to her ancient possessions, and receive the blessings which had been promised. History has verified the fulfilment of the first condition, and if the Scriptures are true the second must now be in the process of realization. The question of intense interest then is. How near may be the third?

The terms of this covenant should effectually dispose of the sentimental belief that God forgives sin without reformation. The Israelites were to be held as strictly to the actual performance of their part as God was looked to to perform His. It was a question of being true or untrue to their knowledge of God's laws, of being righteous or unrighteous. Hence the Promised Land signified more to this people than a mere place of habitation or a source of subsistence; its possession stood, and will so stand to the end of their history, as the token of their loyalty to God and of His presence with them. Wherever Israel is there will be found an affection for the land of Canaan, or Palestine as it is now called, different from that felt for any other portion of the globe; not alone because it was the birthplace of Christianity, but because it was the homeland of her national childhood, the land where God revealed Himself to Abraham, Isaac, and Jacob, and about which cluster the associations of her sacred writings.

The time had now come for Israel to enter this land for the first time as a distinct race. Joshua of the tribe of Ephraim, of whom it had been said, "he shall cause Israel to inherit it," had been selected to succeed Moses as leader of Israel. And never was land invaded in such strange fashion. It presented the appearance of a religious pilgrimage rather than a military campaign, and a religious pilgrimage in reality it was, whose beginning dated back to the first Passover feast in Egypt. And never was river forded by an army in such strange manner as the Jordan was that day. When the feet of the priests bearing the ark touched the water the river parted, and remained thus until the Israelites were safely across, although it was the flood time of year. Again they had abundantly proved the word of the Lord as given in the third sign to Moses, namely, that man, when governed by the Spirit of God, has dominion over so-called physical laws.

The first move of Joshua was to subdue the city of Jericho, and it is highly significant that he was instructed to conquer this city by mental instead of military means. Not by battering rams or engines of war, but by the united thought of the Israelites were the walls of Jericho cast down, recalling the words of the great Prophet of Israel, that if one had faith he could say "unto this mountain, Remove hence to yonder place; and it shall remove." It was the conquest of material resistance by the power of right thought. Israel had thus entered the Promised Land through spiritual ascendancy, and it is a logical inference that she will realize her restoration in the same way. It will not be by material might, physical force against physical force, but by reason of her spiritual conquests, that Israel will come to know herself again as God's chosen people, chosen, that is, to bear the lamp of spiritual illumination to the world.

But when Israel reenters the Promised Land in the latter days, it will not be as the slayer of women and children, nor as the wanton destroyer of men and cattle, for they read the word of the Lord differently in these days. Both Moses and Joshua misinterpreted the divine will concerning the people of Canaan. It seemed that they could conceive of no other way to possess the land except by destroying the inhabitants, a course evidently in keeping with the customs of the times, and which does not appear to have impressed the Israelites as Inconsistent with the character of Jehovah. Naturally we must judge them by the standards of their age rather than of our own, although it is not so very long since human life has been assessed at a much higher valuation than that which obtained during the conquest of Canaan.

The modern student reads with horror of the outrages perpetrated by the victorious Israelites, as they supposed at the command of the Lord, but it is questionable whether even the better nations of today are as far in advance of these people as we have fondly believed, when we remember that the cruelty of selfish indifference is not greatly removed from the cruelty of perpetration. When the great Anglo-Saxon race can witness for a generation the deliberate and unspeakable outrages which Turkey has inflicted upon the innocent Armenians, in contrast with which the Israelites' treatment of the Canaanites was tender mercy; when our enlightened and Christian governments stand blandly on one side while these outrages continue, without more than formal protests, without lifting a finger to suppress them, any criticism on our part of what the Israelites did in Canaan were as well left unsaid.

One thing we do know, that Israel does not make war that way today, although the nature of Deity has not changed, nor have His commands been altered; therefore we may know that the slaughter of the people of Canaan was not divinely inspired. The divine Spirit never prompted the doing of evil, and never sanctioned the misdeeds of Israel, albeit the leaders thereof regarded their course as authorized by God, and notwithstanding that the writers of the Old Testament have so recorded It. The absolute proof against It Is in the nature of God Himself. The bloody course pursued by the Israelites simply proved how finite and human was their concept of Deity, and how little they really understood of the divine nature.

Such affirmations as "The Lord said," can be true only of that which, If obeyed, would promote the activity of goodness, of that which would result In blessing to others as well as to the Israelites themselves. Whatever else has been recorded as God's command was but the outgrowth of human belief and superstition. The God of Israel, as we know Him today, was not behind the annihilation of the people of Jericho, or behind the other pitiless massacres which attended the conquest of this land. To the power that made a way for the Israelites through the Red Sea, that fed them forty years in the wilderness, that gave them water from the rock, there must have been a more

81

humane means of removing the Canaanites from the land than by killing them. And there was, if Joshua and the people had been prepared to see it. The command to have no mercy or pity upon the women and children of the cities which they conquered could not possibly emanate from Him who is the giver and preserver of life. It is absolutely futile, therefore, to attempt the reconciliation of these things with the will of God concerning Israel's entrance into Canaan. It is better to see these misdeeds for what they were — the outcome of that crude misconception of Deity on the part of the early Israelites which led them to believe they were the only people in the world whom He cared for, and that He approved the utter extermination of those nations which disputed their possession of this land.

The children of Israel made the too common mistake of regarding their enemies as human beings, instead of as the enmity to good which existed in their own thoughts, a mistake which the Master rebuked in directing his followers to love their enemies and to do them good. While it may not seem possible, even at this late date, to adjust human differences entirely on that basis, to the prevention of all national wars, the case of the Israelites was radically different. They had been brought from Egypt, as was believed, at God's direct command, land were to obtain possession of this land under divine guidance and protection. It was not a war of defence on their part, but of direct invasion, entirely unprovoked by the Canaanites, and justified only by the belief that this land had been bestowed upon them by God, a belief which, of itself, should have removed all occasion or excuse for improper conduct.

Under divine providence there must be a better way of conquering an enemy than by depriving him of life, for under God's direction men are inspired to do good, not evil. If the thought of the Israelites had been as united in observing the spirit of God's commands as it was in encompassing the material walls of Jericho, they would have been prepared to see that His way of giving them possession of this land included justice to all, and that in following that way they would hold the land in perpetuity and peace. Had they been prepared to see this, they would have gained control of this land by the law of right rather than of might, and the inhabitants of Canaan could have gone out in peace to lands they might call their own, impelled by a divine impulse that is gentler than human mercy and mightier than the force of arms.

It has been said in extenuation of the Israelites that they were ignorant of better things, and did the best they knew; but while this may be true, and we should not demand of them more than they possessed, this fact does not bestow God's sanction upon murder and rapine, nor does it divinely authorize what is morally unjustifiable. It will not help the cause of Israel nor illumine her return pathway to try to transform her past sins into righteousness, or to cover her moral shortcomings with the mantle of God's word. The Israelites expressed their views of Deity according to their habits of thought and feeling, and, although their recognition of God's oneness was no doubt genuine, it was very limited and imperfect, and more or less influenced by the superstition of the period. Because they lightly esteemed the lives of the Canaanites, whom they believed to be their enemies, they assumed that God delivered them into their hands to be exterminated, and they thus transcribed it; but advancing human thought has largely abandoned that cruel concept of Deity, although there is much progress yet to be made before the revelation of God as "Love" will be seen in its full glory and significance. In reading these early records we need to discriminate between that which was inspired by divine revelation, and that which merely reflected the Israelitish conception of Jehovah as the Lord of their nation alone, a conception which gave the color of divine sanction to the inhuman treatment of their foes, but which shut out the recognition of the impartial goodness of God.

But when all this is said, and despite their lack of refinement, we must admit that the Israelites, in comparison with other nations, were still the people of the Lord, and that His presence was with them in a different sense than can be said of others of that time. But that does not necessarily mean that the conduct of this people was above reproach. In many ways their example is valuable as a warning rather than as a model. The truth about God was slowly finding its way to human recognition through Israel, because, as has been repeatedly said, there was less opposition there; but there was much in the human side of Israel, and still is, to obstruct and delay the full recognition and acceptance of that truth. What is particularly helpful in these early records is their unmistakable unfoldment of man's spiritual relation to God, whose readiness to respond to the appeal of righteous faith was repeatedly exemplified throughout the career of this people. These evidences of divine power gave a glory and a value to the Hebrew Scriptures which all the enmity of the carnal mind has been unable to lessen or obscure, and they attach an interest to the present and the future status of this people which time has not succeeded in destroying.

At the time of the conquest Israel had not yet emerged from the dim twilight of tradition. We have no contemporaneous account of these occurrences. The records of the Pentateuch were apparently gathered from various sources, and were put together with none too nice regard for their proper order or the danger of repetition; and with interpolations and annotations by the compiler or transcriber inserted as original text, a clear and comprehensive reading is sometimes difficult. But there is no reasonable ground upon which to question the substance of these narratives. Because we know God is now, we know that He was then; and the experience of this people after coming into the light of history tends to confirm the great things which their traditions say God did for Israel in her earlier years. If we accept these past proofs of divine power, we may be sure that in the present and in the future God will do all that has been promised in His name by His inspired messengers.

We are here following the course of Israel from the beginning in order to get the true perspective of what lies behind, that we may thereby be helped to a true perspective of what lies before, and to some true idea of the infinity of the circle in which we now stand. Israel's tomorrows will be the development of her yesterdays; not that her past errors will continue to be repeated, but that the good which is enfolded in her history will serve to prepare the way for the coming of the day of the Lord. "Every plant which my heavenly Father hath not planted shall be rooted up," said Jesus; therefore the evil and the superstition which so beclouded the early glory of Israel will disappear with progress, but the good which was implanted there will bear its fruit in due season, to increase and replenish the earth. Truly Israel should know about her yesterdays if she would recognize herself today, and prepare for the great work which is awaiting her tomorrow.

Chapter Twelve - The Perils of Disobedience

If ye be willing and obedient, ye shall eat the good of the land. — Isa. 1: 19.

He hath shewed thee, O man, what is good; and what doth the Lord require of thee, but to do justly, and to love mercy, and to walk humbly with thy God? — Mic. 6: 8.

AFTER seven years the Israelites became weary of the conquest, and the land already taken was divided among the tribes. While the seven nations comprising the Canaanites proper were subdued they were not entirely driven from the country, about one-fourth of the land remaining in their possession. This failure fully to occupy the land of Canaan was in direct violation of their instructions, and left the covenant with Abraham only partially fulfilled; but the Israelites were too impatient to enjoy the bounties of this fertile country to consider seriously the danger of sharing the Promised Land with their enemies, a mistake for which they dearly paid in later years.

If there was one thing more than another that Moses urged upon the attention of the Israelites, it was the necessity of obedience to God as the indispensable condition of their safety and prosperity. This had been proved to them in some measure while they were yet in the wilderness, and the incident at Ai, in the early days of the conquest, again emphasized the demoralizing influence of disobedience. When they were unable to stand before their enemies they knew that they had transgressed against the Lord, and the nation mourned in humiliation. This lesson, however, needed to be repeated many times, and still continues to be repeated, for the human mind is slow to learn and take to heart the impossibility of disobeying the law of good and at the same time enjoying the fruits which come of righteousness. The blind expectation of the Israelites, that they could transgress God's commands and escape punishment, still survives in the prevalent belief that the sins and errors of mortals will be finally passed over and forgiven without their individual reformation.

While the terrible sentence against Achan and his family appears altogether out of proportion to the offense, it was not more inconsistent than the view of divine justice which in the later Christian centuries was embodied in the doctrine of eternal punishment; but it was imperative that the accepted belief concerning the administration of God's law, crude though it was, be carried out until a better understanding of that law was reached. It was their necessity to progress from where they were, and to put faith fully into effect what they conscientiously believed to be the divine will concerning the punishment of transgressors, else they would have remained stagnant or have degenerated into worse conditions. It was the carnal sense of the Israelites, the "old man" of the earth, not the offspring of God, that sinned and was punished; and the legitimate design of that punishment was to show the unprofitableness of fleshly servitude.

Moses had set before them the blessing and the curse that they might make their choice, but neither the promise of material blessings nor the threat of material curses has ever Impelled men to seek good for Its own sake; and without that selfless seeking, human peace and prosperity can have no permanent basis. The logical necessity of the truth, that good Includes all that Is substantial and enduring, Is that the delusion of satisfaction In evil must sometime be broken, If need be by the reaction of suffering. Thus In these experiences of Israel the human mind was becoming slowly aroused to the consciousness that evil carries Its own chastisement. The world has consumed a long time over this simple lesson in ethics, and there Is little to indicate that the lesson has yet been very well learned.

The Old Testament records devote considerable space to Israel's wrongdoings, not for the mere purpose of recounting evil or to inform future generations, but to show the consequences of sin and the wisdom of avoiding them. The passing of Joshua had left the Israelites without a leader, with their religion as the chief bond of union, but this bond began to weaken as they mingled with the Canaanites and were beguiled by their idolatries. The decline of their allegiance to Jehovah was naturally followed by dissensions and disunity, until "every man did that which was right in his own eyes," and as the carnal mind thus asserted its sway, the glory and prosperity of Israel relatively faded.

The worship of materiality, which is embodied in the idolatry of all ages, necessarily deadens the spiritual sense, and brings the idolaters into subjection to the evil they exalt. The conditions of which Moses and Joshua had repeatedly warned them, in the event of their serving false gods, now began to come upon the Israelites. The generation which had come into Canaan, which had seen the great things God had done for Israel in the wilderness and in subduing their enemies, had passed away, and another generation had arisen "which knew not the Lord, nor yet the works which he had done for Israel." Not having these proofs in their own experience, they turned the more readily to the deities of the Canaanites, which appealed to their lower senses, and thus placed themselves on the same level with the people whom they had been commanded to drive out of the land. They were to have no intercourse with these people, or even to make mention of the names of their gods. It is easy to understand the deleterious effect this condition would have upon the morale of the Israelites, which their enemies were quick to perceive and take advantage of. It was well known that Israel had obtained possession of this land through some means associated with their religion, and when they became apostate to that religion, the Canaanites seized the opportunity to attack and defeat them.

After several years of servitude to their enemies, the Israelites cried unto the Lord, and a deliverer was raised up for them. This recurrence of apostasy, disaster, repentance, and deliverance was repeated seven times between Joshua and Samuel, occupying altogether a period of more than four hundred years. It was a continual round of crying unto the Lord when they were sore oppressed, and of forsaking Him in time of safety; but God never failed to help them as often as they turned to Him in sincerity. These generations of sinning mortals might come and go, but there was that which remained unchanged from age to age, and that was the God of Israel. "For what nation is there," asked Moses, "who hath God so nigh unto them, as the Lord our God is in all things that we call upon Him for?" It is not recorded that any other nation recognized and acknowledged the same relationship to Deity. One might well ask why all this should be so when the Israelites proved so fickle in their allegiance, so unmindful of their privileges, and so forgetful of their blessings. Why, indeed, should God continue to succor and deliver this people, with all their wickedness and ingratitude, whenever they turned their faces towards Him?

Very obviously because He could not be untrue to Himself. As St. Paul said, "If we believe not, yet He abideth faithful; He cannot deny Himself." God cherished no resentment against the Israelites because of their backslidings and idolatries, for the simple reason that resentment, anger, and revenge are entirely foreign to the character of Deity. If it were possible for these qualities of the carnal mind to become identified with God, and thus to become part of the divine activity, His divine nature would necessarily be subverted and destroyed. It is the possession and practice of these evil qualities that constitute the sinfulness of mortals, and their need of redemption and regeneration; therefore it were impossible for God, who is the Redeemer of men, to express the qualities that make up His unlikeness. The superstition and ignorance of the time might think and write of Him as being hot with anger against the Israelites, or as selling them into the hands of their enemies; but Isaiah had a more enlightened sense when he said, "Ye have sold yourselves," since it was their own defection from good which delivered the Israelites into the hands of evil.

The chronicles relating to this period indicate how intensely human was the Israelites' conception of Deity. While they acknowledged God as their king, He was a king with the attributes of earthly rulers, the chief distinction between Jehovah and human beings seeming to be of degree rather than of quality. The thought of God as the sender of evil as well as good, as the destroyer as well as the giver of life, continued up to the time of the Messiah,

and to some extent still remains. A degraded view of Deity is the logical corollary of a degraded view of man; therefore, as a perfect and wholly good
creator was absolutely incompatible with an imperfect and sinful creation.
Deity was believed to be also conscious of evil, and to permit its defiling
presence throughout His universe. It was but a step from that belief to the
supposition that God Himself expressed evil in His dealings with men. This
conception was not indigenous to Israel, it was and is the doctrine of the carnal mind; and the carnal mind, by its very nature, is incapable of revealing
the truth about either God or man.

It will be remembered that when Jesus was once on the way to Jerusalem,
one of the Samaritan villages refused him hospitality, and some of his disciples asked, "Lord, wilt thou that we command fire to come down from heav-
en, and consume them, as Elijah did?" But Jesus rebuked them and said, "Ye
know not what manner of spirit ye are of. For the Son of man is not come to
destroy men's lives, but to save them." If, then, he who came forth from God
to do the will of the Father rebuked the suggestion of taking the lives of of-
fenders in return for their wrongdoing, we may know without a doubt that
God had nothing to do with bringing misfortune upon either the Israelites or
their enemies, beyond the fact that men may not transgress the law of His
infinitude and not experience the consequences.

As already stated, in reviewing the history of the Israelites we should consider the mental status of their times, and not expect their beliefs and practices to measure up to the better spirit which came in with Christianity. If the
qualities and activities ascribed to God by the early writers and compilers of
the Old Testament had been actually true, the world could not have progressed beyond them, for man may not become more excellent than his Maker; but human betterment has kept pace with improved thoughts of Deity,
and it must naturally so continue until God is perfectly understood in His
true character and being, and man is understood to be His likeness.

There is no doubt that the cause of true religion has been seriously imped-
ed by the superstitious assumption that every thing recorded of God in the
Hebrew Scriptures is divinely authorized, and must be accepted as infallible
truth. As Dean Hodges points out in his work, *How to Know the Bible,* Jesus
reproved the disciples for supposing that Elijah's interpretation of God's will
was applicable to their own time. In this instance the Master clearly implied
that each period must be judged by its own thoughts of good and evil, and its
own degree of enlightenment, not by the attainments of later ages. Thus the
beliefs entertained by the early Israelites as to the nature of God and His
dealings with men cannot be held as applicable or acceptable to the Christian
thought of the present day. While perfection has been the standard of Truth
in every age, the progress of humanity towards its attainment has been slow
and difficult, and is still far from the ideal presented by the Founder of Christianity.

The records of the Israelites during the period of the judges point to the
truth that a period or a people cannot rise higher than the ideals entertained

of Deity. The materiality of the human mind had been too dense to permit the line of spiritual illumination to continue unbroken.

There was a stretch of approximately six hundred years between Eve and Enoch, another gap of about a thousand years to Noah's building of the ark, then four hundred years to the covenant with Abraham, and four hundred years between Joseph and Moses. The contact of the Israelites with the people of Egypt, and afterwards with the people of Canaan, naturally left its influence upon their religious life. While they continued to acknowledge God as One and supreme, they had come under the suggestion that evil was part of the divine plan, and that view quite naturally influenced their intercourse with one another and with the neighboring peoples. This concept necessarily inspired fear of both God and man, and prompted the offering of sacrifices for the propitiation of Deity.

It should be readily seen that the true Israel was wholly separate from these pagan beliefs, for they were of Gentile origin, and hid from human view the true nature of divinity. Abraham's recognition of the demand for perfection could only have emanated from some glimpse of the perfection of Deity, but during their sojourn in Egypt the purity of this ideal was not preserved by the Israelites, becoming more or less corrupted by the polytheism of that country. The revelation of God's perfection came again to Moses at Horeb, and the light of that revelation illumined all their way from Egypt to Canaan. It was their sustenance in the wilderness and their protection in danger. But because of the disobedience of the Israelites in mingling with the people of Canaan and participating in their idolatry, the light again became obscured, until they saw God only through the lens of their own earthly nature, and believed Him to be like men. This supposition, that God possesses qualities which are morally wrong in human beings, would necessarily prevent human beings from overcoming these errors in themselves, and must continue to be inimical to the well-being of mankind.

But however imperfectly they represented in their lives the spiritual meaning of Israel, it is evident that the highest thought of their time was always to be found among them, the discrepancy between their practices and what had been taught and proved to them of God being no greater than now obtains between Christians and Christianity. The ancestry of the Gentile races, and their development and history, are not such as to warrant a belief that they ever replaced Israel as God's medium of revelation. It is true, as their own records testify, that the Israelites were continually straying into forbidden paths. Over and over again we find them in rebellion against the commands of the Lord, or bowing themselves to the gods of the heathen, but to none of their Gentile neighbors could one turn with the hope of discovering the light which seemed to be darkened in Israel. And when the time is come for the reappearing of the Christ, it must needs be in Israel that the full shining of the light will be seen, and whence it will send out its rays to all mankind; for it were not possible that this light should first appear in other than the most spiritual consciousness.

The raising up of the obscure individuals known as the judges to redeem the fortunes of Israel, and to restore some degree of national unity, furnishes a notable chapter in the history of this people. Notwithstanding her sins, God had not wholly forsaken Israel, nor was He without a witness in her. Although the mission of the judges mainly appeared to be to deliver the Israelites from their enemies, and was therefore more military than religious, they nevertheless stood for God's supremacy. The case of Gideon is notably interesting because of his demand for signs from the Lord before he would undertake the national cause. The first sign, that dew should be on the fleece only and not on the ground, was reversed in the second sign, that he might be sure it was not a coincidence or chance event. His remarkable victory over the Midianites with the mere handful of men whom wisdom had selected for him has continued an inspiring illustration of what a few can do when relying upon God.

The signs which Gideon asked of God, while apparently irrelevant to the circumstances, and the mere whim of a sceptic, were nevertheless indicative of the fundamental purpose of Israel's existence, namely, the conquest of materiality. In each instance Gideon was asking that the so-called laws of nature, as he had observed them, be set aside as a token that it was God who was directing him. The selection of the fleece and the dew was merely incidental. What Gideon was dimly seeking after was what humanity today is dimly seeking after, and that is the satisfying consciousness that there is a divine power which can be laid hold of and utilized to overrule the seemingly fixed modes of material sense, which today may seem beneficial, but which tomorrow may hold one in oppressive bondage. This was set forth in the Master's declaration to his disciples, "Behold I give you power...over all the power of the enemy," and this enemy is the carnal mind, the mind which claims to be material and to rule man by material law.

Gideon undoubtedly showed himself to be a true Israelite in seeking a token of this nature. He knew that Israel could only be saved by the aid of spiritual power, as had been the case from the beginning; and he wanted some visible assurance that the same Presence which had been with Moses in his undertakings, and which had been with Joshua, would also be with him. He naturally felt that if he were being inspired by the God of Israel to do this work, he could surely discover it by some sign which involved the setting aside of what the human mind regards as law. What the world has been slow to perceive is, that the salvation of national Israel from the varying conditions indicated in the Scriptures, and the salvation of the human mind from error, are identical. Their belief in material power and intelligence holds mankind in a bondage as hard and unrelenting as that of the Israelites in Egypt, and it was this idolatrous belief in a power and intelligence apart from God that the line of the woman started out to overcome and destroy. Gideon here proved, as Moses did before him, that the material conditions which are named laws exist only in the carnal mind, and do not therefore belong to God's creation and government.

The spell of heathen idolatry does not appear to have been entirely broken under any of the judges. The influence of the belief in false gods had become so tenacious that the inconsistency of serving them, while at the same time formally acknowledging the national Jehovah or Lord, had ceased to be recognized. The punishment which came upon one generation did not deter the next from following the same course, until the lofty concept of God and of fidelity thereto, which distinguished the early patriarchs, had almost disappeared.

Unfortunately the practice of idolatry has by no means been confined to the age of the judges, nor to any or all of the ages preceding or succeeding it. The Israelites fell into the snare of idolizing the sensual concepts of the carnal mind, and so do we today. Under the spell of the serpent, they bowed down to other gods besides the one God of Israel, and so do we today.

It is true we do not offer sacrifices or burn incense to Baal or Moloch or Ashtoreth, but the difference is only one of name or form; the spirit is the same. Sensuality, in its various types and phases, has ever been and is the avenue of all idolatry, and its images and groves have not yet disappeared from the lands we call Christian. We have but to examine the creeds and doctrines and practices of most of our modern religions to find evidences of an idolatry as pernicious as any that ever invaded the land of Israel, inasmuch as they set aside the sovereignty of God and endow the powers of darkness with the prerogative of Deity. The more subtle and refined expression of this idolatry is the more dangerous, since it encourages the delusion that one is worshipping God the while he is bowing down to the asserted law and government of the carnal mind, the acknowledged enemy of all that is good.

We are not to assume, however, that the errors of the Israelites of this period were less evil because the same errors in other forms hold sway today. Then, as now, the effort of the serpent was to destroy the seed of the woman, but while the carnal mind seemed for long periods to have held the ascendancy, and the light of Israel to have well-nigh gone out, the precious seed was rooted in the soil of spiritual consciousness and could not be destroyed.

Chapter Thirteen - The Coming of Prophets and Kings

And I will make thee exceeding fruitful, and I will make nations of thee, and kings shall come out of thee. — Gen. 17: 6.

I have also spoken by the prophets, and I have multiplied visions, and used similitudes, by the ministry of the prophets. — Hos. 12: 10.

THE last of the judges marked the beginning of a new order in the religious and political life of Israel. The priesthood had been losing much of its earlier prestige, because the moral standard demanded by that high office had not been consistently maintained, and the priest was now to make way for the prophet, both as the chief religious authority and as the revealer of God's messages to Israel. Beginning with Samuel, the prophet as a teacher and interpreter of the word of the Lord became a new and notable factor in the nation; not that the priestly functions were to be superseded, but that a more definite mode of communication, so to speak, between God and His people was to be established.

The priests instructed the people out of the law, but could not properly be regarded as teachers in the same sense as were Moses and the later prophets. The monotonous repetition of formal codes, which exercised no regenerative influence, was not of the sort designed to further the purposes of Israel's existence. The Israelites had continued to revolve religiously around the Mosaic utterances, and punctiliously to observe all the requirements of outward forms, but without making any general spiritual progress. It is evident that something more vital than these repetitions was essential for the development of the Israel-idea. The recognition of the moral law was, undoubtedly, a pronounced step in the line of human awakening, but this naturally revealed the necessity of taking the next step, and so on, since human consciousness will not realize the second birth through morality alone, but through the entrance of spirituality.

If Israel was ever to justify her existence, the time had to come for a broadening and rising in her mental life. The repeated backslidings of her people, and the disasters which as repeatedly followed, indicated the necessity for more spiritual light rather than for more law and ritual. The real nature of the God declared in the First Commandment was obscured by the ordinances of the priestly office. The surrender of animality for spirituality, which was the metaphysical import of their sacrifices, was lost sight of in the mere shedding of blood; for the attempt to appease a supposedly offended Deity by the sacrifice of another life than that of the sinner was intensely selfish on the human side, and never brought the worshipper one jot nearer the divine nature, nor made him one jot less sinful. It was imperatively necessary, therefore, before Israel could hope to possess her spiritual inheritance, that a less heathenish concept of God and of His attitude towards men, than was expressed in the practice of animal sacrifices, should begin to be formed in the national consciousness.

From the nature of her religion the government of Israel was theocratic, but it necessarily called for human administrators to whom the interpretation and execution of God's laws were entrusted; therefore the success of such a form of government depended upon the purity of the human instrument. The frailty of this instrument, when animated by selfish purposes, made the step between theocracy and autocracy but a short one, as Israel discovered in her subsequent career. Although the highest ideal of government is, undoubtedly, theocratic, its attainment calls for a common ground of understanding upon which the governed can mutually recognize their relation to divine authority, and by which they may determine the fitness of the human administrator. This naturally brings theocracy and democracy to an inevitable meeting-point in human affairs, and while such an ideal of government is not yet fully realized, it points to the course along which humanity must progress before the reign of harmony can be established in the earth and among its peoples.

While the lessons of experience would point to democracy as vastly preferable to other systems of human government, it is not the panacea for the world's ills, since it has been found to produce about as many problems as it solves. Democracy will have to establish its superiority by giving the divine qualities in man their practical place in human affairs, and by testing and choosing men on the ground of their moral and spiritual suitability.

In the preface to his translation of the Scriptures Wycliff wrote, "This Bible is for the government of the people, by the people, and for the people," showing that the only right basis of government is the Word of God; and government upon that basis is democratic because in it the individual cannot evade his responsibility. Right law and right government separated from God is impossible; hence the obvious conclusion, that democracy can succeed only as it maintains its essential relation to divine things.

It naturally follows that until obedience to divine Principle as the supreme authority, becomes the ideal and rule of democracy, its highest possibilities cannot be realized. Democracy and theocracy must, therefore, sometime meet in the recognition that the law of good is the one law of the universe. Then will heaven mingle with earth in an increasing consciousness of God's kingdom.

Between Joshua and Samuel the political affairs of the nation were more or less chaotic, all that preserved Israel from destruction as a separate people, and from consequent absorption by the Gentile nations, being the fact that the seedling of spiritual truth which had been implanted in her, and which antedated the formation of the nation, was never wholly uprooted. The sensualism of the human mind might seem at times almost to smother it beneath the ashes of indifference, or well-nigh to consume it with the fierceness of its enmity, but it unfailingly reappeared. Terrible things had been declared as the doom of this people if they should prove false to their God, and terrible things had been experienced by them, but the presence of a spiritual remnant made complete destruction impossible; and that there will always be this spiritual remnant is made certain by the immortal nature of good. A genuine perception of divinity, once incorporated in human consciousness and experience, has never been destroyed, and never can be while God's omnipotence remains.

At the time of Samuel, affairs in the nation had reached a crisis. Enemies were threatening from without, while within, the country was bordering upon a state of anarchy and disruption. The climax came when the Philistines defeated the Israelites and captured the ark of the covenant, a calamity which fell upon the people as a national disaster, for the ark was to them the visible token of Israel's glory and protection. It was a memorial of her many deliverances, a sign that Jehovah dwelt among His people, and in its loss they felt bereft not only of their glory but of their safety. Like mortals of a later and more enlightened day, they mistook the shadow for the substance, attaching virtue and power to the symbol instead of to the idea which it represented. Had they been faithful and obedient to the divine commands, His presence and protection would have been realized independently of the ark; while their belief that His favor could be obtained, irrespective of their moral inconstancy, simply by taking the material symbol into battle, was abject idolatry. God's covenants were always conditional upon Israel's fulfilment of their terms, and without this fulfilment, the external token was as meaningless as the idols of their enemies.

The incident in the house of Dagon, as recorded in the Scriptures, illustrated the infinite distance between the living God of Israel and the mythical deities of paganism. Although but a material symbol, the ark of the covenant represented something more than superstition and delusion, and that was the presence of divine power among men. Now Israel, be it always remembered, was God's witness among the nations. Jeremiah wrote of her, speaking as the voice of the Lord, "Thou art my battle ax and weapons of war," — and for what purpose? Not for the slaughter of human enemies, but for the destruction of the false beliefs about God which have deceived human consciousness. It was her explicit purpose to overthrow idolatry, and to that end, as Israel awakens to her meaning and destiny, all that stands for other powers and other minds than God will have to be broken in pieces. In this Philistine temple, the great work of Israel was too plainly exemplified to be mistaken or forgotten.

The person of Samuel, last of the judges and first in a new line of prophets, stands out at this critical time as one of the great figures in Israel's history. Born in response to a woman's spiritual desire, he was dedicated before birth to the service of the Lord, and set apart as a Nazarite according to the prevailing custom. His purity of thought was early seen in his sensitiveness to the divine call. As prophet, priest, and statesman, he guided the affairs of Israel throughout one of her most trying periods, and left a name for unselfishness, patriotism, and magnanimity which has not been excelled. His career inaugurated a succession of prophets whose lofty ideals and spiritual teachings have been an inspiration to all subsequent ages, and whose visions of the events of the latter days have served to preserve the hope and sustain the faith of a conquered and scattered people.

Samuel's attempt to transfer the reins of government to his sons did not prove acceptable, because they did not walk in the ways of their father, nor did they manifest his spirit of devotion to the well-being of Israel. The experiences of the nation under the rulership of the judges did not inspire the Israelites with a desire for its continuance, and, although the cause of their misfortunes lay in their own disobedience to divine law, they took advantage of the disordered state of the country to ask for a king. Samuel earnestly endeavored to dissuade them from this course, but the determination to be governed after the manner of other nations remained unshaken, despite his gloomy picture of their conditions under kingly rule.

It will be remembered that the covenant with Abraham included the promise that kings should come from him, and that Jacob in his final blessing designated Judah as the kingly tribe. Moses also referred to the time when Israel would choose a king, and even gave instruction as to his selection. It is unlikely that the Israelites were ignorant of these things, and it was not surprising, in view of the chaotic state of the country, that they should believe the time opportune for the setting up of a monarchy. Just where lay the inconsistency of being under the temporal sovereignty of a king in place of a judge, and especially a hereditary judgeship such as Samuel seemed to be desirous of establishing in his own family, is not readily apparent. The attitude of the Israelites towards God would be as good or as bad under a judge as under a king. The precise form of acknowledged authority was of minor importance so long as both ruler and people were loyal to the divine commands, and without this loyalty, the character of their political administration could make little difference.

The theocratic system went reasonably well when administered by such men as Moses, Joshua, and Samuel, because their eye was single for the glory of God and the well-being of Israel; but with men of inferior type, the element of religious authority afforded opportunities for an abuse of power and position that the self-seeking could not resist. Entrusting the human with unqualified power in any direction has always resulted disastrously, and especially so when entrenched behind religious sentiment or superstition. Time has rounded many cycles since the Israelites asked for a king. Kingdoms and empires have come and gone; revolutions have upset governments and set up others in their places; but the world still waits to be ruled by him "who hath not lifted up his soul unto vanity, nor sworn deceitfully," who "despiseth the gain of oppressions, that shaketh his hands from holding of bribes"; and no other's right it is to exercise authority over mankind.

Ever since their entry into the Promised Land, the Israelites had been mingling and intermarrying with the Canaanites, and imbibing their religious and political ideas, all of which was contrary to Moses' instructions. Their offense in demanding a king apparently lay in the choice of un-Israelitish ideals, that is, in preferring a course to which they were not divinely directed, rather than in the desire for a new system of temporal government. If, as a people, they had been obedient to their covenants, and had maintained in its purity the monotheism of Israel, they would have had a priesthood and an administration to correspond; but the Israelites had only themselves to blame when the pernicious seed which they had scattered throughout their nation brought forth its evil fruit.

Whether Israel should be a monarchy or a commonwealth was relatively unimportant. If her people were loyal to the divine requirements, all would be well with them, but if they gave themselves over to the worship of other gods, no form of government known to men could protect them from the consequences. Because the truth of the one infinite God had been, to some extent, revealed to Israel, it would necessarily devolve upon her to make this truth known to the rest of mankind, not simply in the line of religious teaching, but to make a knowledge of divine power available in human affairs. It is obvious that the best way to do things must be learned from good, not evil, and this fact naturally applies itself to every department of human activity, whether it be in politics, economics, education, or religion.

It is certain that there could be no just or permanent apprehension of law, or any beneficial expression thereof in government, apart from divinity. No nation could wholly separate itself from the influence of virtue and truth, and survive. The ruins of kingdoms and empires that strew the path of history bear emphatic testimony to this momentous fact. The specious argument of the carnal mind, that life, intelligence, and power exist independently of good, is the lie which has deceived every generation of mortals, and which continues its deception in the very shadow of our schools and churches.

In Young's Concordance the literal meaning of the word Israel is given as "ruling with God," and this is plainly what the government of Israel was designed to express. The human mind, on the contrary, believes it can govern by other means than the divine. It assumes the right and the power to rule by material force, willpower, and other phases of evil, ultimating in the worst forms of tyranny and despotism. Israel was the one nation which acknowledged God's supremacy, hence the commandment forbidding the acknowledgment of any other god, or any other governing power. Translated into impersonal terms, the meaning of Israel, according to the above definition, and as applicable to all earthly governments, was that men were to exercise authority by means of good alone, and that the law of righteousness must be recognized and adopted before any human government could approximate the divine ideal.

If the foregoing is true, and it undoubtedly is, the right idea of government, with all that that term includes, must come out of Israel, out of the truth of man's divine sonship. No matter what may be the name or aim or composition of any system of human government, it cannot be acceptable to God or a blessing to men unless its ruling power and animating influence proceed from goodness. The adoption of anything less worthy as a means of influence or control is, for that very reason, a usurpation of rightful authority. It is clearly the prerogative of every individual and of every nation to be governed by good alone; and no governing power, whether civil, political, or religious, can justly assume to control the destinies of men by any other means. This idea was inseparable from national as well as spiritual Israel. It was the chief cornerstone of the national structure, and, although it has been rejected by the carnal mind, it must be found in its place at the final restoration of all things.

What Samuel was endeavoring to impress upon the Israelites was that a king, such as they had in mind from their acquaintance with the Canaanites, would rule them according to the dictates of the carnal mind, and not accord-

95

ing to the divine ideal which their nation represented. To his understanding they were turning their backs upon God in thus looking to the outside nations for their political models. It was certain that what God had done for them and had given them were vastly more vital and important to their present and future welfare than anything which the Gentile nations could teach them. Were the great things which had glorified their past history to be set aside, that Israel should now seek to be governed after the manner of those nations which acknowledged not the true God?

The evident mistake of the Israelites was in abandoning the ideal of divine government which preceded their national existence, and their acceptance of which was to distinguish them as the people of God. They fell into the common error of seeking a remedy for their troubles in external things, instead of correcting their own failure to fulfil their covenants with God. Under these circumstances, the mere substitution of a king for a judge would not lessen their difficulties, but would rather tend to increase them, as the prophet pointed out, by the exaltation of human authority. While it was plainly possible for Israel to exist as a monarchy without sacrificing her allegiance to Divine sovereignty, the present agitation was very evidently not the outcome of progress but of chaos, and was not, therefore, likely to benefit the nation permanently.

But since a king they were determined to have, a king Samuel gave them. Notwithstanding his strong personal disapprobation, the prophet assured them of the divine protection if both they and the king obeyed the voice of the Lord. The experiment seemed at first to be a success. Saul broke the power of their enemies and consolidated the tribes into some degree of unity, but his reign became clouded by evil influences and ended in pitiful tragedy. It had been verified to Israel that, without God, all human sovereignty is abortive and vain.

Chapter Fourteen - The Throne of David

Of the increase of his government and peace there shall be no end, upon the throne of David, and upon his kingdom, to order it, and to establish it with judgment and with justice from henceforth even for ever. — Isa. 9: 7.

He shall be great, and shall be called the Son of the Highest; and the Lord God shall give unto him the throne of his father David:

And he shall reign over the house of Jacob for ever; and of his kingdom there shall be no end. — Luke 1: 32, 33.

BY this time Samuel had apparently become reconciled to the establishment of a monarchy in Israel, and was in consequence more open to God's direction in the choice of a king. In his second attempt the prophet was guided at once to the tribe of Judah, in evident confirmation of Jacob's foresight.

The simple but impressive anointing of the youngest son of Jesse deeply touched his spiritual nature, for it is recorded that "the Spirit of the Lord came upon David from that day forward." Thus was instituted a royal dynasty that was never to be wholly overthrown until the reign of the Christ should ultimately supersede it, as it is naturally destined to do, for divine Truth must sometime reign supreme in the halls of government as well as in the hearts of men.

The meagre and somewhat confused records of the time leave much to be supplied by inference, and too often by the imagination, but it appears that David accepted, his high destiny in all seriousness, believing that God and not man had chosen him to be king over his people. This solemn conviction, imparted to him by the prophet of the Lord, and doubtless accepted by many of the Israelites, gave a higher meaning to the throne of Israel than mere political sovereignty. It can be seen that the oneness of God, as He was revealed to the founders of the Hebrew nation, could never be dissociated from the sovereign power, no matter how disloyal to the divine idea some of its administrators might be, or how blind the people to the spiritual genesis of Israel.

The newly anointed king-elect gave early promise of the courage and resourcefulness which were to stand him in such good stead in the stormy period that lay between him and the throne, and which later won recognition in the palace of Saul and in the affection of the people. In his famous duel with Goliath, David's challenge indicated the spirit of the man: "I am come to thee in the name of the Lord of hosts, the God of the armies of Israel...this day will the Lord deliver thee into mine hand...that all the earth may know that there is a God in Israel." He had already acknowledged God as his deliverer from the lion and the bear, and he was now to prove to the whole nation, to use his own words, that "the battle is the Lord's." This recognition of divine power as at hand to deliver from the enmity of the carnal mind at once marked him as a true Israelite, and gave him his large and enduring place in the history of the nation.

Although first crowned king over Judah only, David was later acknowledged as king over the whole nation, and continued thus to the close of his reign. So far as the thought and customs of the age made possible, he appears to have exemplified the true monarchic ideal, that the king is the servant rather than the master of the nation, and derives his real authority, not alone from family inheritance or the will of the people, but from his own moral and spiritual qualities. This fact naturally discloses the weak point in all hereditary rulership, since it is necessarily a matter of individual consciousness and attainment, not the accident of birth, which decides one's fitness to govern. Israel was to learn through many bitter experiences, as other nations have had to learn, that the son does not always possess the worthiness or the wisdom of the father. True kingly succession belongs to type rather than to person, and it is in this higher or spiritual sense that the throne of David is frequently referred to in the Scriptures.

David apparently recognized that he held his throne by the grace of God, and that his kingly power was to be exercised in trust for his people, rather than to further personal ambition or aggrandizement. While there was a show of similarity to his predecessor in the means and manner of his selection, there the similarity ended. Saul's idea of kingship partook more of the type of his Gentile neighbors, whereas, despite the rude conditions of his time, David approximated a more spiritual conception of his position and its responsibilities, and of Israel's peculiar place among the nations. Early in his experience he had come close to the fact that God is a source of strength and protection in the hour of danger, and he doubted not that God would preserve his people from evil while they served Him in sincerity. He was not unmindful of Israel's divinely appointed destiny, and that unless he proved faithful to her ideals, his reign would be a failure as Saul's had been before him.

When Jacob prophetically designated Judah as the holder of the sceptre he did not necessarily imply royal honors for the whole tribe, but that out of it, by the process of mental selection, Israel's kingly line would come forth and remain until the coming of Shiloh, an event which evidently belongs to the period of the restoration. Israel's destiny was not to remain a perpetual monarchy, under a human king, but to prepare God's throne in the earth, and to prepare the earth for His supreme government. Israel will not vacate her place among the nations until this is accomplished, and her heavenly King is acknowledged and enthroned, for if this people were to become absorbed by the Gentile races, and the line of the woman ceased to have a human instrument and representative, it would mean a return to pre-Israelitish barbarism and idolatry.

The coming of Shiloh indicates that era of peace and good will towards which the faces of mankind are eagerly and anxiously turning, when the Christ shall reign upon the earth, and God's will be done as in heaven. This new era, wherein the new heavens and new earth are to appear, can begin its course, and open a new history for the race, only as the human or material sense gives place to the divine or spiritual sense, and all forms of despotism and self-seeking give up their fear-hold upon mortals.

But in the meantime, while mortal passions so readily sway the multitude, and while the sensual takes precedence in human thought over the spiritual, the Judaic line of kings, the line of David, is to continue in Israel. And the Judaic line of kings, as named in David, stood for something more than political dominion or authority, for from the beginning it shadowed forth the absolute sovereignty of God, although somewhat obscured by the Hebrew concept of a national Jehovah. It is true this ideal of divine sovereignty in the nation was at times submerged to the point of apparent extinction, but it always reappeared, because it was incorporated in the very nature and constitution of Israel. In its progress towards spiritual awakening, human thought must go on with its turning and being overturned until the reign of Truth appears, and man's control over man shall cease.

All this of course means that, even on earth, kings are to be eventually dispensed with, and all selfish or unlimited exercise of human power will disappear when good is understood to be the equal possession and protection of all men, and no other government than divine Love will be needed. Conditions in Israel at the coming of her prophets and kings indicated a tremendous distance from that ideal state, as they did during most of her later history, but to consider this subject justly we cannot afford to lose sight of the fact, at any point along the way, that Israel's spiritual mission was not intended to be absorbed in the functions of her nationhood, but to be preserved and promoted thereby. It is this great mission to make God known to all mankind which links up the future with the present and the past, which shows the whole question of Israel to be inseparable from the salvation of the world, and therefore as one with the Christ.

David was enough of a seer to recognize these things, and not to be deceived by any earthly glory that might attend his kingdom. He appears to have grasped, in a measure at least, the significance of both literal and spiritual Israel; and while not minimizing or neglecting the former, it is plain that he looked to the latter to declare and embody the real greatness of the nation. This discernment qualified him to be the founder of the greatest and most enduring dynasty the world has known, and it was to endure and be exalted to honor because of the germ of spiritual truth which had been implanted in Israel, and which was to grow and increase until it replenished the earth. It was the royal line of "the woman," and as such could never wholly pass away until the Edenic prophecy be fulfilled.

It should be becoming continually clearer that, if we separate her from her spiritual meaning and mission, Israel would be but one among other groups of mortals, with nothing to lift her above the general level of humanity. We have seen the divine hand unmistakably indicated in the spiritual selection which led to the rise and development of this people, in the wonderful events of their early history, and confirmed by the fact that in no other nation was God's oneness truly known or acknowledged. Thus it can be said that Deity was literally the substance of Israel's history, and that her obedience or disobedience to the divine commands was always the determinative factor in her destiny.

What else was there to endure, or that merits endurance, about this or any other race or people, except their godliness? Disloyalty to the highest known good, whether in the case of a man or of a nation, is not real history, since nothing is worthy to be remembered that is not fitted to survive. The evil things recorded of the Israelites did not pertain to or proceed from the real Israel, but from that which was foreign to it, !as expressed throughout the Scriptures in the word Gentile; and unless we make this discrimination, and separate the sensual from the spiritual, we shall fail to discern Israel's real identity, and her place among the nations of today. It is the writer's aim to keep these facts well to the front lest they become obscured in the accumulating details of persons and events, humanly interesting in their historical relation, but important chiefly as evidence corroborative of higher things.

David's influence upon the thought of Israel was such that henceforth the royal line was to be named in him rather than in Judah. The tribe became eclipsed in the greatness of the man, and in turn the man disappeared in the type for which his name became a synonym. Standing midway between the traditional beginning of human history and the present age, David is easily the central figure in Israel's national life. While he did great things for the nation in subduing her enemies, and in completing the conquest of Canaan according to the instructions given to Moses and Joshua, he is most widely known because of the sacred writings with which his name has for ages been associated. The mention of David at once calls to mind those wonderful Hebrew hymns which have stimulated the hope and inspired the faith of both Jew and Christian, although modern scholars and critics tell us that the great founder of the royal line of Israel was the author of only a few of the psalms which bear his name.

This disappointment, however, serves to turn our thoughts the more from the man to the type. It is obvious that many of the promises and prophecies regarding David do not refer to his person but to that which he represented. This is illustrated, for example, in the case of Abraham. The promise that in Abraham all the nations of the earth were to be blessed clearly could not refer to his personality, but to that which he so exemplified in his life as to become synonymous with his name. Thus Abraham is the heritage of all mankind as an ideal of loyalty to one's highest conception of good, in the sense that Paul wrote to the Galatians, "they which be of faith are blessed with faithful Abraham."

The circumstances attending David's anointing at the hands of the prophet Samuel, while he was yet a stripling on his father's farm, the many remarkable events leading up to his coronation, his dramatic victory over the Philistine giant, all appealed strongly to the romantic nature of the Hebrews, and to the hero-worship which is inherent in the human mind. Added to this were the conspicuous prosperity of his reign, his passionate devotion to the national religion, and the high position achieved by the nation under his leadership. In view of all this, the idealization of David as a man and a king "after God's own heart," and as representing the divine sovereignty over His chosen people, can easily be understood, despite his occasional lapses into gross error which, while inexcusable, were less inconsistent with the moral standards of his time than with our own.

Thus the exaltation of David as a type in Israel is not without ground or reason. There had been many periods of disorder, defeat, and national humiliation since the passing of Joshua left the Israelites without a head and surrounded by hostile neighbors. Under David, whom they had accepted as their divinely chosen king, they had become united and prosperous, triumphant over their enemies, and an acknowledged power among the nations. What more natural than that the name of David should come to stand in the nation for the highest expression of Israel, and for the embodiment of her ideals? And what more natural than to conclude, in the light of Israel's extraordinary origin and history, that the divine kingship foreshadowed in David would never be without its rightful representative on the throne, and that that representative would always be of his own lineage? It will be remembered that the blind man appealed to Jesus as the "son of David," which shows that the Jews attached a higher significance to that name than is implied in the human thought of royalty or of personality.

The prophet Nathan apparently referred to this when he announced the perpetuity of the house of David: "and thine house and thy kingdom shall be established forever before thee." David's kingdom certainly could not be established forever before him in any personal or literal sense, so that here the name evidently expressed more than the personality of the man. The student of prophetic Scripture sometimes has in mind an unbroken line of kings, extending from that time to ours, all of the lineage of David, as the proper fulfilment of this and similar passages, and it is not denied that that may consistently be looked for; but even if that conclusion were historically verified, it would simply prove the case by external evidence which, of itself alone, is always inconclusive. The ripening process of time has reached the point where the need is to break open the outer protective shell which has served its purpose, and disclose the satisfying kernel. Unless we get at this inner meat, this "hidden manna," we shall spiritually starve on the husk of the letter, the literal or human side of Israel.

It was very clearly the recognition of God's government in the earth, as typified in the kingdom of David, which was to be maintained, and which alone could link up the kings of the nation with the spiritual mission of Israel. Therefore what is called the Davidic covenant had a much broader significance than the securing of the throne for David's descendants, or than the preservation of the national integrity or existence. Its predominant feature was the perpetuation of Israel itself, not as a nation merely but as an idea, the idea that was faintly discerned by the woman in the story of Eden, and that had been steadily growing to human perception. It was this dawning spiritual sense of being, as contrasted with the materialism of the carnal mind, which was the real chosen of the Lord, and which could not be destroyed because its seed was in itself, in its inherent truthfulness.

Without the recognition and acceptance of the truth about God, as the foundation and support of the nation and of her institutions, it could matter little whether any of David's descendants occupied the throne or not, or whether the nation itself endured. On the other hand, the preservation of this truth in human consciousness would necessarily involve the right vehicle for its human expression and activity.

The position of Israel in these days of prophetic fulfilment will not be weakened or obscured by keeping the spiritual and the material aspects of this question where they belong. The last should not be put first and the first last. Material conditions must always be secondary to the spiritual, and the human to the divine. The one obvious purpose of a vehicle is that something may be conveyed by means of it, not that it should obstruct or take the place of the thing to be conveyed. In other words, it is valuable for its service rather than for its own sake. In like manner, as before pointed out, but which like some other things will bear much repetition, Israel came into existence as a separate people or nation to be a vehicle by which the truth perceived of God might reach the rest of mankind; but the incidental details of this human vehicle, interesting as they undoubtedly are and important in their place, should not be allowed to overshadow the larger and more vital issues. Thus the identity of Israel in the latter days must be sought for and tested by the fact of her being the vehicle to humanity of the truth about God, rather than by mere external or historical evidences.

The throne of David, which was to be "established forever," logically signified more than political power or authority, since all human things are temporal, and must have referred to a realization of power and authority that transcends the material. What could this be but that consciousness of divine power which gave Jacob his new name, and which was Israel's national birthmark? This everlasting throne was not, therefore, the expression of human authority, nor did it belong to David or his descendants in any personal sense, but represented the eternal sovereignty of the God of Israel. Because it was true that there was no other God, the power vested in a right perception of Him would necessarily endure and have some form of expression, despite the lapses and backslidings which might temporarily darken that perception. Earthly kings and kingdoms continue to come and go, and their glory and their greatness are as the grass that withereth and the flower that fadeth away, but only that which declares the glory of God can abide forever.

To suppose, however, that God enters into unconditional covenants with sinning mortals, in order to bring about certain human ends, is to misunderstand the absolute nature of Deity. God's ways and means are necessarily divine, not human, otherwise He would Himself be human. Reading into the letter of Scripture what is contrary to its spirit only serves to defeat the purpose of divine revelation. It is impossible to think rightly of the Infinite as making terms with the finite, for this would leave us without a conception of infinity, and therefore without a true sense of the oneness of God.

It is the so-called carnal mind that argues for unconditional and unmerited favor and protection at the hands of the Almighty, that would blend good and evil as one intelligence, and name God as consenting to this monstrosity. Throughout the inspired Scripture runs a line of absolute separation between what is and what is not of God; and between these opposites there is and can be neither affinity, sympathy, nor communion.

It was what David manifested of the divine nature which constituted his greatness and made him beloved of the Lord; whereas the evil in his carnal nature, which constituted his human weakness, was neither condoned nor compromised with by God, but was left to its own self-punishment and final destruction. From the beginning Israel stood for the overcoming of evil, not for its acknowledgment. Fidelity to the First Commandment, which denied the existence of other gods, was sure to work out in the experience of Israel the self-destruction of whatever would oppose the reign of good in human consciousness, a process which ignorance or superstition might attribute to an angry God, but which is simply the result of the falsity and groundlessness of evil coming to light. All this is related intimately to the question of David's throne and to the succession of his line, because no sovereignty could be consistent with Israel's history and destiny which did not rest upon God's supremacy and infinitude.

'The "throne of David" is without doubt used in Scripture with a metaphysical meaning and should be so understood. Like all human terms it naturally has a literal application, but its higher import possesses our chief interest, and embraces much more than the personal kingship of David or the fate of his posterity. It goes back to the time when it was said to Jacob, "As a prince hast thou prevailed." In that experience was laid the foundation stone of the spiritual kingdom of Israel, and every later instance of subduing the carnal mind served to strengthen this throne, which was to stand in the symbolic language of the Scriptures, not for man's dominion over man, but for man's dominion over evil as the son of God.

The greatest honor that could rest on the Davidic line was the appearing in it of him who was preeminent in Israel, of whom Pilate asked, "Art thou a king?" Although a thousand years distant, the resplendent glory of that event, "the brightness of his coming," was already prophetically lighting up the mountain tops of Israel. Greater than the promise of the perpetuity of his kingdom was this selection of his house as the lineage of the Messiah, which established the fact beyond question that David represented the direct line of "the woman," both literally and spiritually.

Chapter Fifteen - A House Divided

Whereas there is among you envying, and strife, and divisions, are ye not carnal, and walk as men? — I Cor. 3: 3.

For the kingdom is the Lord's: and He is the governor among the nations. — Ps. 22: 28.

WITH peace established throughout his reign, Solomon raised the kingdom of Israel to its highest point of material prosperity and national influence, although it is not shown that these became a blessing to himself or to the nation. It is recorded that in a dream of the night God offered the new king his choice of what He should give him, and that he named wisdom as the thing he most desired. Because he had chosen well, and for the sake of his people rather than for himself, he was also to receive both riches and honor. While his dream came true in respect to the latter, and great possessions

103

were his in abundance, the history of his reign does not disclose the wisdom to be expected from one divinely endowed. The record of David's youngest son, brilliant though it was in some respects, does not point to the wisdom which the apostle describes as coming from God. His enormous revenues were recklessly squandered in the extravagant appointments of his court, and in the unrestrained indulgence of his whims and desires. What men count honor came to him, it is true, chiefly because of the external glories of his kingdom, and because of the intellectual astuteness which passed for wisdom; but withal he did not prove wise enough to shape his reign to the best interest of himself or of his kingdom.

Had Solomon -indeed possessed "a wise and understanding heart," he would surely have been aware of the folly of forsaking the pure monotheism of Israel for the gods of his Gentile wives. While his reign began most auspiciously with the building of the great temple, the first known building erected for the worship of the one God, and while his prayer on the occasion of its dedication gave promise of a noble career, it was not long ere his kingly bark grounded in the shoals of sensuality, and his light went out in the temples of his idols. Truly was it fulfilled in him that "the wisdom of their wise men shall perish." It would seem that the superior understanding with which he has been credited must have been reversed in his later life, else his career would not have ended with the wail of disillusionment which we find in the book of Ecclesiastes, for divine wisdom does not lead mortals into "vanity and vexation of spirit."

The first ray of true wisdom which lighted human consciousness was the recognition that only good should be believed and obeyed; and, as the nature of God became better understood, the folly of going contrary thereto became correspondingly more evident. In common with other mortals, the Israelites were besieged by the suggestion, put forward continuously by the carnal senses, that there was something outside the spiritual consciousness of being which they were justified in taking into their experience. The way of wisdom was stated with unmistakable clearness in what is called the First Commandment, first in order and importance, obedience to which would have saved Israel from her failures and misfortunes.

We read that Solomon so far succumbed to the allurements of evil as to erect altars in the midst of Israel for the worship of strange gods. The writer of the book of Ecclesiastes discloses the motive of the king's idolatrous course, namely, that he might indulge his physical desires to the full. This does not necessarily apply to Solomon more than to the average mortal, except that his position enabled him to gratify his passions without restraint. This course naturally led him to exalt other gods, or other sources of good, than the "Holy One" of Israel. The consequences of taking this course revealed, not only how absolutely at variance it was with the will of God, but how absolutely at variance with the divine reality of things were the senses which led him and his people into idolatry. The acknowledgment in Israel, that Deity is one, and therefore all, was as inseparable from the throne as from the temple, from the king as from the priest and commoner; and king and priest and commoner found to their cost that they could not set aside this corner-stone of their nation. This truth of God's infinitude was the stone spoken of by Jesus, when he said, "Whosoever shall fall on this stone shall be broken; but on whomsover it shall fall, it will grind him to powder."

The experience of Solomon reveals sensualism as the underlying motive of idolatry, therefore that what mortals name evil is but the enthronement of matter as a source of life and intelligence. The king was plainly lured into recreancy to the God of Israel through the old-time suggestions, of the serpent, alias physical sense, or a perverted sense of being as physical instead of spiritual. This perverted sense is not, therefore, the mode of good but of evil, or the deception by which the carnal mind asserts itself to be something, and to exercise power over men. The altars which Solomon set up to strange gods merely evidenced his mental apostasy. In Sinai, Moses realized that loyalty and obedience could not be divided between the God who had revealed Himself as the eternal I AM, as the one Mind or self-consciousness, and the belief that something else also had self-existence and intelligence. Between these mental opposites there never has been and never can be mutual sympathy or agreement. It had been repeatedly urged upon the Israelites, that God required their obedience to good alone, but what they apparently failed to recognize was, that the way of evil always lay through the appeal of the carnal senses.

The human consciousness had been feebly groping its way towards the spiritual or immortal sense of being, and, although the founders and leaders of this upward movement had been men of exalted vision, the general thought of the Israelites at that time had risen little or no higher than a recognition of the law of morality, a recognition which also obtained, to some extent, among the Gentiles. -The first and great commandment of her law forbade the acknowledgment of other gods, but it was not then fully seen that the universal idolatry of the race is the carnal-mindedness that would clothe man in the garb of flesh, and hold him under its debasing claims? The subservience of the Israelites to these lower demands led them into agreement with what the Scriptures call "strange gods," in other words, with beliefs about God and man which were incompatible with the oneness of God as taught in Israel. This sense idolatry, symbolized in all idol worship, had permeated even the priesthood, and now invaded the throne itself, the concept of good as physical was exalted to its pinnacle by the "wise man," who only began to enter the way of wisdom when he discovered "no profit under the sun" in the choicest things of material sense.

It had been proved over and over again throughout her history that Israel could not thrive in an idolatrous atmosphere. Her very existence depended upon her spirituality. Because Solomon had utterly failed to appreciate this, his kingdom was now to be divided. The king had burdened the people for the means to gratify his desires, and when his son Rehoboam would have increased these burdens, ten of the tribes revolted and formed a separate kingdom, to be known by the name of Israel, leaving Benjamin and Judah to continue under the reign of the Davidic line, to be known as the kingdom of Judah. This division of national Israel continued up to the final captivity, and, so far as Judah is concerned, still exists. The house of Joseph representing Israel, and the house of Judah representing the kingly line of David, from now on went their separate ways.

The nation thus divided began to drift further and further from her allegiance to God. Kings and people turned to the carnal mind and followed its evil counsel. Jeroboam led the northern kingdom of Israel into such excesses of idolatry that his name became a byword and a reproach in after generations, while we read that in Judah they "built them high places, and images and groves, on every high hill, and under every green tree." This continued with more or less variation during the history of these two kingdoms. Of the nineteen kings that ruled over the ten tribes of Israel, not one followed the example of David in adhering loyally to the one God, and for some two hundred and fifty years the northern kingdom, under its idolatrous rulers, lapsed deeper and deeper into the worship of evil. Jehovah was supplanted by the gods of their enemies. Israel had played false to her God, to her ideals, to her high destiny, and was plunging recklessly and blindly into the darkness ahead.

During these evil days there were notable attempts to recall the nation from her apostasy and impending calamity. There is nothing finer in the records of her prophets than the efforts of Elijah and Elisha to redeem the Israelites from their idolatry. The challenge of Elijah to the priests of Baal still retains its inspiring appeal for loyalty to the God of Israel, while his marvellous triumph, in face of the apparently overwhelming impossibility of achievement from a material standpoint, should reassure the timid faith of all after ages that the divine Spirit is omnipresent as the only power, notwithstanding the cold stubbornness of material testimony to the contrary.

In this incident Elijah presented the third sign which Moses was commanded to show to his brethren in Egypt, namely, his control over matter and its asserted laws. This sign of man's spiritual dominion was interwoven with. Israel's history, and must also be found in the latter days as one of the proofs of her identity. It was employed by the prophet during the famine which came upon Israel in the reign of Ahab, when the widow of Zarephath, and Elijah, and her house, subsisted upon "an handful of meal in a barrel and a little oil in a cruse"; and we read that "the barrel of meal wasted not, neither did the cruse of oil fail, according to the word of the Lord, which he spake by Elijah." The verity and importance of these proofs were later verified in the work of Christ Jesus, thereby establishing beyond question, not only the absolute supremacy of Spirit, but that Spirit was and is the one God of Israel.

All these things serve to illustrate the apostle's meaning when he said, "The carnal mind is enmity against God." They also corroborate the conclusion that all forms of idolatry rest upon a denial of the infinitude of Spirit, and the exaltation of matter or the flesh as possessing divine qualities and attributes. Sensuality and spirituality are found in human experience to be mental opposites, the latter always leading mortals to good and the former to evil, and this simple fact will serve to guide us in discriminating between the real and the unreal Israel, or between that which is of God and that which contradicts His oneness or infinitude.

The true understanding of man's spiritual dominion as the son of God, enabled Moses to subdue material conditions, and the accumulated evidences of this power which were furnished by Elijah and Elisha survive the denials of the carnal mind. These proofs of the amplitude of Mind in supplying the needs of men were confirmed and extended by the Messiah, thus establishing their rightful place in the mission of Israel, and their scientific relation to human salvation. It is by these waymarks alone that we can trace the footsteps of Israel, and not by mere racial distinction or descent. Let us, therefore, look for and welcome these spiritual footprints, if we would not lose our way amid the mass of material literalism w4th which human thought surrounds the saving truth of divine revelation.

That the healing of the sick by spiritual means alone was also at this time naturally associated with the religious thought of Israel, was made manifest at the healing of the son of the widow of Zarephath, when she said to Elijah, "Now by this I know that thou art a man of God, and that the word of the Lord in thy mouth is truth," in other words, she knew by what he had done that he was a true exponent of the divine Word. And again, when Naaman the Syrian said to Elisha, "Now I know that there is no God in all the earth, but in Israel." And why so? Why should these people say, "Now I know," if there was not something in what had taken place that was particularly pertinent in establishing the verity of the God of Israel? That this was true the records bear testimony, and the student of Israel's destiny in the world, today and tomorrow as well as yesterday, must follow along this line of research, until he perceives that the true idea of Israel is identical with the healing Christ, so abundantly expressed in the life and work of Jesus, and without which human regeneration would be impossible.

Thus in the midst of the darkness of this terrible time, when the nation was heedlessly working out its own damnation, Israel was not left wholly without a light and a witness of the power and presence of her God. During these evil days, when idolatry held its paralyzing grasp upon the thought of the people, it was the work of the prophets to keep the spiritual lamp of Israel from going out, a work whose value cannot easily be overestimated, but which in the larger light of Christian revelation and accomplishment we are sometimes apt to overlook. The perception of the true God which had reached human consciousness through Abraham, Jacob, and Moses, could not be destroyed by the overwhelming tide of infidelity which was engulfing the nation. It was whispered to Elijah, in a moment of extreme loneliness and despondency, that there were still seven thousand in Israel whose thoughts were uncorrupted with idolatry. This was God's census of His people. The names of this remnant have not come down to us, but their influence has remained un-wasted, for it was their spirit of quiet devotion to the true ideal that kept the salt of Israel from losing its savour, and that nourished and preserved the spiritual seed of the woman.

In reviewing this period one might well pause in contemplation of the character and experiences of Elijah, so fully did they interpret the inner meaning of Israel, and so clearly did they indicate its utter oppositeness to materiality. Although Elijah belonged entirely to the northern kingdom, and contributed not a word to the sacred literature of the Hebrews, he has been regarded as the greatest of the prophets, and took his place in the thoughts of the Jews as the forerunner of the Messiah. He was the link between the law and the gospel, since it was he who appeared with Moses on the mount of transfiguration. His remarkable work betokened a nearness to God, and a comprehension of the spiritual facts of being, which are not encountered elsewhere between Moses and Christ Jesus. Here was an Israelite indeed, not because of birth or residence, but because of his close acquaintance with the God of Abraham, an acquaintance which enabled him to expose the iniquity of the carnal mind and the illusion of its gods.

Let us accompany this prophet to the famous "mount of God," where Moses so wondrously glimpsed the nature of Deity as the eternal I AM, and grasped something of the supremacy of Mind. We learn from the record that as Elijah was fleeing from the vengeance of Jezebel he was visited by an angel from God, by whom he was miraculously fed, and the inspiration of that experi-ence sustained him during the forty days' journey to Horeb. Here it dawned upon his consciousness that God is not present in the so-called forces of na-ture. He w-as not in the earthquake, the wind, or the fire: He was not in mat-ter at all. It was surely worth that long and perilous journey to learn this fact, and that man may commune with God in the quiet of spiritual desire and un-derstanding. It was here impressed upon Elijah that the Supreme Being is not revealed through material sense, but that He is to be worshipped in spirit, or spiritually, as Jesus afterwards taught. That the prophet was faithful to his higher sense of Deity is implied in the account of his ascension above the reach of mortality. Be that as it may, there was that about this remarkable man that breathed the spirit of Israel as transcending the expression of race or nationality, even as that which was preparing the way for the full appear-ing of the Christ.

The impression produced by Elijah's denunciation and exposure of Baalism was not lasting. The southern kingdom of Judah for a time main-tained the worship of Jehovah, but it was not long until practically the whole nation had succumbed to open idolatry. Incense to Gentile deities arose from every part of the land. It is evident that this state of things could not long en-dure, since neither individuals nor nations can obey evil indefinitely and re-main immune from its evil consequences. The outcome of the course they were pursuing had been placed before them, and was again foreshadowed by the prophet Ahijah to the wife of Jeroboam: "For the Lord shall smite Israel, as a reed is shaken in the water, and he shall root up Israel out of this good land, which he gave to their fathers, and shall scatter them beyond the river." It is apparent that nothing else could logically happen. If their covenant with God required obedience to His commandments as the condition of continued occupancy, as it plainly did, it would naturally follow that their persistent disobedience to these commandments, and the repudiation of their covenant, would forfeit their right to remain in its possession.

The long standing judgment against Israel began to be finally administered in the reign of Hosea, king of the northern division of the nation, when he was defeated and carried into captivity, with many of his people, by Shalmaneser, king of Assyria. About one hundred and thirty-four years later a similar fate overtook the southern kingdom of Judah, when Nebuchadnezzar, king of Babylon, carried the main portion of the people into his own country, although the execution of this sentence upon the whole nation consumed many years.

Chapter Sixteen - In Exile

For, lo, I will command, and I will sift the house of Israel among all nations, like as corn is sifted in a sieve, yet shall not the least grain fall upon the earth. — Amos 9:9.

And I will scatter thee among the heathen, and disperse thee in the countries, and will consume thy filthiness out of thee.

And thou shalt take thine inheritance in thyself in the sight of the heathen, and thou shalt know that I am the Lord.

Thus saith the Lord God; Although I have cast them far off among the heathen, and although I have scattered them among the countries, yet will I be to them as a little sanctuary in the countries where they shall come. Ezek. 22: 15, 16; 11: 16.

And the remnant of Jacob shall be in the midst of many people as a dew from the Lord, as the showers upon the grass. — Mic. 5: 7.

To all appearance the national existence of the Hebrews had come to an end. The people of both the northern and southern kingdoms, with the exception of some of the poorer classes, had been literally rooted up and transported to the lands of their conquerors. Let it not be supposed, however, that the conquest of Israel had been accomplished from without. Although the northern kingdom had been completely subdued by the Assyrians, and although Judah had been at the mercy of her enemies on either side for some time prior to her final defeat, this humiliating condition was not due to the superior physical force of their adversaries, but to the weakening and demoralizing effect of their own disloyalty to God. They had reached the place where they no longer relied upon divine protection. One has but to recall the occasions in their history, from the conquest of Canaan to the defeat of Sennacherib, when their enemies were miraculously delivered into their hands, to realize that their subjugation in the present instance was not brought about by military force. The vision of the servant of Elisha at Dothan, when his eyes were opened to see the mountains round about full of horses and chariots of fire, showed that Israel need not fear the armies of her enemies, however formidable they might appear to be. Her divine protection had been proved so often and so decisively, that there was absolutely no danger to her national safety so long as she remained loyal to her covenants.

It is true, however, of any nation whose moral qualities are held in subjection to evil, and whose highest rule is worldly self-interest, that it will meet eventual defeat and downfall. History furnishes undoubted proofs that unless good holds the balance of influence in the councils of a nation, and in the thoughts of its citizens, its final ruin is inevitable, because of the unescapable and omnipresent law that good is all that can endure. In the present instance, the Assyrian invasion was the occasion but not the cause of Israel's conquest and captivity. "O Israel, thou hast destroyed thyself," was Hosea's verdict of what had taken place, and his view coincides with the lessons of human experience. The evils that men do become their captors and executioners, while, conversely, the good which men do is their liberty and their defense.

With the brief account of their deportation into Assyria, the ten tribes which had constituted the northern kingdom of Israel disappear from history ac abruptly and as completely as if they had been annihilated. But they were not to be annihilated, for Israel's work was not yet done. The judgment against her did not call for extinction, but for banishment, and for dispersion among the nations of the earth; which obviously means that they were not to remain permanently in Assyria, nor to return to their own land, but were to go out into other countries. It is not difficult for the imagination to accompany them in their subsequent wanderings, which were strongly suggestive of the wanderings of their ancestors in the wilderness, when an improved generation was being fitted to take possession of the land of promise. We can see them gradually recovering from the mesmerism of their heathen idolatries, shaking off the cruder superstitions about the nature of Deity, and of His relation to man, which they had imbibed from their intercourse with the Gentiles, and which had adulterated and defiled the purely monotheistic religion of Israel; and we can see their eventual awakening to again recognize and acknowledge the one God.

The situation of the people of the southern kingdom of Judah was somewhat different. Their immediate exile in Babylon was comparatively brief, lasting not more than seventy years, and one can glean from the Scriptures a reasonably clear understanding of what transpired there, and of the circumstances of their return. From that time on, with the exception of about two hundred years, the Jews have left an almost uninterrupted trail through history, so that while they too were finally dispersed, they have remained in the world's observation, detaining their racial identity and their national religion. Their census can be taken today in every country where they have found refuge. They have been unable to lose themselves if they would, or to erase the evidence of their lineage, or to dissociate themselves from the shame and the glory of their past. The preservation of this division of the Israelitish race, scattered for twenty centuries in nearly every country of the globe, without a national head or recognized government, is one of the most striking confirmations of prophetic Scripture which modern history affords. In view of the literal fulfilment of prophecy in this notable instance, one not unnaturally looks for the same literal fulfilment in respect to the other and major portion of Israel, and there is no valid reason to believe that the Scriptures will not be confirmed in this also until the "final restitution of all things" shall be accomplished.

It was a natural result that the continued disappearance of the Ten Tribes would eventually divert attention to Judah as the only representative of Israel, so that in time the word Jew came to be used as synonymous with the word Israelite, until practically no distinction was made in the general thought between these designations. The former word, however, was originally used only of the members of the tribe of Judah, or the inhabitants of Judea, and was not given any broader application until after the captivity; but the distinction in correct usage necessarily remains, notwithstanding the general custom to the contrary, and this distinction must be carefully maintained in order correctly to understand the subject of Israel. The mystery which surrounded the subsequent career of Ephraim and Manasseh, the birthright house of Joseph, did not dispose of the fact of their existence, or lessen the importance of their destiny in the world, nor did it make the Jews the sole representative of Jacob's seed. The doom of exile which fell upon Israel was not declared to be final, nor was she to be deprived, except for a time, of her national identity. Therefore, while general ignorance of the whereabouts of the Israelites may serve to explain the misuse and misapplication of the word Jew, the careful student will discover that this is not warranted by the Scriptural records nor by the facts of history.

In the sense that he was a descendant of Jacob, a Jew was an Israelite; but an Israelite was not a Jew unless he was a member of the house of Judah. A Californian, for example, is an American, but an American is not necessarily a Californian unless he is a resident of that state. When the division of the kingdom drew the line between Judah and Israel, it drew the line of distinction between Jew and Israelite, and the same national and racial distinction exists today; so that when Israel is restored to her former position and identity it will not be as Jews, as some mistakenly suppose. The Scriptures indicate that the restoration will find Israel bearing a new name, and that will necessarily be neither Israel nor Judah.

The tribe of Judah did not lose her identity as descending from Jacob, nor was she ever lost historically or geographically, but she did lose her national unity and the possession of her tribal territory in Palestine. But Palestine, as a country, never was hers to any greater extent than America can be said to belong to California, therefore to say that Palestine was the national home of the Jews presents only a portion of the facts, and is apt to be misleading. An

111

intelligent perception of these distinctions is essential in order to understand the relative positions of Israel and Judah in the present and future problems of the human race.

It will be remembered that early in the history of the two kingdoms, before Judah had herself fallen under the spell of idolatry, the Levites separated themselves from Israel and united their fortunes with the Jews. The presence of the official priesthood, and the possession of the national temple, thus gave the southern kingdom a decided advantage, but an advantage which depended entirely upon the strength of the religious sentiment among the Israelites. It proved insufficient to restore the unity of Israel, and may even have contributed towards weakening the resistance of the northern people to the appeal of foreign religious influence. The Jews, on the other hand, holding the high place of the national religion, the Mecca of all Israel, developed an exaggerated belief of the importance of ecclesiastical formalities that in time became a stumbling-block to their spiritual freedom and progress.

The temple was a visible token to Israel of the Divine presence, as the tabernacle had been before it, and there is no doubt that its location in their own territory exercised, for a time at least, a compelling restraint in the thoughts of the Jews in face of the steadily increasing influence of idolatry. Although the elaborate ritual and ceremony of the temple worship appealed most strongly to the senses and emotions, and enshrouded the true concept of God in mysticism, there was that about it all which reminded the Jew of God's wonderful dealings with Israel. The very thought of the temple, even when it was destroyed and but a memory in his exile, brought before him the cherished glories of his race, so that he could say in the words of the Psalmist, "If I forget thee, O Jerusalem, let my right hand forget her cunning."

The Jews were apparently more mindful of God during the captivity than they had been in Jerusalem, and we need not doubt that the Israelites in their Assyrian captivity also thought longingly and remorsefully of the religion they had betrayed. Without in any sense condoning their infidelity, it seems inconceivable that one could be a descendant of Jacob, with a knowledge of the sacred traditions and records of his race, and not feel that God meant something to him which was beyond the power of evil to destroy. It is because of this that the banishment of Israel would be corrective rather than punitive. Although the vicious elements of the carnal mind had apparently overwhelmed and submerged the spiritually awakening thought of this race, we may still know that whatever is derived from God is imperishable. Notwithstanding their vicissitudes, their lapses into error, their sheep-like wanderings into the byways of sensual allurements, underneath it all they were still the people of Israel. The spiritual qualities which they had possessed were still there, and it only heeded the tribulating process of evil's self-punishment to beat the encumbering chaff from the precious grain.

No one who looks at these events from the viewpoint of divine revelation, so closely linked up as they are with the present and future of human salvation, can suppose that the tribulations which came upon Israel, prolonged though they were, were intended to end her great mission or to blot out her place in human destiny. This mission was to be none the less hers because evil had temporarily triumphed, or because she had disappeared into an age-long obscurity. What are ages to divine Truth! "A thousand years In Thy sight are but as yesterday when it is past, and as a watch in the night" (Ps. 90: 4).

We have read of the seed which had lain hidden in a mummy's hand, and which when planted responded to the warmth of the sun — that had been shining on during the ages of darkness and concealment — and brought forth its increase of grain. And so will it be with Israel. The eclipse of her long exile has not signified decay. It only means that the "mills of God" have been grinding on with their patient exactness. Israel's hard experiences have been surely working out the self-destruction but not the self-perpetuation of evil, and the spiritual seed of the woman has been as unharmed through it all as the seed which lay through thousands of years in an Egyptian sarcophagus. The tribulations of Israel, as the word itself implies, have been the means of liberating the grain from the chaff, the true from the false, and in the ripeness of time we shall see the precious seed breaking forth into its increase of living grain, warmed by the rays of that Light which St. John tells us is God.

Let us, then, dismiss the too popular delusion that when Israel disappeared from the eye of history she lost her existence as a nation, or her place in God's plan, or that she became merged with races of inferior ideals. Let us not believe that the glorious things spoken of her, and revealed in her, were as the passing breath of human emotion, or as the inconsequential happenings of dreams, for they were the voicings to human consciousness of the Divine presence. They pointed to a spiritual quality of thought which could not be dissolved in the furnace of sensuality, or be deprived of its vital energy in the shadows of obscurity. Although Israel disappeared in an exile which has apparently been prolonged to the present period, the light which was aflame in her, weak and flickering though it frequently appeared, was one with its divine source, and could not be extinguished by all the darkness that ever blinded mortal eyes.

We feel assured that the inhabitants of Paris, New York, or London, or the natives of South Africa, continue their round of activity, progress, and experience whether we are present to witness it or not. Although human beings are transported from one locality to another, or although they may even pass entirely out of one's earthly focus, we still know that they are expressing what they are,; irrespective of their environment, and are moving steadily on to the fulfilment of their being. By the same rule, therefore, we may be assured that, when the Israelites passed out of the world's notice, or when in other lands as the generations went by they even passed out of the knowledge of their former identity, they still continued to "carry on" with the best they had. Notwithstanding changes of time and place, they were working out the destined end and purpose of their race, because these outward changes had not separated them from the Father, or from the spiritual good which had been incorporated into their national consciousness. Thus they would go on and on in their appointed course, because they could not escape from what they were, or from what they were yet to be.

The fact evidently is, that Israel in her exile was no further removed from her rightful place in the human drama than if she had continued her career in the land of Canaan. Although Judah has remained out in the open, she is apparently no nearer the fulfilment of her share in Israel's promised destiny than if she had shared the same obscurity. It is not the simple fact of being in the eyes of the world that fits one for his work in it, but what is being accomplished in one's own consciousness. Whether the whereabouts of Israel were known to the rest of the world or not is a matter of small moment beside the question of her moral and spiritual recovery, a work that could go on quite as well in one place as in another.

Inasmuch as the government of God expresses the only power there is, and operates impartially and universally for the good of all men, it necessarily follows that there was no power operating anywhere to prevent the Israelites from recognizing this fact and throwing off their subservience to evil. Wherever they might be, their sense of good was still there. The worst that the fiery experiences which followed her wrongdoing could do to Israel, would be to consume the human satisfaction in sin's delusions, and prepare the way for her return.

It is certain that evil cannot destroy any portion of God's creation, otherwise man and the universe would be in danger of ultimate extinction. The consciousness in man which reflects God, and which He acknowledges as His own likeness, can neither be atrophied nor destroyed, but remains to shine forth at every opportunity. It should be self-evident that it is not the spiritual side of a man's being which sins and suffers, but the mistake of a selfhood and mind which God neither fathers nor supports. As St. John wrote, "He that is begotten of God keepeth himself, and that wicked one toucheth him not." The son of God, because of his very divinity, can neither sin nor be punished, and that man is spiritually the son of God was the glimpse of heavenly glory which changed Jacob to Israel, and which appears in ever increasing volume and emphasis throughout the subsequent Scriptures.

Races and peoples are differentiated by their mental rather than their physical characteristics, and these remain and are perpetuated and renewed although individuals and generations pass away. The spiritual origin and development of Israel, and the high destiny assigned to her in the inspired visions of the prophets, imply the necessarily temporary nature of her exile, and the certainty of her return chastened and purified. We may well believe that the nation in whose consciousness came the revelation of the spiritual creation of man in God's image and likeness, and of the consequently false nature of His unlikeness, could not be held in continual captivity. The perception of the spiritual idea of being which came to Abraham, Isaac, and Jacob, and to the inspired leaders of Israel, which moulded and preserved the nation's ideals, which illumined the visions of her prophets, and led human thought "to where the young child lay," could not fail to bring back this race to the realization of her true identity, and to "restore again the kingdom to Israel" both spiritually and nationally.

The comparatively speedy return of Judah to Palestine did not indicate that she was less involved in error than her brethren in Israel, as one may conclude from her later record. The destruction of the temple seems to have aroused a more or less sincere desire to return to the worship of Jehovah, and the way was consequently opened for its rebuilding and for their return to Canaan. It would seem, however, that the tendency towards any general or sustained restoration of the worship of the true God of Israel was soon smothered by the cold ecclesiasticism and stern application of the letter of the Mosaic law, such as prevailed after the captivity, and which laid the mantle of severity and formalism upon the gentler impulses which true religious feeling should call forth. Judaism exalted the form of religion in place of its spirit, and magnified the importance of external observances, until the Jewish thought became spiritually benumbed and unresponsive to any glow of divine inspiration. Thus while it is true that the Jews came out of their Babylonian captivity, and have since maintained their identity, they entered a spiritual exile from which even the coming of the Messiah was unable to recall them, and which still holds them as completely as does the national exile in the case of Israel.

This spiritual exile of the Jews is not the least important or interesting aspect of Israel's captivity, and of the breach between Joseph and Judah. It will probably be found that the spiritual exile of Judah and the national exile of Joseph will end at approximately the same time; and that when Ephraim and Manasseh awaken to their national inheritance in Israel, Judah will awaken to see her spiritual inheritance and freedom in the "Son of David." To lose the sense of one's racial identity is not more obscuring than to lose the perception of man's spiritual identity as the son of God. The dense ritualism of the Judaic religion, with the mystifying influence of a localized and tribal Jehovah, so beclouded the spiritual perception that when the Messiah came the Jews were unable to see him except as an Impostor, showing how effectually they had been driven into exile by their false concept of Deity.

But while the nature of the captivity and exile of Israel and Judah is thus contrasted, it will be found equally true of the latter that the sufferings and persecutions which have attended her dispersion will serve to grind out the rebellious unbelief which has held her in bondage, and prepare her thought to welcome the things which belong to her peace, And who can say that it may not be Israel's opportunity to lead Judah into the vision of the long expected Christ! The indications are that the exile of both Israel and Judah has about spent itself, and that we are on the eve of the realization of reunited Israel, and the world's recognition of the reign upon the earth of her divine King.

We cannot consistently close this chapter without noting some of the remarkable events which Daniel records of the Babylonian captivity. The escape of the three young Hebrews from the fiery furnace, and of Daniel from the lions, are among the most familiar of Bible incidents, and furnish additional proofs of the Divine omnipresence when men are ready to acknowledge and understand it. The failure of the attempt to destroy these young men because of loyalty to their God illustrates the impotence of evil to interfere with His creation and government. The calm and steadfast refusal of these Jews to forswear their allegiance to the God of Israel, in face of what appeared certain death, is perhaps the most sublimely heroic incident of the Old Testament records. So clearly did they realize the divine power to annul the material law of fire that it was impressed upon the vision of the king as a fourth figure in the flames, described by him as like "a son of the gods" (Isaac Leeser's translation).

Here again was a demonstration of man's spiritual sovereignty over matter, a demonstration so intimately associated with Israel's history and development. If it were true that man is formed of dust, and therefore in subjection to material conditions, these three Hebrews would have been as helplessly at the mercy of the fire as other mortals, even as men today are taught to believe themselves helpless to overcome adverse physical conditions, as if the God of Israel were no longer a factor in preserving the lives of men. The Scriptures plainly show that it was the mission of Israel to bring to human consciousness the perception of spiritual law, based upon man's indestructible sonship with God, and which is capable of nullifying the operation and effect of what is called material law. It were well if those who are attempting, and very properly so, to establish Israel's identity in the present day, took more account of these things; for as surely as Israel began with the first human perception of man's spiritual being as the son of God, and gave proofs of this truth all along the way, so will she be judged and tested in the last days.

"My God," said Daniel, "hath sent His angel, and hath shut the lions' mouths, that they have not hurt me," — and what did he mean by "my" God, if it were not that the God declared and revealed in Israel was the preserver and not the destroyer of men? Isaiah gives a vision of the time when the supremacy of Spirit will be so understood that the lion will lie down with the lamb, showing that the unthinking cruelty of the beast, and the unthinking cruelty of material laws, never were a part or a feature of God's creation, and will disappear with human progress.

Surely, it must be in these things that we shall find the true glory of Israel, and her true identity, and not in great number, material prosperity, military dominion, or political supremacy. What can be more applicable to this whole subject than these words of the prophet Jeremiah: "Thus saith the Lord, Let not the wise man glory in his wisdom, neither let the mighty man glory in his might, let not the rich man glory in his riches: but let him that glorieth glory in this, that he understandeth and knoweth Me."

Chapter Seventeen - "The Times of the Gentiles"

Though Babylon should mount up to heaven, and though she should fortify the height of her strength, yet from Me shall spoilers come unto her, saith the Lord. — Jer. 51:53.

These great beasts, which are four, are four kings, which shall arise out of the earth.

But the saints of the most High shall take the kingdom, and possess the kingdom for ever, even for ever and ever. — Dan. 7:17, 18.

JESUS' statement, that "Jerusalem shall be trodden down of the Gentiles, until the times of the Gentiles be fulfilled" (Luke 21:24), directs the attention of Christians as well as Jews to this subject. In Weymouth's translation the passage is rendered, "until the appointed times of the Gentiles have expired." This prophetic statement clearly referred to a definite period, which apparently began before and would continue after the events of the age in which it was spoken. One might well ask. What are the times of the Gentiles to which Jesus referred, and what is their prescribed course or "appointed times"?

There seems little doubt that Jesus was thinking of the duration of Gentile world-dominion, spoken of in the book of Daniel, which began approximately with the taking of the Jews to Babylon, an event which completed the captivity of Israel. It is not the present purpose to enter into the details of the prophetic dates outlined in Daniel; suffice it to say that the "seven times" mentioned therein as passing over Nebuchadnezzar is interpreted by many writers as defining the period indicated by our Master. Prophetic time is usually reckoned on the year-day plan, with a year of 360 days; and a "time" is understood as a year of such days, or 360 years of actual time. Thus the "seven times" would be equivalent to 2520 years, and are therefore due to end sometime in the near future, if they are not, as some contend, already ended. The conquest of Jerusalem by British troops in 1917, and the recent establishment of an English protectorate over Palestine, naturally point to the probability that the times of the Gentiles, at least in their external aspect, have about run their course.

In chapters 10 and 11 of Genesis we have the first Scriptural account of the division of the human family into races and peoples, and although, as time went on, these increased through self-division, they retained the characteristics of their root origin. Later on in the Scriptures, mankind were more broadly divided into Israelites and Gentiles, and these two divisions of humanity continued to flow side by side, one as an almost insignificant rivulet and the other a mighty stream, with Israel spiritually in the ascendancy. The Assyrian and Babylonian conquests and deportations of the Israelites inaugurated the period spoken of by Jesus as the times of the Gentiles, or the times when national types of thought foreign to Israel would have dominion over the Land of Promise and over the people of the covenant.

After the destruction of Jerusalem by Nebuchadnezzar, the name Babylon became a symbol or a synonym in the prophetic writings for all that was inimical to the spiritual life and freedom of Israel. The original of this word in the Hebrew is Babel, or confusion. We read in Genesis 10 that Nimrod, the reputed first king of Babel, was the son of Gush and the grandson of Ham. Ovid, an early Roman poet, as quoted in Hislop's *The Two Babylons*, represents Janus, the "god of gods," or the beginning of gods, as saying, "The ancients called me Chaos." Authorities may be found in the same work for the following statements regarding the origin of Babylon and her line of kings. In the Chaldee, chaos is said to be the pronunciation of Gush; thus it would seem that Ham's firstborn corresponded with Belus or Bel, the mythological founder of Babylon, since Bel signifies "the Confounder." Thus if Janus, as is claimed, is identical with chaos, Cush, or Bel, it is evident that the first god of mythology was identical with confusion, and that confusion, or ignorance of the truth, signified the beginning of pagan idolatry.

An ancient representation of the god Janus gives a club as his symbol, and this word in the Chaldee means to break in pieces, or to scatter abroad. It is interesting to note that the word in Hebrew, from which a club derives its name, is the same as that used to denote the scattering abroad of the people, following the confusion of tongues. (Gen. 11: 9.) A club was the symbol of physical force, and physical force is what the ancient rulers worshipped and sought after, that they might scatter their enemies and break them in pieces. That this was still the Babylonian ideal at the time of the captivity is seen in Jeremiah 50: 23, where the prophet says of Babylon, "How is the hammer of the whole earth cut asunder and broken!" The hammer of Vulcan and the club of Hercules show how the worship of physical power had permeated the Gentile world; and the line of kings that descended from Cush, as well as the later Babylonian dynasties, found their greatest glory in wielding this club in the effort to bring all the nations of the earth to their knees.

These things indicate to some extent the nature and character of the beginnings of the Babylonian race, and of the Assyrian race which later came out of it. While the true God was being revealed to Abraham, the Gentile nations were deifying their material concepts of man and woman. The moon-god of the Assyrians, identified with the Phoenician Ashtoreth, the Roman Venus, the Grecian Aphrodite, and the Egyptian Hathor, was the goddess of sensual love. The sun-god of the Babylonians was in reality the counterpart of the same deity, and was symbolized by a serpent coiled about a shining disc. The figure of a serpent or dragon was sometimes placed on their military standards. This deification of animality thus became the framework of the Babylonian and Assyrian national consciousness.

The mythical deities of other nations were the outgrowth of Babylonian mythology, and in the last analysis they all centered in the worship of the serpent. Cradled in the darkness of this spiritual ignorance, and held fast in the grasp of superstition and fear, the pagan peoples came to regard evil as the supreme power on earth, and the procurer of human success as well as of woe and disaster. This canonization of the carnal mind eventuated in a demonology and a mystic priestcraft whose incubus the world has not yet shaken off, but which is doomed to be destroyed as not the least evil feature of the times of the Gentiles. The sensual religion of Babylon, breathing out selfishness and cruelty, and minus any touch of genuine goodness, was the antipode of that spiritual inspiration which was beginning to be humanly felt in Israel. As the latter prefigured, prophesied, and prepared the way for the coming of the "Son of the Highest," the Redeemer of men, so Babylon prefigured and ultimated in that curse of diabolism which would bind men forever to the beast, and which the apostle called the "son of perdition," the "mystery of iniquity," whose end St. John so graphically describes in the Apocalypse.

The nations which sprang from such a source were not likely to express even the human ideal of liberty and righteousness, much less to illumine the human pathway to God. Their ambition was to conquer and oppress, never to make free or to uplift mankind. Their highest creed appears to have been the right of the sword, in their devotion to, which the basest passions of mortals were given license. Their worship of the heavenly bodies gave them no glimpse of heaven or of divinity, but shut out the godlike from earthly vision, and fostered and encouraged the indulgence of inhuman cruelty and unspeakable licentiousness. One can well understand the edict of Moses forbidding the Israelites to intermarry with these nations, or to acknowledge their gods; and why darkness and defilement overspread Israel and Judah when they disobeyed his injunction.

It is not surprising, therefore, that Babylon, where evil was endowed with supernatural powers, should be the birthplace of sorcery, witchcraft, and the black art, which infected the life of the ancient world with their baleful influence, and which continued their activities under the cover of secrecy or the cloak of religion. In the eighteenth century these destructive agencies came into more public notice in the so-called discovery of mesmerism, under which name evil claimed to have normal and legitimate powers. These occult practices were interdicted in Israel under penalty of death, and this ban was never removed. The use of any form of enchantment belonged wholly to Gentiledom and accompanied its world-course, but occultism was inherently antagonistic to the true idea of Israel, and never had a place in it, nor can its more recent activity under the name of hypnotism be reconciled with the Israel of today. No "ravenous beast shall go up thereon," said the prophet, and nothing "that defileth, neither whatsoever worketh abomination, or maketh a lie," can make its home with God's chosen people. "They shall not be found there." The new faces in which necromancy and witchcraft appear today belong to the dominion of the Gentiles, as surely as did the occultism of Egypt and Babylon.

Let us not overlook this feature of the restoration. Restore means to bring back to a former state of excellence or soundness. To restore Israel, then, would mean something more than the bringing back of her national integrity and self-recognition. It would involve the restored consciousness of what she stood for in the beginning, and the restored fitness and ability to fill the place and accomplish the work that had been assigned to her. Anything less than this would not be restoration. She could not bring back her acknowledgment of other gods, and yet be restored Israel. She could not arise from her grave, as Ezekiel pictures the restoration, and bring the things of death along with her. Speaking of the return of the Israelites this prophet says, "Neither shall they defile themselves any more with their idols, nor with their detestable things, nor with any of their transgressions." Thus the Israel of the latter days will surely have to forswear her false gods, her idolatries and adulteries, before she can again be known as God's chosen people, or be entitled to claim that designation. The New Jerusalem is not a myth, nor a mere figure of speech, but the purified consciousness of humanity, wherefrom the errors that defiled and betrayed her have been cast out, and wherein good alone is known and acknowledged. St. John makes it unmistakably plain that sorcerers and idolaters are not to be found within that heavenly city.

The Babylonian empire continued to increase in power as Israel declined, and practically reached its zenith at the latter's downfall and captivity. The dream of (the image, which Daniel revealed and interpreted to Nebuchadnezzar, pointed to the constitution of Gentile dominion and its final destruction. The four kingdoms composing the image are generally understood to mean Babylonia, Medo-Persia, Greece, and Rome. The king also saw in his dream "that a stone was cut out without hands, which smote the image upon his feet that were of iron and clay, and brake them to pieces. Then was the iron, the clay, the brass, the silver, and the gold broken to pieces together, and became like the chaff of the summer threshing-floors; and the wind carried them away, that no place was found for them: and the stone that smote the image became a great mountain, and filled the whole earth."

This dream-prophecy has been literally fulfilled up to the present period. These four kingdoms arose, and in their day typified the dominion of the carnal mind, and perpetuated the Babylonian ideals; but one after another their day as world-rulers declined and faded into night. "Though Babylon should mount up to heaven, and though she should fortify the height of her strength, yet from Me shall spoilers come unto her, saith the Lord" (Jer. 51: 53). The doom of destruction and desolation pronounced by the prophets against Babylon and Nineveh was literally carried out. Their ruins became so completely buried under the debris of the passing centuries that even their sites became lost to the knowledge of men.

It has been found that the most enduring achievements of the carnal mind carry the germs of their own decay, and that its greatest glories eventually pass and are forgotten. If it were possible for the nations that knew not God to prosper and endure despite their idolatry and their iniquity, there would be no distinction between good and evil, and the story of Israel would be one of the passing fictions of history; but the glorious revelation of the first chapter of Genesis, and the light of spiritual truth which continued to shine forth in Israel, assured the ultimate downfall of Gentile materialism, even though the people of Israel should come under its ascendancy for seven times, or for seventy times seven.

There is no doubt that, when Jesus spoke of the treading down of Jerusalem by the Gentiles, he used the word Jerusalem as typifying human consciousness, as well as in a literal sense. The Master would hardly have voiced a prophecy of this nature if it had no connection with his mission and with the work of his followers, since it was only the demonstration of his teachings that could bring the end of Gentile dominion in the earth. As the word Israel, applied to a nation, meant something more than racial distinction, so the word Gentile had a deeper significance than the distinctive term for one who was not an Israelite. Naturally it is the metaphysical sense of Scriptural statements and designations that we most need to understand. As Israel signified a perception of the spiritual facts of being, the word Gentile, or foreigner, signified the opposite or carnal sense of things. Not one city alone, or one nation, but the human consciousness was under the oppression of the carnal mind, claiming that intelligence, power, life, substance, and happiness are material; and this Gentile thought, foreign to the true idea of Israel and to human salvation, would keep the human mind in subjection until the spiritual sense of thing's should be restored, and the truth of man's divinity bruise the serpent's head.

Gentile dominion was the expression of autocracy in all its aspects. The belief that might is right, and that this might is physical, had held the thoughts of mortals from the most primitive times, and reached the acme of its development in the Babylonian monarchy. To become military master of the world was the unscrupulous ambition of that and following ages, and the phrase "Gentile dominion" was truly and terribly earned and maintained. Brute force was the god to whom the Gentile world burned incense, but the "Confounder" in every case was sooner or later confounded and broken in pieces by his own weapons. Egypt fought against the God of Israel, and became the conquered dependent of other nations. Babylonia and Assyria laid their hands upon the Lord's chosen people, taking them into captivity and profaning the temple, and their high places became the abode of the owl and the bat and the beasts of the desert. Persia helped the Jews to rebuild their temple and permitted their return from exile, and although her power was broken she never lost her national existence. Rome gave God's anointed into the hands of the Jews to be crucified, and she went down and out despite her tremendous power.

But for all this, Gentile dominion had not yet passed. With the fall of the Roman empire, the "seven times" had about half their course yet to run. There was still "a time, times, and half a time," which were apparently reserved for other phases of Gentile ascendancy. Heretofore the world had been under a military or political autocracy, which, in its more general application, came to an end with the downfall of the Western Roman Empire; but from that time forward, Gentile dominion began gradually to take on the aspect of an ecclesiastical autocracy, which, in its cruelty and inhumanity, eclipsed any military despotism that preceded it. The fourth kingdom of Nebuchadnezzar's dream, which coincided with Rome, had simply changed its face; it was still Rome, and would so continue to the end of its course when the whole image and all it stood for would be ground to nothingness by the stone cut out of the mountain without hands, that is, a kingdom not of human origin.

The Babylon of the Old Testament was the type of Gentile dominion in its relation to Israel. The Babylon of the New Testament typified the same dominion in its relation to Christianity. Although the second appeared in history under the name of Rome, the two were undoubtedly identical, and were so treated by St. John in the Apocalypse. The carnal mind might change its spots but its evil nature remained the same, whether it held its grasp upon humanity as a false expression of government or a false expression of religion. There was to be no respite from oppression. The hand of ecclesiasticism that fell upon a war-trampled and suffering race was hard and heavy, and the weary heart of humanity groaned under its pressure for twelve hundred years.

That the Roman hierarchy was the counterpart or completion of the fourth kingdom of Nebuchadnezzar's image, and the fourth beast of Daniel's own vision, history grimly testifies. The evidences in its support, both internal and external, are too strong and numerous to be seriously questioned. A Roman Catholic writer of the last century is quoted as saying: "The rise of the tem.poral power of the popes presents to the mind one of the most extraordinary phenomena which the annals of the human race offer to our wonder and admiration. By a singular combination of concurring circumstances, a new power and a new dominion grew up, silently but steadily, on the ruins of that Roman empire which had extended its sway over, or made itself respected by, nearly all the nations, peoples, and races that lived in the period of its strength and glory; and that new power, of lowly origin, struck a deeper root, and soon exercised a wider authority, than the empire whose gigantic ruins it saw shivered into fragments, and mouldering in dust."

But autocracy in religion, under whatever name, is not the expression of God's government on earth. The deeds of violence and torture perpetrated in the name of religion, the unspeakable outrages committed in her name, covering every conceivable form of cruelty, far exceeded and outrivalled the worst that has been recorded of Assyrian despots. One has but to read the history of the Dark and Middle Ages to realize the depth and extent of the infamy of the carnal mind, assuming to occupy "the temple of God," and to be His representative upon the earth.

The stone cut out of the mountain has surely struck the feet of the image, but the grinding process referred to by Daniel is yet to be completed. The liberation of Jerusalem points to the fulfilment of Jesus' prophecy in its purely external aspect, but a greater freedom remains to be won before the times of the Gentiles are fully ended, and men come to realize their liberty as sons of God. "For the earnest expectation of the creature waiteth for the manifestation of the sons of God" (Rom. 8:19).

Chapter Eighteen - The Covenant of Prophecy

Think not that I am come to destroy the law, or the prophets; I am not come to destroy but to fulfil. — Matt. 5:17.

And when they had appointed him a day, there came many to him into his lodging; to whom he expounded and testified the kingdom of God, persuading them concerning Jesus, both out of the law of Moses, and out of the prophets. — Acts 28: 23.

FROM the beginning of human discernment between good and evil, followed as it naturally was by the realization of the necessity for salvation, there has been a steady looking forward to something better. Without this desire and expectancy for a more harmonious and enduring consciousness, prophecy would have found a barren and unpromising field for its ministry. Every improvement effected in human experience is in itself a prophecy of perfection, since the achievement of better conditions in any direction not only proves the possibility of continuing this progress until the ideal is reached, but the certainty of its realization, for the impulsion of the race forward has its source in the truth of man's original divinity, and will not cease until perfection is realized.

In its earlier use in the Old Testament, the word prophet signified a spokesman, that is one who was delegated to speak for God; and although the word was later used chiefly to denote a foreteller of future events, its original significance naturally remained with it, for unless the Hebrew prophets had been so divinely illumined that they felt commissioned to speak for God in human affairs, their utterances would not have been received as bearing the stamp of authority. These men were undoubtedly inspired to lift a comer of the veil, and disclose something of the course and destiny of Israel, and her relations with the Gentile world.

The Hebrew Scriptures present in progressive order and degree the unfoldment of the truth of divinity. God was being revealed to humanity through the only avenue available, — namely, the spiritually awakening thought which was given the name of Israel. If there had been found elsewhere a greater responsiveness to spiritual truth, it would naturally have become God's medium of revelation, since it was not a question of preference or privilege, but of opportunity. The spiritual facts of being had been coming to light along the line of least resistance, and without this illumination the night of materialism would have been without a star to bespeak an approaching dawn. It was this star of Israel, the star of prophecy, which led the wise men to "the young child" at Bethlehem, and which, during the succeeding centuries, has ever cheered the watchers on the hilltops of Zion.

If men were more alive to the wondrous messages which the Hebrew prophets voiced to the Israel, not of their day only, but of our own day and time, there would be less indifference concerning this subject. Many seem unwilling to acknowledge any connection between the prophecies of the Old or the New Testament and the present age, assuming that they are chiefly or wholly concerned with a remote past or a remote future, forgetting that today is the connecting link between yesterday and tomorrow. It is our own period of history that is linking up the prophetic vision of the past with its fulfilment, and which points to the relation of the prophets' messages to the political and religious life of today. The value of the inspired utterances of the prophets is not lessened because they may be denied or ignored by those who should be awake to their importance, for whatever of God's government is unfolded to men will sometime be universally acknowledged.

To minimize the value or to deny the validity of the prophecies indicates a lack of appreciation of the design of the Scriptures, and shuts from view the wonderful perspective of a perfected Christianity and a perfected humanity, or the perfect understanding of God and man, as that towards which the eyes of all peoples have been turned in hope, and which the prophets foresaw and foretold from Genesis to Revelation. Those who depreciate the Scriptural prophecies, and by this is naturally meant the prophecies that await fulfilment, should bear in mind that the Scriptures are themselves a prophecy. The Old Testament was a prophecy of the New, and the New Testament is a prophecy of that which is to come after. No book of the Bible is complete in itself, but points to or implies the coming of that which is to carry on the work. What Moses and the prophets accomplished was not final, or independent of relations. They filled their parts in a great scheme. Their work foreshadowed the teachings and miracles of Jesus, while he in turn pointed to the Comforter for the completion of his ministry. The last chapter of the Bible is a glorious summing up and amplification of all preceding prophecy, and prophecy will continue its God-appointed task until the dream of materialism is dispelled, and no sense of evil remains to deceive or becloud human vision.

It may be well here to recall the Master's rebuke of his disciples' dullness, after his resurrection, when he said, "O fools, and slow of heart to believe all that the prophets have spoken! ...And beginning at Moses and all the prophets, he expounded unto them in all the scriptures the things concerning himself." And again, "These are the words which I spake unto you, while I was yet with you. that all things must be fulfilled, which were written In the law of Moses, and in the prophets, and in the psalms, concerning me." It is equally important, is It not, if present-day disciples would not be dull or slow of heart to believe, that they should also understand the things which are written In the Scriptures concerning the reappearing of the Christ and the conditions which are to Indicate Its approach? It should "be of some consequence to understand what is to usher in the consummation of the story of the past six thousand years, when the kingdoms of this world are to acknowledge the government of God, and bow the knee in allegiance to Christ.

Unless one gets the true perspective of any subject, the vision is either limited or indistinct. We naturally look to history for the right perspective of Israel's origin and development, but we must look to prophecy and revelation for the right perspective of her destiny. Her history in outline was pre-written in her prophecies and in her covenants; all that remained was the filling in of details; and the course which yet remains may be found, in general outline, in the writings of the prophets. We must look beyond today or tomorrow or next year or the next decade for the full vision of the glory of Israel as the chosen of God; and where shall we find this vision indicated save in the prophecies of the Old and New Testaments?

But, one may ask, why this pre-statement of future events, with its apparent prearrangement of the fate of mortals? Did the Supreme Being provide beforehand for the terrible occurrences of history? Did He prearrange the times of the Gentiles, the idolatry and captivity of Israel, and the betrayal and crucifixion of Jesus? Did the divine plan of creation include a place for the serpent and the fruits of his deceptions? The God of Israel forbid! It is the sophistry of the carnal mind which argues that, because sin and suffering, disaster and death, have attended human existence in the flesh, God must have provided and planned for them. If this view were to be accepted, it would implicate the Almighty in a chain of events down the ages that could have its origin only in an inversion of divinity, a thing impossible.

The time has come, surely, for this relic of paganism to be banished from the advancing thought of the age, for to those who accept it there can be no reasonable hope that the universe will ever be free from evil, inasmuch as God is revealed to be eternally the same. Although the prophets were surrounded by pagan influences, and their manner of speech was largely moulded by the primitive traditions of their race, their inspired utterances did not proclaim a God of good and evil, or of love and hate. While a superficial reading of the Scriptures might lead one to suppose that God inspired the prophets to foretell evil, the reverse is the case, as a more careful reading will disclose. It should be self-evident that good, not evil, constitutes the only possible sphere of divine activity; for even omnipotence could not hallow an evil deed, or transform revenge into a heavenly grace. We are taught that the Messiah came to do the will of the Father by destroying the works of the devil, not by consenting to them; and the will of the Father is as changeless as His own being, however dimly it has been perceived or grossly misinterpreted.

The prophetic gift of the ancient Hebrew seers was no more allied to occultism or divination than were the marvellous works of Moses to the jugglery of the Egyptian magicians. Their nearness to God so illumined the perception of the prophets, and so enlarged their mental focus, that the course of truth and the course of error in human consciousness were brought within their view, and they uttered as much of what they saw as the conditions and thought of the age permitted. Speaking after the custom of their time and race, they voiced their messages as communications from the Lord, and they were received as such, notwithstanding the obvious fact, as we see it today, that it was their own approach to God in spirit that lifted them above physical limitations and revealed the secret things.

The chief event upon which the eyes of the prophets were fixed was the ultimate deliverance of Israel, and through Israel of the rest of mankind. What the prophets did not always keep clearly before them was, that the oppressor of Israel was not a man or a nation, but the human sense of evil; and that deliverance was to be brought about, not by the conquest or overthrow of nations but by the overcoming of this sense of evil in the thoughts of their own people. The conflict in human consciousness between the forces of good and of evil, personalized as these seemed to them, were much in the thought of the prophets; and in their jealousy for the vindication of Jehovah, the doom of the oppressor, as they saw it foreshadowed, was not an unpleasant thing for them to picture.

But the prediction of the doom of their enemies, and of the terrible things which were to accompany it, by no means implied that they were to take place simply because they had been foretold, but because of the certainty of the eventual self -punishment and self-destruction of evil, and were to be viewed as proofs of the sovereignty, not the vengeance, of God. The spiritual illumination which enabled the prophets to pierce the shadows of futurity unveiled the evil as well as the good of the latter days. They saw the onward development in human consciousness of the spiritual idea, and its resistance by the carnal mind; but it was plain that this resistance would ultimate in its self-destruction, since Truth, in its very nature, is irresistible. The woes which the prophets foresaw as coming upon the Gentile nations, or upon Israel herself, as the case might be, were not acts of God, but the reaction of evil upon those nations in consequence of their consent to be its instruments.

No enlightened student of prophetic Scripture anticipates the occurrence of disturbing events merely because they were foretold, but because they are harbingers of the triumph of good in human experience. Jesus described the great commotions that would herald the reappearing of the Christ, but he pointed to them as cause for rejoicing, not for dismay. "And when these things begin to come to pass, then look up, and lift up your heads; for your redemption draweth nigh." (Luke 21:28.) His words were plainly intended to comfort his followers, not in that age only, but in subsequent ages, and to stimulate human expectation of his coming.

The bright vision in the mental horizon of the Hebrew prophets was the final restoration of Israel. Because the prophets were able to foresee the restoration of Israel, in other words the restoration of the Messianic idea, they were able to foresee the tremendous commotion which the approach of that great event of all the ages would produce in human consciousness. But Jesus understood better than the prophets why these disturbances would come, therefore he was able to read them as the signs of the near approach of hu-

126

man redemption. He saw them as the pangs of a world awakening from the sleep of materialism, to behold and to welcome the dawn of spiritual being.

It was to find a spiritual sense of being that Abraham left his parental home, and having found it, he laid thereon the foundation of Israel. The prophets, ever mindful of this spiritual foundation, looked forward to the time when the knowledge of the one true God should fill the earth, and that "day of the Lord" was the converging-point of their prophecies. All the truths uttered in the Scriptures necessarily lead to that point, and when they are fully proved, as all truth must sometime be, the covenant of prophecy, spanning the age-long interval like a bow of promise, will be abundantly fulfilled in Christ's universal kingdom.

The Apocalypse, which begins with the statement that it is the "Revelation of Jesus Christ," devotes many chapters to the description in metaphor of the events which were to occur during the period before the Millennial Age, but there is always the glow of the bright picture at the end, and which is the chief feature and object of that revelation. This drawing back of the curtain of futurity had reference only to human progress, or mortal's emergence from a false concept of life into the true, and was intended to encourage those who were looking forward and upward. It is self-evident, before a realization of the infinity of good could become humanly universal, that the human sense of evil, of that which denies God's allness, would have to be seen as unreal; and this is plainly what is to constitute "the end of all things," that is, of all things false. It is very clear that this process of human emancipation can be perfected only at the full appearing or reappearing of the Christ.

The prophets of the restoration had a glimpse of this I culminating event of history, and they saw also the disturbing influence of that event upon the carnal mind. They foresaw the tremendous conflicts which would take place in human consciousness between the flesh and Spirit before the former would be finally overcome, or laid off, as the apostle terms it. These disturbing conflicts were desirable only because through them it was possible for the human sense to rise higher. The stubborn determination of the carnal mind to retain its influence in human affairs has resisted every step of spiritual progress, and has been the underlying cause of national turmoils and world-wide disorder; but when the ability to separate good from evil came to human consciousness, the doom of this so-called mind became unquestionable. The onward course of the true idea, although apparently slow, has been irresistible; and while the prophets foresaw that the conflict would go on for ages, they also foresaw and foretold the absolute triumph of that idea, and, as inseparable from it, the overthrow of the oppressor.

This prophetic gift or faculty followed the line of spiritual enlightenment in Israel. By it Noah became aware of the outcome of the evils of his time, and the means of his escape. Abraham's perception of the unity of God, and the facts of His spiritual nature and presence, revealed to his consciousness what the development of that perception would be in its relation to the human race. He foresaw his seed, as spiritually named and perpetuated in Isaac, become a mighty people which would bless all the earth, not on account of material greatness, but because of their spiritual knowledge of God. This prophetic vision was to Abraham as God's covenant, and it was so designated and accepted by the Jsraelites, His experience was renewed in Isaac and Jacob, thus confirming "the covenant which God made with our fathers, saying unto Abraham, And in thy seed shall all the kindreds of the earth be blessed."

All the inspired prophecies of the Scriptures are but different chapters of God's covenant with men. They all point to one ultimate fulfilment, although they deal individually with various phases of human progress out of error. They are links in that one great chain of prophecy which runs throughout the Scriptures, and which finds its ultimate fulfilment in the universal redemption of the race. While many of the prophecies outwardly relate to material disturbances or commotions, it is always the self-destruction of error that is typified or indicated. As human consciousness approaches nearer to the discernment of God's infinite nature, it increasingly awakens to the deceptiveness of His unlikeness, and to that degree the evil in human belief dissipates into nothingness.

It is sometimes argued that, if these things were to occur anyway, wherefore the purpose of foretelling them. Peter spoke of prophecy as "a light shining in a dark place," or, as in another version, "in dimly lighted places." Thus prophecy undoubtedly served to illumine the long ages of paganism through which human consciousness passed, and is still passing, in its travail with the carnal mind. It was apparently in line with the divine plan that the human pathway should be thus illumined by the light of what lay ahead, just as a distant light guides the traveler on his course. It rested with mankind to throw off the yoke of evil and destroy its works, and this required spiritual illumination. It could not be accomplished in the dark, "when no man can work." It needed, and still needs, the revelation of the promises and prophecies to give rest and inspiration to human faith for the long journey to the Heavenly City.

But there was another and equally important part which prophecy was to fill in the working out of human salvation, and that was to supply Truth's affirmative to error's negative. The carnal mind was continually pouring its suggestions into human consciousness, denying the law which prohibits the knowing of evil, denying man's spiritual origin and divine sonship, denying his immortality and ability to overcome the flesh. The tendency of these immoral suggestions would be to induce such a subservience to sensuality as to sink the race into spiritual oblivion, and the inspired prophecies and promises of the Hebrew Scriptures were voiced and preserved in human consciousness to counteract this propaganda of error, and to prepare the way for the coming of the Lord.

It is impossible to conceive the difference in human history and progress if the prophecies had never been uttered. If one could subtract the influence of Hebrew prophecy from the character and lives of the Master and his disciples, of the great men who succeeded them, or from the thoughts and conditions of our own time, would we find that they had served no good purpose, and would have been better unsaid? Would we look forward with the same assurance of God's reign upon the earth, and the enthronement of love in the hearts of men, if the prophetic Scriptures had been a blank, and we were without the record of their fulfilment up to the present time? Would Jesus have found the same place in the thoughts of mortals without the confirmation of prophecy in his advent and experience? If we would hesitate to obliterate their place and influence in the work of the past, shall we not be glad to accord the same importance and value to the prophecies which are still awaiting their fulfilment, standing, as we seem to be, upon the very threshold of that fulfilment?

Jesus' indorsement of the prophecies was so unqualified that those who acknowledge the authority of his utterances have no ground upon which to belittle the importance of what yet remains to be fulfilled. "Surely I come quickly," is the message of the last of the Biblical prophecies, a message that should open the eyes and quicken the understanding of all who are watching the signs of the times. The most significant feature, however, of the conditions pertaining to the so-called latter days will not be found in world-wide disturbances or in fearful events, but in the manifestation again of that divine power which so mightily accompanied the Messianic teaching and ministry.

Every glimpse of the glory that was to come, of the certainty of evil's overthrow, and the triumph of righteousness, which came to the prophets and was recorded by them in the mental life of Israel, declared God's eternal fidelity to His own changelessness, and was plainly not of human origin or invention. As St. Peter wrote: "For no prophecy ever came by the will of man: but men spake from God, being moved by the Holy Ghost" (Revised Version). These prophecies have shone like beacon lights over the turbulent sea of human existence as constant reminders of God's covenants of peace and safety.

Chapter Nineteen - The God of Israel

And God said unto Moses, I AM THAT I AM. — Ex. 3: 14.

Unto thee it was shewed, that thou mightest know that the Lord He is God; there is none else beside Him. — Deut. 4: 35.

This then is the message which we have heard of Him, and declare unto you, that God is light, and in Him is no darkness at all. — I John 1: 5.

THE remarkable history of the Hebrew nation, as recorded in the Scriptures, her many miraculous experiences, her distinguished place among other races, and her unique destiny in prophecy, were all due to her truer conception of God, and not to anything superior in herself. Other nations had their own particular deities, but they were the outgrowth of superstition and imagination and were as far removed from any helpful relationship to the needs of their worshippers as intelligence is removed from non-intelligence. That this was clearly recognized by the Israelites is evident from such passages as these: "For what nation is there so great, who hath God so nigh unto them, as the Lord our God is in all things that we call upon Him for?" "Who is so great a God as our God?" "We know that an idol is nothing in the world, and that there is none other God but one."

This practical nearness of the God of Israel to His people was a feature that pertained to no other race. The absolute oneness of Deity, His inseparable unity with His creation, and His unfailing readiness to supply human need when sought in sincerity, were what differentiated the "living God" of Israel from the mythical gods of the Gentiles. These characteristics belonged to Him alone, and we should remember this, not only in thinking of the God of Israel, but in thinking of Israel herself, her history and her destiny, because it was what she knew of God that gave Israel her peculiar place among the nations. It was what she knew of God but did not obey, that left her a prey to her enemies; and an awakening love for the God of her fathers is all that can restore her to her covenant heritage.

Darkness and mystery have ever enshrouded the human concept of Deity. While everything visible points to an origin or creator, there is nothing to indicate the what or the where of this great Unknown. The allegory of Eden illustrated the crudeness of primitive thought in attempting to account for the origin of man, but there is nothing inspirational about the dust of the ground as a medium for the expression of God's immortal thoughts, and men have never learned to know Him that way. Jesus rejected this idea of the creation when he taught that men must be born again, that is, reach a new and spiritual sense of being, before they could have a place in God's kingdom.

Following mortals' recognition of the unlawfulness of evil, came the desire for salvation, and there began a movement in human consciousness to find God; ever since, in one way or another, mankind have continued that great quest. According to the allegory of Eden, this movement began in the consciousness of woman, and brought forth the prophecy regarding the enmity between her seed and the seed of the serpent, and this movement is to continue until evil shall "deceive the nations no more."

The lives of the great Hebrew patriarchs had been moulded and exalted by their higher ideal of Deity, so that the God spiritually perceived and made known by them has never been superseded by the gods of other nations, but is still acknowledged throughout the civilized world. The transformation which came to Jacob at Peniel brought divinity nearer than ever before to the thought of humanity, and imparted to that revelation a warmth and a tenderness that have never faded, but which still make the God of Israel the name by which Deity is best known, not only as the God who was worshipped by the nation of Israel, but as the God who walks and talks with men today. The Messiah later glorified Him as the Father, a term which naturally includes the spiritual identity of men as sons of God.

The provable character of the God of Abraham, Isaac, and Jacob was early recognized. He was so real to these patriarchs that they could hear His voice. Moses discovered that God could be absolutely and literally relied upon, under all circumstances, when He was sought with a pure heart. There was not much said then about waiting for a hereafter in which to know Him. They looked for His help in their present conditions and environment, and they knew it would be forthcoming, no matter how great the need, or of what nature it might be, so long as they fulfilled their part of God's covenant.

It was, undoubtedly, this demonstrable truthfulness and goodness of the God of Israel that made Him the "God above all gods." It is also strikingly obvious that without this practical or demonstrable feature the Hebrew religion would have been as devoid of spiritual life or of real service as were the religions of paganism. This point cannot be emphasized too strongly, for it is the vital element concerning Israel, her religion, history, and destiny. It was the recognition of man's intimate relation to God, as practical rather than theoretical, which constitutes the chief value of the Hebrew Scriptures, that prepared human thought for the coming of Christ Jesus, and that so wondrously vivified and glorified his ministry. At no point in her history can the subject of Israel be rightly treated independently of her relation to God. Her very nationhood, as we have seen, came into being to be the vehicle by which a knowledge of God might eventually be brought to all mankind. Eliminate this great purpose of her existence, and the subject of Israel would lose its interest and value.

The God of Israel is the designation by which the concept of Deity, as one and supreme, became impressed upon human consciousness, and this term, or any of its Scriptural synonyms, will not be exchanged for another until the "new name" spoken of in the Apocalypse shall be revealed. It is significant that Israel is the only nation to which God's name has been attached, because it was in Israel that the truth about Him was first known and demonstrated.

The religious concepts of what we call the pagan nations, or the Gentiles, rested upon a human basis, hence the attempts of these nations to embody their concepts of Deity in material forms or images, and after the pattern of human and animal types. The apprehension of the nature and presence of divinity which came to the Hebrew patriarchs was, however, so purely a thing of consciousness, that they recognized the folly as well as the impossibility of attempting to give it outline and form. The divine Spirit was to them something to be felt and adored, not to be humanly seen save in effect upon life and character; hence the command given through Moses against the making of graven images to represent their concept of Deity. The Israelites were reminded that they saw no manner of similitude on the day when the Lord spake to them in Horeb, and that any attempt to make an image of their God would result in disaster; and thus it always proved.

The First Commandment plainly exalted Deity above all comparison with human thought or things. As the prophet Isaiah pointed out with unanswerable finality, there was nothing beside Him to which He could be likened. God existed by Himself alone, the one I AM THAT I AM; and a perception of this truth is in itself a commandment against all forms and phases of idolatry. The knowing of something beside good was all that mankind were warned against, and in itself and in its consequences it constitutes the whole of evil. Hence the sinfulness of the idolatry which has beset all people of all times. The Scriptures give the God of Israel a position that admits the truth of nothing else. "I am God, and there is none else." The entire course of Israel was designed to be the development of this ideal of Deity, until nothing unlike Him remained in consciousness. What else could Israel mean as the chosen of the Lord?

Naaman the Syrian dimly recognized something of this all-inclusiveness when he said, "Now I know there is no God in all the earth but in Israel," because he knew that the gods of other nations could not have healed him of his disease. This idea of Deity was the dominant note in the sacred writings of the Hebrews. They knew there could be but one power capable of the great things which had been done in their history, and it was this recognition that made idolatry in Israel so "exceeding sinful." In their defection from the one God, they were sinning against the light of revelation which had been given them, hence the heavy price they were repeatedly called upon to pay.

Although the Israelites suffered severely in consequence of their idolatries, it was only because they had themselves opened their experience to the entrance of evil. The God of Israel was not as a mortal, to be swayed back and forth by human caprices. Such a statement as, "God is angry with the wicked every day," simply expresses the lowest human belief about Deity, and is manifestly unjust to His divine nature. The prophet Isaiah declared His thoughts to be as high above those of mortals as are the heavens above the earth, and this seems the only rational viewpoint for an enlightened age. We should form our thoughts of God from the highest point of revelation, and not from the lower plane of anthropomorphism, the outgrowth of the crudest superstition.

The prophet Isaiah represents God as saying, "My thoughts are not your thoughts, neither are your ways My ways." How, then, can one describe Deity from any human standpoint? Mortals can reach a true perception of the nature of God only through goodness, and goodness is a divine, not a human, quality. It is the carnal mind that has argued to both Israelites and Gentiles that Deity is human as well as divine, and has sought to excuse or justify its own evil propensities on that ground; but the God of Israel is not an amalgamation of opposite qualities, as were the gods of the heathen. The source of the inspiration which animated and illumined the Hebrew patriarchs and prophets was not human but divine, and could not have embodied the qualities which make mortals mortal, unless He were Himself mortal.

In reading the Biblical records, it should be remembered that what Israel received of the truth about God came through human avenues, and that these human revelators were still, to some extent, under the influence of racial traditions and habits of thought, and the phraseology of their messages was naturally somewhat colored thereby; so that, in some instances, their statements, as they have been repeatedly copied and translated, apparently imply a human side to God's character. From the standpoint of primitive mortals, evil, in all its forms and phases, appeared to be so tangible and universal, that they did not suppose for a moment that Deity had nothing to do with it. Believing themselves to be a compound of spiritual and sensual qualities, having a sense of both good and evil, they reasoned backward and assumed the Creator of man to be similarly endowed. To be aware of a power and presence besides good appeared so natural to them that they did not question the incongruity of the belief that God possessed the same dual consciousness.

But the God of Israel could never be anything different from what He eternally is; and is not, and never was, what imperfect human beliefs have pictured. It were morally and spiritually impossible for Deity to redeem mortals from evil, if He also believed in its reality and power; for in that case their thoughts would be His thoughts, and their ways His ways. "Your iniquities," said Isaiah to the Israelites, "have separated between you and your God, and your sins have hid His face from you"; and the Scriptures imply that all men must sometime overcome their false knowledge of anything beside Him in order to become conscious of man as God's likeness.

It is apparent from the records that the revelation of the Divine nature came gradually to the consciousness of Israel, and that, in the earlier periods of her history, God's infinite goodness was not clearly seen or acknowledged. To the thought of the early Israelites, it was God who sent evil upon their enemies, or upon themselves as the case might be; they did not then conceive of Him as the perfect Father, yet the God of Israel was not a being whose nature changed with changing ages; He was the same in the time of Abraham as in the days of the Messiah; the only difference was that Jesus knew Him better.

Israel denoted that point in human consciousness where the light of divine revelation was beginning to shine upon the darkness of mortal ignorance and superstition, but the full dawning of the "day of the Lord" had not then come. Moving about in their mental darkness, believing it to be the natural condition of their existence, primitive mortals imbibed the belief that it appeared the same in the sight of Deity as to themselves, until this belief became fixed in the thoughts of mankind. If they knew of evil as a dread and mighty power, why should not God know this also? If they saw themselves bound in sorrow and affliction, God must surely see them in the same way. Would not everything, the evil and the good, appear the same to Him as to themselves?

This view of Deity is one of the densest shadows that has lain across human vision because it has hidden from humanity the true perception of God's absolute perfectness; but we learn from the Master's exposure of the devil, or evil, as a liar, that its arguments and suggestions must be reversed to find the truth. Therefore, for men to know evil makes them unlike God; and this is the verdict of experience and enlightened reason. It was an unfathered evil sense, which came not forth from God, that assumed to see and know something beside Him; then to affirm that God is conscious of a reality and being beside Himself, or that He is aware of a creation in addition to His own, would be equivalent to affirming that Deity Himself entered the deception of the serpent, and believed a lie.

In a moment of great illumination, the prophet said of God, "The darkness and the light are both alike to Thee, and the night shineth as the day." That is to say, to the Divine consciousness there is neither darkness nor night, neither evil nor error. If human sense beheld the universe to be full of God's glory, as it surely is, or if men knew God so perfectly that only good was present in their thoughts, there could be to them no consciousness of aught else. Then shall we say that God does not yet know Himself perfectly, and is not yet aware of His own omnipresence and omnipotence, that we practically endow Him with the distorted and finite vision of mortals? From these logical and unavoidable conclusions, it is inevitable that human thought and understanding must sometime rise to the recognition that God, to be God, can know good only, and be conscious only of light. "In Thy light," said the Psalmist, "shall we see light," — not darkness, since, in the words of St. John "in Him is no darkness at all."

This is without doubt the most important point involved in man's understanding of Deity. The earlier thought of Israel was too immature to grasp the facts of God's perfection in all their significance; and in the light of subsequent progress, we know that the limited concepts which they handed down in their traditions, and which became embodied in their sacred literature, did not include the most or the best that could be known of Deity, nor are we justified in regarding them as complete statements of truth. Some of the later prophets received such glimpses of the Divine being that they were inspired to utter things beyond ordinary human comprehension, the full import of which they themselves probably did not perceive. While the Biblical writers sometimes spoke of God as if He were a man, the highest sense of what they were endeavoring to teach does not so reveal Him, and it is the highest, not the lowest, thought of God which we must have in mind to understand the vital meaning of their messages. In reason, we cannot read parables and symbolic pictures or metaphors as literal statements of truth, else our ideas of Deity will be more human than divine.

It should be clearly apparent that to personalize the being of the Infinite, as we are accustomed to think of persons, or to bring divinity down to the level of human beings, springs from the idolatry that acknowledges more than one God, a position whose logical effect is to limit the presence of good to the absence of evil, instead of repudiating evil on the ground of her omnipresence of good. All that Deity can consistently recognize or acknowledge in His creation, or as His creation, is that which expresses Himself, His own nature and character, else He would be a transgressor of His own law in acknowledging other gods, a position that is unthinkable and therefore untrue. It is impossible to define God as the one and only source of intelligence, and then think of Him as crossing the mental line between good and evil, between the true and the false, and holding converse with the carnal mind, and making terms and conditions with it.

The one God whom Israel acknowledged has been conceived and written of differently in different periods of her history, according to the beliefs and needs of the time. Moses saw Him as the changeless identity of being, the I AM THAT I AM; while to the Israelites in their bondage He appeared as their liberator, and the punisher of the Egyptians. When they came to enter the land of Canaan, He became the fighter of their battles and the destroyer of their foes. To the Philistines who took possession of the Ark of the Covenant, He was the sender of disease and pestilence. To Naaman the Syrian, to the Psalmist, to the Master and his disciples, God was one "who healeth all thy diseases." To St. John, God was Love.

Matthew thus wrote of the "son of David," the promised deliverer for whom Israel had looked and waited: "And great multitudes came unto him, having with them those that were lame, blind, dumb, maimed, and many others, and cast them down at Jesus' feet; and he healed them: insomuch that the multitudes wondered, when they saw the dumb to speak, the maimed to be whole, the lame to walk, and the blind to see; and they glorified the God of Israel." Let us note the connection. These people at once recognized that the God of their fathers, not Beelzebub, was the power behind these great things, and divine healing was there affirmed as an indelible sign of Israel. No matter what may be our particular phase of religious belief, if we accept the records of Israel we cannot evade or deny the fact that the divine healing of disease has woven itself into the very fabric of her history. It first appeared at the healing of Sarai's barrenness, when the so-called laws of nature, supposed to produce infirmity and decay, were proved to be not the laws of God. And from that recorded beginning it continued to be repeated, in varying forms, during the course of Israel, until it was so abundantly exemplified in the ministry of Jesus that he made it a definite and enduring sign while Israel should endure, — "And these signs shall follow them that believe."

Let it be said again, that it was the work of Israel to make God known, and to establish His way upon the earth, and nothing else. Without the spiritual and literal witnesses of God's presence and power, there were no means by which humanity might become acquainted with Him, and lay off mortality for immortality. "Ye are My witnesses, saith the Lord, and My servant whom I have chosen: that ye may know and believe Me, and understand that I am He: ...I have declared, and have saved, and I have shewed, when there was no strange god among you: therefore ye are My witnesses, saith the Lord, that I am God."

Does Israel today realize what it means to be witnesses of her God, of His oneness and allness, of His power and goodness, as in the former times? When Israel ceased to witness to her God, she became a false witness for strange gods, and was taken into captivity; and she will return from that captivity only when she resumes her place as His witness.

The obvious meaning of witness is to bear testimony. Men are constantly bearing testimony in their lives to what they know of God, to their ignorance of Him, or to their indifference about Him. When the Israelites in Egypt turned their thoughts towards God, Moses was raised up to lead them out of bondage, and he bore remarkable testimony to the divine power in delivering this people. And during their sojourn in the wilderness, and in the land of promise, they were witnesses of His goodness and greatness, and their testimony is still accepted as valid. And on through the times of the prophets, of Jesus and the apostles, God was not altogether without His witnesses in Israel; and this rule cannot fail in the last days, when the people of Israel are to be brought out of their obscurity into the realization of man's divine sonship.

All along the footsteps of Israel we may find the signs which prove the reality of her God, and these signs have never lost their interest or their intense significance. Expunge this testimony from the Bible and from human history, and what would there be upon which to build our hope or sustain our faith? Without them how would one verify the truth of the Scriptures, or what would there be left to lift it above the realm of mere earthly history? If God's covenants had proved to be but a form of words, if His promises had not worked out true under test, if it had not been demonstrated over and over again, that the way to God was abundantly open to the honest heart, the Bible would be the greatest mockery of human need in all the world's literature.

Everything dear to human welfare and aspiration has rested upon the proved faithfulness of the God of Israel; and what her mission has been in past ages, is hers in a larger sense today. The witnesses and the signs must be known and seen in our own day and generation. Israel cannot be resurrected to her true identity and destiny by virtue of the wonders wrought in Egypt more than thirty centuries ago, or by the works of the prophets, or by the many glorious proofs of Gods power in the days of Christ Jesus. As surely as the same sun that shone on the Hebrews in Egypt still gives light today, so surely the same God of Israel must be found glorifying His name before His people and before the heathen.

Let this feature of the restoration of Israel be given the place of first importance in the consideration of this subject, otherwise we shall miss the grand purpose of that event. But this shall not be. God will come into His own as the God of Israel as certainly as all true Israelites will come into their own as children of the Highest, and the earth will rejoice because of them; for in Israel, in her witnessing of the one God, shall all the nations of the earth be blessed.

Chapter Twenty - The Rise of Christianity

Then took he him up in his arms, and blessed God, and said,
Lord, now lettest Thou Thy servant depart in peace, according to Thy word:
For mine eyes have seen Thy salvation,
Which Thou hast prepared before the face of all people; A light to lighten the Gentiles, and the glory of Thy people Israel. — Luke 2: 28-32.

Of this man's seed hath God according to His promise raised unto Israel a Saviour, Jesus. — Acts 13: 23.

ISRAEL had been exiled from her home for seven hundred years, and the land given to Abraham and to his seed for an inheritance had passed under the dominion of the Gentiles. The first three of the kings described in Nebuchadnezzar's dream had lorded over it in turn, and it was now under the heel of Rome. The people of the northern kingdom of Israel, after their captivity in Assyria had run its course, had, for the most part, found their way into adjacent countries, or were slowly trekking through Europe toward the isles of the sea which are now known as Great Britain; while those of the southern kingdom of Judah which returned from their exile in Babylon remained in Canaan as vassals of their conquerors.

We shall not attempt to follow the history of the Jewish remnant during this troubled interval. The voices of the prophets had been silent for five hundred years, but their impassioned exhortations and admonitions, both before and after the exile, were not wholly barren of results, in that the open indulgence of idolatry was discontinued. The spiritual quickening which had been felt in this nation was the natural outcome of her reception of divine revelation, and however overwhelming might seem the resurging tide of materialism, it could only obscure for a time what had been achieved in her. The necessity for progress, stronger than evil's delusions, would in due season ensure the ebbing of this tide, and the emergence again to human view of the spiritual line of Israel.

In his memorable prophetic analysis of his sons' destinies, Jacob had designated Judah as the holder of the sceptre, which was fulfilled in the setting up of the Davidic line to be an enduring dynasty; and carrying this into the spiritual realm, the later prophets foretold the coming of the Messiah from among David's descendants. Not, however, with blare of trumpets nor with worldly display did this Prince of the house of David make his appearance, but in the lowly fashion of a babe, heralded, it is true, by songs of angels, but humanly unnoticed more than other babes, except for the adoration of the shepherds, and the homage of the three unknown wise men, guided thither by a heavenly constellation. As the child Moses was divinely preserved from the jealous fear of Pharaoh, for the deliverance of the Israelites from Egypt, so the child Jesus was protected from the murderous fear of Herod, that he might lead Israel and all mankind out of their captivity to the carnal mind.

The star, or conjunction of stars, which brought the Magi to Bethlehem, betokened the advent of that to which the spiritual experiences of the Hebrew patriarchs and prophets had clearly pointed. A new order of things was dawning in Israel through a woman's receptive recognition of the fatherhood of God and the spiritual sonship of man, a recognition which points to the fundamental truth of Christianity. "The woman" was disproving the age-long claim that the life of man is derived from matter, and her discernment of the spiritual idea of creation had so far developed as to be made cognizable to the human sense in the babe Jesus. No wonder that the watching shepherds caught the songs of angels, for heaven had come nearer to earth than it had ever been.

In his Gospel, Matthew accepts Isaiah's prophecy to the "house of David," — that a virgin should conceive and bring forth a child, and that his name should be "Immanuel," that is, God with us, — as being fulfilled in the birth of Jesus, a conclusion which was doubtless derived from the Master himself. In the Gospel of Luke the spiritual conception of Jesus is treated in greater detail, and if we accept his subsequent record of the events in the life of our Lord, there is little room to question the authenticity of his opening narrative. Materialistic philosophy has persistently scouted such a fundamental departure from its established and revered canons, for the simple reason that it has no apprehension of spiritual realities, and was then and is now unprepared to admit the existence or operation of the spiritual law of creation.

The age which witnessed the advent of Christianity was not, however, characterized by any greater degree of spirituality than is the thought of the present day. There were but a few men and women sufficiently awake to recognize the significance of Jesus' nativity, and that it was in direct fulfilment of the prophecy uttered in Eden. The religious thought in Judah was too materially deadened to hear the song of the angels, or to perceive even dimly the great glory of what was taking place; but Mary, the chosen Mother in Israel, recognized it in adoration, and pondered it in her heart. She steadfastly recognized Jesus' "high calling" even through the ordeal of the crucifixion, not because of any maternal instinct, but because she knew that her child was "of a truth" the Son of God.

If we have carefully followed the footsteps of Israel up to this point, we shall be ready to see that Isaiah's prophecy of the virgin mother did not in any sense contravene the nature and order of divine revelation, however radically it opposed the conventions of the human mind. Looking out across the mental distance, the prophet saw the Redeemer of mankind, appearing in the flesh but not of it, as the embodiment or idea of the truth of man's spiritual sonship.

The scepticism which denies spiritual causation naturally discredits the record of Jesus' supersensual origin, but this same scepticism has been carefully explaining away all that is humanly miraculous in the Scriptures, from the passage of the Israelites through the Red Sea down to the spiritual healing of the present day. This class of criticism has proved itself to be neither constructive nor inspiring, and leaves mortals helpless and hopeless in the grasp of materiality, with no brighter or higher vision of life than animated dust.

"And the angel answered and said unto her, The Holy Ghost shall come upon thee, and the power of the Highest shall overshadow thee: therefore also that holy thing which shall be born of thee shall be called the Son of God." And the angel said to Joseph also, "that which is conceived in her is of the Holy Ghost." Long afterward Paul asked of Agrippa concerning Jesus, "Why should it be thought a thing incredible with you, that God should raise the dead?" And why should it be thought incredible with other mortals that the highest revelation which had come from God to man, that spiritual impartation which was to be the Saviour of the world, should appear to human sense without the impulsion of animality? The law of corruption had no dominion over Jesus, because he had been virtually raised from the dead before he was born; in other words, he was not born of "corruptible seed." If we are to accept the testimony of angels, such as we find in the legendary records of the prophets, and which have come to us out of the dim ages of tradition, we cannot consistently turn from this testimony in relation to the coming of the promised Messiah, recorded two thousand years later, simply because this testimony contradicts human law and precedent. Has not every step of human progress towards the understanding of God been a growth in spirituality, and therefore a step away from the laws and precedents of the carnal mind? In what other way could the woman, the purest type of thought expressed in the human, bruise the serpent of sensuality except by attacking its claim to be the creator of man, and to be indispensable to the expression of life?

But however much the lower or higher critics might dispute the unprecedented manner of his coming, it was a fact that the hope and glory of Israel, the light that was to "lighten the Gentiles," was here, and the world could never be the same again. Enough of truth had been perceived to ensure the final leavening of the human mass. The first act in the restoration of Israel had begun, a new day had dawned for the race, as indicated in a new reckoning of time; and however long and troubled might be the interval, the final act in the great drama of Israel, namely, the spiritualization of human consciousness, was from that time assured.

It soon became apparent that Jesus was not the kind of deliverer which the Jews were expecting. They were not looking for a Saviour from sin, but from Roman oppression. As in the days of Saul, they were still asking for a king after the manner of other nations, hence they were not prepared to recognize the real King of Israel when he came. What did they want of a man who rebuked them for their sins, and who was supposed to be the son of a carpenter, when they desired a princely descendant of the great David?

Jesus' advent was the natural outcome of that spiritual sense of things of which Israel was designed to be the human vehicle or expression. Although what Jesus taught and practised far transcended the best which had preceded him, it was the advancing spiritual thought from Eden to Canaan, and from Abraham to the last of the prophets, which led up to and made possible the appearing of the Messiah. This appearing was a light to lighten the whole world, that is to bring to men the freedom of spiritual enlightenment. It was not, therefore, the setting aside but the glory and crown of Israel, and was not succession as much as fulfilment.

The Judaic religion had become little more than a strict observance of empty forms and ceremonies. It cannot, therefore, be looked upon as either the foundation or the forerunner of Christianity. The Jews were frankly not watching for a spiritual Redeemer. They were for the most part satisfied with their religious beliefs and practices, and, to that extent, w-ere not open to the appeal of the great Teacher. Their utter failure to respond to his message was a sore disappointment, and called forth Jesus' touching lament over Jerusalem, but Judah's spiritual apathy towards the Christ was by no means representative of Israel. Their cruelly tragic rejection of the Messiah, of him whom God had sent to be the king of Israel, served more than anything else to isolate them from their brethren, and caused them to be a reproach and a byword among the nations where they were afterwards dispersed.

Jesus was thoroughly familiar with the history of his race, and his thought turned yearningly to those who where then in exile. "Other sheep I have which are not of this fold," he said, "them also I must bring." And again, "I am not sent but to the lost sheep of the house of Israel." These were not the narrow views of one who could see nothing good outside of his own nation, but of one who realized that his message would be accepted only by those spiritually prepared for it. It was plainly because of this, and not from any bigoted or prejudiced sense, that he at first refused the appeal of the woman of Syro-Phoenicia. It is evident, from the impartial nature of truth, that the Messiah did not belong to one people more than to another; but the thought of Israel, on account of her origin and experience, was more spiritually susceptible, and therefore more open or receptive to divine revelation, than the thought of other nations. It was solely because of this that the Christ came to humanity through the consciousness of Israel, and pertained more particularly to her, or to the spiritual status of thought which she typified. To Israel alone had come the revelation of the oneness of God, and while as a nation she had again and again proved disloyal to her heavenly trust, and was even then enduring the penalty for her idolatries, she was still the guardian of that revelation.

Jesus announced that his mission was "to seek and to save that which was lost." If we read this in conjunction with his statement that he was "not sent but to the lost sheep of the house of Israel," it will be seen that his mission had to do especially with Israel, although it is apparent that he was speaking more metaphysically than literally. If his meaning was that he had come to seek and to save persons, he would naturally have used the word *those* or *them* instead of *that,* but he made no attempt to find the lost Israelites, or to bring them back to their own land. His work plainly had to do with Israel's spiritual significance and purpose in their relation to human salvation. He came to save or to restore that which had been temporarily lost sight of in Israel, and that was the spiritual sense of God's omnipresence and omnipotence, the spiritual perception of man as the son of God.

If the Israelites had not relinquished what had been revealed to them of God, they would not have lost their national independence and freedom. As has been pointed out again and again in these pages, it was her spiritual knowledge or perception of truth that alone had made Israel the chosen of God, that had gathered her into a distinct people, and that was her only means of becoming a blessing to the world. When she was enticed from this position, and despoiled of her chief possession by the deceptions of the carnal mind, she lost her unity and Identity as a people and became scattered among the Gentiles. This state of things had existed for seven hundred years. Did, then, the coming of the promised Messiah have nothing to do with bringing back these "lost sheep"? Was the great Son of David chiefly concerned with the few Jews who remained in Palestine, and who would have none of him?

If this were to be the case, how was Jesus to be "the glory of Thy people Israel," as Simeon said of him? Or how was he to fulfil the declaration of Nathaniel, "Thou art the King of Israel," an acknowledgment which the Master neither denied nor rebuked? When the disciples asked him after the resurrection, "Lord, wilt thou at this time restore again the kingdom to Israel?" he did not reprove them, nor did he imply that that had nothing to do with his work, but he enjoined them to leave the question of time to the Father. His reply plainly indicated that at the proper time her kingdom would be restored, but his special mission was to redeem the Israel of Spirit, knowing that in due course this would result in the literal restoration.

There is no doubt that Jesus had talked with his disciples about these things else they would not have questioned him as they did, but what they apparently failed to grasp was, that the spiritual restoration in Christianity would have to be established first. From his reference to the "times of the Gentiles" and their fulfilment, we may gather that Jesus was familiar with Daniel's prophecies, and was aware that these times had still a long course to run, but he saw also that, running concurrently with the Gentile course would be the new leavening force of Christianity, before whose influence the whole structure of Gentile dominion would finally crumble.

Another point of vital interest, in connection with the long interval before Israel would come into her own again, was Jesus' intimation that the Messianic prophecy was not to be completely fulfilled in his present ministry. Jesus foresaw that his teachings would not be fully understood, and that a second appearing of the Christ would become necessary before his kingdom could be finally established in the earth. The intimate relation of that event to the restoration of Israel, as plainly implied in both the Old and New Testaments, points to the necessity of an adequate and just knowledge of this subject if

141

one would have a just appreciation of the scope and purpose of the Hebrew Scriptures.

Throughout his whole career Jesus proved himself to be a true Israelite, departing in no wise from the best traditions and ideals of his race. He not only confirmed "the promises made unto the fathers," as Paul said of him, but he confirmed and amplified the proofs of God's power which were so distinctively associated with Israel's history. He did this to such an unprecedented degree that he asked the Jews to believe in him for what he did, if they could not believe in him for what he was. He linked the human appearing of the Christ with the early development of Israel when he said, "Abraham rejoiced to see my day, and he saw it and was glad," and then he announced the eternal nature of the truth which he represented, saying, "Before Abraham was, I am."

The birth of Jesus, as recorded in the Gospels, was unquestionably the most momentous event, not only in the history of Israel but of the world, and is generally acknowledged as the beginning of a new era for humanity, and a new starting-point for the dating of time. The old chronology began with the "first Adam," and rested upon a wholly sensuous conception of life; the new chronology began with the spiritual conception of man as the son of God, as having no other father or source of life, and rested upon the regeneration of humanity as expressing the true sense of existence, even upon the earth.

The evidence of God's spiritual fatherhood, which the birth of Jesus afforded, superseded the mythology of a material origin of life, and turned human attention towards the possibility of attaining a perfect and enduring consciousness of being. The transforming nature and effect of Christianity had in some degree been experienced, and this fact could never be obliterated from the consciousness of humanity, neither could its mighty significance be ever wholly set aside. The new idea in Christianity had its roots in divine reality, and the withering blasts of evil could not destroy its vitality. It were not possible that the spiritual light which had been seen in Israel, and which shone out in its greatest glory in the advent and ministry of Christ Jesus, could be put out, although it might again flicker feebly in the densely materialistic atmosphere of coming centuries. The actual truth of man's spiritual being, the truth of Spirit's supremacy over the flesh, had been seen and tangibly felt in the life of Jesus of Nazareth, and the false philosophy of evil could no more destroy the spiritual gain which had come to men, than darkness could destroy a single ray of light.

Jesus was aware of all this. "Heaven and earth," he said, "shall pass away, but my words shall not pass away." And again, "I beheld Satan as lightning fall from heaven." "What have we to do with thee, Jesus, thou Son of God?" cried the devils before he cast them out. What, indeed! But Jesus had this to do with them, that his mission was to destroy evil and its works. To this end he taught men the necessity of regeneration, or their awakening to the spiritual truth of being. He laid bare the metaphysical secret of evil influence by showing that men are defiled by their own base thoughts, and not by something external to their consciousness; but he did not leave the matter there. He exposed the falsity as well as the subtlety of the serpent. He declared of the devil that he "abode not in the truth, because there is no truth in him." Why, then, should men accept its arguments or obey its suggestions, since they were not true?

This was the master-stroke which pierced the serpent in its most vulnerable point, namely, its unreality, and clearly indicated the line along which Christianity would have to go in redeeming mankind. "Ye shall know the truth," Jesus had said again, "and the truth shall make you free" — free from what? From what else could a knowledge of the truth free a man except from his belief in what is false, or from what else do men need freedom? Truth frees from the lie, when the truth is understood, but from nothing else. Christianity could not be more than the truth about God and man, and it needed to be nothing more in order to make men free from error. The Messiah did not come to the world with a human doctrine, or a creed, or a set of dogmas. He did not come to teach men that there is a good and a bad creator and power, for that belief had been accepted for ages before him, and was the nightmare which had so long oppressed the race. He came to rouse men from this nightmare, to teach them of the perfect Father and the perfect Son, to bring back the lost consciousness of man in the image and likeness of God.

There was very plainly no devil, no debasing bondage to the flesh, no law of suffering, in the truth which Jesus said would make men free. He was in the world to demonstrate the infinite goodness of the Father, and he did this by destroying the evidences of evil, disease, and death. He was here to free men from everything which God did not make or authorize, from the fear, the sin, and the mortality of the fleshly sense. And he did all this, not as a privilege peculiar to himself, or as due to a power exclusively his own, but as the natural result of his understanding of God, and of his obedience thereto. More than this, he designated the "signs following," enumerated in the last chapter of Mark, as the proof of Christianity in all after ages.

Although in the literature of other races the coming of a Deliverer had been foretold and described, more or less after the manner of pagan mythology, in Israel alone were these prophecies fulfilled. In Israel alone, out of all the nations, the one true God had been made known in a long series of signs and wonders, too often repeated to be classed as coincidences, and too diametrically opposed to the assumed laws of nature to be set aside by any material inference or deduction. These were the real heralds of Christ's coming, and they will continue the distinguishing mark of Israel's mission to the end.

Chapter Twenty-One - The Woman Driven to the Wilderness

I beheld, and the same horn made war with the saints, and prevailed against them — Dan. 7: 21.

Let no, man deceive you by any means: for that day shall not come, except there come a falling away first, and that man of sin be revealed, the son of perdition. — II Thess. 2: 3.

And to the woman were given two wings of a great eagle, that she might fly into the wilderness, into her place, where she is nourished for a time, and times, and half a time from the face of the serpent.

And the earth helped the woman, and the earth opened her mouth, and swallowed up the flood which the dragon cast out of his mouth. — Rev. 12: 14, 16.

THE supreme tragedy in the history of religion was the crucifixion of Jesus at the instigation of the Jews. The God-crowned Prince of her royal line was insanely set at naught by Judah, and executed as a criminal and an impostor, but his teachings and example have remained the greatest spiritual force in human consciousness, and are destined so to remain, until the restoration of Israel shall be fully accomplished.

It was soon apparent that the spirituality of the new religion came too strongly into conflict with the passions and appetites of men to find a smooth and unobstructed course. History records that every effort to exalt the spiritual above the material has been stubbornly and viciously opposed by the animal nature of mortals. The natural outcome of practising Jesus' teachings would be the subjugation of sensuality, and mankind generally have not yet found themselves ready to undertake this; hence the resistance which every spiritual movement has encountered, not only from its open antagonists, but from the materiality of its own professed adherents.

The new religion, in virtually setting aside the rites and ceremonies of the old, looked upon as sacred from time immemorial, and in requiring repentance and reformation as the price of salvation, was plainly not acceptable to the religious prejudices of the Jews. While there continued to be many and notable exceptions, they were not sufficiently numerous to conclude that the Jewish branch of Israel would be readily Christianized. Following the destruction of Jerusalem by Titus, the Jews rapidly lost what semblance of national existence they had retained, and became dispersed among the nations as had been foretold by the prophets. All hope for the establishment and promulgation of Christianity thus lay between the Gentiles and the scattered tribes of the northern kingdom. Would the latter, chastened by their experiences, again resume the great task of carrying on the line of the woman, a task which Judah blindly repudiated when this line came so gloriously to light in her very midst in the advent and life of Christ Jesus?

144

There seemed little to warrant the expectation, if such there were, that the outside nations were to be the spiritual successors of Israel, and become God's light-bearers to humanity. The thought of the Gentiles had been nurtured in the darkest religious superstition, and although many became touched by the promise and appeal of Christianity and embraced its teachings, it was questionable whether the Gentile type or quality of thought would furnish any permanent avenue for establishing and promulgating the new faith. On the other hand, from her earliest beginnings, Israel had been assigned the great task of proving to the world the existence and goodness of the one God, and this had been repeatedly confirmed at later periods of her history. If the Hebrew prophecies were true, there is no doubt that the work of Christianizing humanity belonged primarily to Israel.

Paul said of Jesus that he was "a minister of the circumcision for the truth of God, to confirm the promises made unto the fathers," and the promises made unto the fathers included the fulfilment of Israel's destiny. In his defense before King Agrippa, Paul said, "And now I stand and am judged for the hope of the promise made of God unto our fathers: unto which promise our twelve tribes, instantly serving God day and night, hope to come." The great promise made unto the fathers was, that in Israel, that is, in the spiritual understanding of God which had been committed unto her, all the families of the earth were to be blessed. In speaking thus, the apostle was not unmindful of the fact that Judah had utterly repudiated the Messiah, and that for many centuries Israel had been an outcast in foreign lands, an unknown people, without national unity or identity; but he was confident that God's plan for His ancient people would not miscarry, and that through the Christ her work would yet be accomplished.

It is not too much to assume that during the long period of her exile Israel was being prepared for her great work. The problem of human regeneration is not to be stated in terms of solar time, but of spiritual awakening. Whether it would occupy two thousand years or ten thousand years to teach Israel the folly of her idolatries, and to bring her back, in the full sense of the word, to her allegiance to the one God, is relatively unimportant. In the nature of things, Israel's backsliding and consequent punishment would necessarily be temporary, and in these fiery experiences only her errors could be destroyed. The revelation of the oneness of God which had come to her, and which she had in part grasped, could not be extinguished by the moral weaknesses and failures of the nation. This revelation came to Israel because an opportunity and a place was there found for it, and although human error might afterwards seem to magnify itself to the heavens, it could not accomplish the recall of divine revelation, reverse the progress of the truth in human consciousness, or remove the place which God had found to set His name there. Let the centuries and the millenniums go by, let the heathen rage, and vain things occupy the stage; the true Israel was only waiting to take up her appointed task at the right time.

Paul was undoubtedly mindful of these things when he preached Christ to the Gentiles, but he knew also that there was no respect of persons with God. The Israelites, because of their past blessings and privileges, did not have a private way, nor the right of way, to the understanding of Deity. The way to God was open to all who were ready to depart from evil, whatever might be their nationality. The apostle had made it plain that in the truth about God and His universe, there was neither distinction nor discrimination between Jew and Gentile; and on that comprehensive spiritual basis he invited all who were ready to enter the heavenly Jerusalem.

The universality of the spiritual appeal of the new religion was made evident at Pentecost when men of differing nationalities understood what was said each in his own language. The Gentile nations which had been contiguous to Israel, or which had come into close association with her, were not entirely ignorant of the nature of her religious ideals, nor of the remarkable events which had distinguished her history. They knew of the wonderful deliverances which the God of Israel had wrought for His people, and they were quite as likely as the Jews to accept the works of Jesus as of divine origin. This was illustrated in the exclamation of the centurion at his crucifixion, "Truly this man was the Son of God." Although the nature of the pagan religions was in no way allied to the new faith, the best in every man only awaits the first genuine divine touch to spring into activity. Those who have awakened to an honest desire for a higher experience than materiality affords are open to the message of Christianity, and Christianity finds no other opening into human hearts, whether they be Jews or Gentiles.

In his vision at Joppa, Peter was taught that in God's sight nothing is common or unclean; and on that broad platform of a common humanity and a common divinity, he forthwith preached Christ to all who would hear. As a result. Christian churches soon sprang up in Rome, Antioch, Corinth, and other Gentile communities, until the growth of the new religion was sufficient to attract the attention of the imperial authorities. Jealous of its rising influence, unwilling to lose her hold upon the superstitious thought of the people, and the power to dictate what they should worship, Rome attempted to extinguish Christianity, both by proscription and persecution. Although these attempts were carried out with the utmost cruelty, they only served to give the new religion a stronger foothold, and to develop a more fearless spirit of loyalty to conscience. The Christians steadfastly refused to abandon their allegiance to God at the instigation of human authority, a state of mind which Rome did not understand, and blindly failed to respect. The First Commandment was enunciated to human consciousness amid such fearful commotion that even Moses said, "I exceedingly fear and quake"; and the carnal mind has met the spiritual demands of Christianity with the same fierce resistance.

But the open antagonism of Rome was the least formidable enemy with which advancing Christianity had to contend. More dangerous because more subtle and unsuspected in their source were the dissensions which arose among the Christians themselves. While they were ready if need be to face the torture or the lions rather than disown their faith in Christ, they too easily succumbed to the carnal elements in their own nature. The apostles had earnestly exhorted them to have the same mind that was in Christ Jesus, to put aside bickerings and disputes, and to be charitable and forgiving towards each other, but their disagreements over technicalities and non-essentials continued and widened. Notwithstanding Jesus' warning, that a house divided against itself could not stand, factions arose and refused to be reconciled. Christianity was of such a nature that attacks from without could never succeed in overthrowing it: its real foes were and always have been those of the Christian household.

Well did the great Teacher say that mortals had to deny themselves in order to be his disciples. When the spirit of the Christ came to be regarded as secondary in importance to the establishment of humanly formulated doctrines and creeds, the vital essentials of Christianity were left unprotected, for the enemy within is ever identical in origin and spirit with the enemy without. The great danger in this situation lies in the fact that it is seldom realized by those most responsible for it. The man who built his house upon the sand was doubtless unaware of the danger until the testing-time of storm and flood. Those who sought to build the Church of Christ upon the foundation of human opinion, creed, or authority, with the internal conflicts which these inevitably entail, were probably unconscious of the insecurity of such a foundation, although later ages saw the wreck of these unstable structures.

It should be obvious that the seed of the woman does not bring forth the same fruit as does the carnal mind. The Christ-vine bears the fruit of the Spirit, but of nothing else. "For whereas there is among you envying, and strife, and divisions, are ye not carnal?" asked Paul of the Corinthians. The schisms and breaches in the early Church, as in every movement intended to redeem mankind, were prompted by the enmity of evil: they have never borne the nourishing fruit of the Spirit, or stimulated humanity to the love of God or man. The warnings of Peter and Paul, and the entreaty of John for brotherly love, were not mere formal precepts and exhortations, they were called forth by repeated breaches of the fundamental law of Christianity. The early Christians were ready to endure martyrdom for the sake of their adopted religion, but, like their brethren of today, they were not as ready to endure the ordeal of following Christ in the denial of self.

During the fierce persecutions which were directed against the adherents of the new faith, the primitive Church felt the impelling necessity of keeping the lamp of spirituality trimmed and burning, but a period was approaching when this impelling necessity would be less keenly felt, a period in which the carnal mind would make overtures of peace to Christianity, and the warfare with the flesh enter its most critical stage. Would the young Church rise to the occasion and preserve herself from defilement, or would she yield to the lure of worldly prestige and popularity?

In the meantime the carnal mind had been striving to deprive humanity of the freedom to "know God aright which was embodied in the Messianic teaching, and it was seeking to accomplish this by an insidious paganization of Christianity. Whenever a more spiritual concept of God and man has appeared on earth, this carnal sense has immediately attempted to fasten its tentacles upon it, and to strangle the awakening better sense. It has ever sought to counteract human progress by insistently holding thought to finite and humanized concepts of Deity, and of His relation to man. According to the allegory of Eden, it led mortals to believe that a knowledge of evil was characteristic of Deity, and therefore a thing to be desired, thus plunging humanity into the darkness of materialism, and the terror of an angry God. It led Abraham to believe that God required the sacrifice of his son's life, a program which, if carried out, would have sent the patriarch back into the paganism out of which he had been called. It flooded Israel with the religious delusions of her heathen neighbors until she was carried into captivity and lost sight of her spiritual inheritance. Was this experience to be repeated?

The concept of God as cruel and vindictive towards man, unless means were found to appease His wrath, arose from the grossest superstition, and found expression in religious practices which went to the length of sacrificing human beings for the propitiation of their deity. Abraham was evidently familiar with this barbaric rite, for he was sorely tempted to show his loyalty to his new idea of God by the sacrifice of his best beloved son, but the better sense of divinity which had been quickened in him prevailed, and he discovered that God did not require the murder of Isaac, either as a proof of his own fidelity or as a propitiatory offering.

The patriarch, however, compromised with the crude beliefs of his time by retaining the sacrifice of animals as a sacred rite, and this primitive custom became forth with a feature of the Hebrew religion, which the Israelites, in their simplicity, assumed to be of divine institution.

In both the Old and New Testaments we may learn the fallacy of the belief that animal sacrifices have any spiritual value, or that they are in any sense acceptable to God. Although transplanted into the soil of Israel, this custom remained what it was, the product and relic of a barbaric age; it was never a factor in revealing or maintaining man's true relation to his Creator. The human mind, frankly stubborn in its materiality, and correspondingly disinclined to exchange it for spirituality, instinctively sought a substitute for its own self-sacrifice, and a scapegoat upon which to lay the burden of its own sins, a weakness which is native to the Adamic race, but which was not indigenous to the regenerative ideals of Israel, and certainly had no place in the spiritual idealism of Christianity.

In his zeal for a corrupt and outworn Judaism, and his hatred of the new teaching, Caiaphas, the high priest, conceived the idea of offering Jesus as a sacrifice. "It is expedient for us," he said, "that one man should die for the people, and that the whole nation perish not." The Hebrew mind was already imbued with the belief in vicarious atonement, for it was the essential element in the practice of animal sacrifices which their nation had copied from heathen religions, and Caiaphas appealed to that paganish belief with the vicious purpose of getting the Founder of Christianity out of the way. The high priest's proposal meant a reversion to the days of human sacrifices, and its adoption and execution by the Jews brought upon them the just condemnation of an enlightened humanity.

Looking at it from this distance we can see that the suggestion of Caiaphas was only the beginning of the carnal mind's attempt to paganize Christianity, for it not only found a response in the thoughts of the Jews, but in after days it bore fruit in the thoughts of Christians themselves, until the belief that Jesus was offered as a vicarious sacrifice for the sins of others became incorporated in the doctrines of Christendom. When fairly and fearlessly examined, one cannot evade the conclusion that the acceptance of this doctrine is a virtual endorsement of the inhuman practices of paganism, and that it springs from the same false conception of Deity. The beloved Teacher of Israel was not a scapegoat for humanity, and it is unjust to the Father to regard Him as a party to the tragedy on Calvary. The abhorrent practice of offering human sacrifices to appease the anger of the gods has been rightly condemned by the advancing thought of the race; but the teaching that the sacrifice of Jesus was necessary to placate an offended Deity, or to reconcile Him with sinful humanity, is on a level with the, worst phases of paganism in its darkest age.

Was the seed of the woman, which had blossomed into such abundant promise in the life and ministry of Christ Jesus, to become a victim of the serpent's enmity, and were the blessings which his revelation of God as the Father held for mankind to be lost in the crude savagery of a pagan sacrifice? This was a momentous question. It is true that Jesus was offered as a sacrifice, but it was on the altar of the carnal mind's hatred of the spiritual truth which he taught, and was of a nature to appease the wrath of devils, not of Deity. Indeed, the latter belief was obviously self-contradictory, since anger, by its own testimony, is not a godly attribute. The theory that the murder of the great Nazarene expiated the sins of mortals is but a repetition of pagan superstition in Christian terms, and has done more, perhaps, than any other one thing to deaden human conscience to the necessity of individual atonement and reformation.

The sacrifice of the human Jesus on the cross was as palpably futile to relieve mortals of their own moral responsibilities as was the blood of a bull or a sheep to absolve the Israelites from their transgressions. It is the sacrifice of their animality and sin, not the life of animals or of men, which God requires of mortals, and this it is certain no vicarious offering can provide. In his crucifixion and resurrection, Jesus furnished conclusive evidence of man's oneness with God, but his individual experience did not lessen the demand that each mortal must sometime and in some way do likewise. The foundation of Christianity was not the martyrdom of its Founder, but the truth which his teaching and example brought to the recognition of humanity. It required no human or animal sacrifice on the part of Abraham to establish the verity of the God of Israel; and it required no sacrifice of human life for Jesus to establish the verity of the Father's presence in healing the sick and in raising the dead.

We learn from the Scriptures that man, in his true estate, is not at war with his Creator, but is the son of God, always inseparable from the Father. To bring to humanity a working knowledge of this saving truth was the Messiah's mission, not to be personally deified, or to be offered as a propitiatory sacrifice. The religion which Jesus taught and practised, and which he expected his followers to practise and perpetuate, was not a sanctified paganism. Christianity was the crown and glory of the highest spiritual thought of Israel which had preceded it, but it had nothing in common with heathen conceptions of Deity, nor with the beliefs and practices which grew out of them. Both the deification and sacrifice of human beings bear the stamp of the purest paganism, and the leopard can change his spots as readily as these practices can transform themselves into the exercises of enlightened religion.

In his vision at Patmos St. John beheld the perils which Christianity would encounter, and a second captivity or banishment which was to overtake the Church, or spiritual Israel. In the twelfth chapter of the Apocalypse, the serpent appears as "a great red dragon," waiting to destroy the child which should be born of the woman. Failing in this, the dragon persecuted the woman, until she fled into the wilderness, where she was to be protected from "the face of the serpent" for a period of 1260 days, equivalent in prophetic time to the same number of years. In this passage, the woman has been interpreted as signifying the spirituality of the early Church, which had been gradually diminishing until it practically disappeared from the external structure or organization.

We have seen how the serpent began to persecute the woman when it was found impossible to destroy the Christ by crucifying the human Jesus. The divine feature of the new faith was its spirituality, and it was naturally against this that the carnal mind would direct its antagonism, for in its spiritual element lay the vital force of Christianity. Let the spirituality of the new religion be submerged in materialism, and its power to uplift and redeem men would be lost. In such an event, evil would naturally find nothing to resist. The aims and tendencies of Christianity and worldliness find no common atmosphere in which to thrive, strive hard as mortals may to mingle them. The carnal mind felt no enmity towards the religions of paganism, human sacrifices and all. It did not oppose the introduction of pagan rites into the religion of Israel. All that evil has opposed is whatever tends to spiritualize the thoughts of humanity, and thus to establish the sovereignty of good in the consciousness of men.

The spiritual decline and captivity of Israel had been accomplished by the inflow of paganism into the inner life of the nation, and the carnal mind was now at work to counteract in the same way the spiritual influence of Christianity, but so quietly and insidiously as to lull Christendom to sleep over what was taking place. Notwithstanding the plain and insistent precepts and injunctions uttered by the Master regarding the essentials of the Christian life, and the indispensable conditions of discipleship, the opinions and interpretations of church leaders became accredited as definitions of Christianity. These personal views, afterwards authorized as creeds of the Church, were more or less colored by influences not derived from the Founder of Christianity, but from the religious traditions and practices of both Jew and Gentile.

The adoption of the ancient pagan superstition of vicarious human sacrifice as a prominent feature of church doctrine, logically led to the belief that human salvation could be realized without individual self-sacrifice and reformation. The deification of the person of Jesus, in direct contradiction of his own statements to the contrary, was another notable instance of pagan influence, as can be seen by an examination of early profane history. This doctrine contravenes the fundamental truth of Israel, that God is One, and soon led to the deification of Jesus' mother as well. This dogma of the divinity of the fleshly Jesus removed him from that human kinship into which he had invited all who follow him in deed, and placed his example upon an altitude to which Christians may not logically aspire. The stamp of evil is plainly visible in the consequences of these teachings. The spirituality of first-century Christianity began to be replaced by adherence to the letter of church doctrines, and by a zealous devotion to the person of its Founder. As the Jews could not see the Messiah because of their hatred of the personal Jesus, so Christians, conversely, began to lose sight of the spiritual Christ in their worship of the man, until their adoration of the great Teacher gradually overshadowed the vital importance of obeying his teachings.

The healing of the sick, which had been such a conspicuous feature of Jesus' ministry, was continued by the disciples after his ascension, and became a normal activity of the Church in its earlier history; but with the injection into its life of false and unregenerative teaching, like unsuspected virus, and torn by contending factions, the spiritual sensibility of the Church became more and more benumbed until its healing office finally ceased to function.

What had taken the place of this vital feature of Christian faith? Turning away from this divine nourishment, this fruit of the Christianity authorized and established by its Founder, upon what could the church feed and prosper?

The formal adoption of Christianity by the Emperor Constantine, and its establishment as the state religion, generally acclaimed as a triumph for the Church, only left it stranded in the meshes of worldly favor and prosperity. It relinquished its purely sacred character to become a political factor in the empire, its offices being the object of ambition and intrigue, while the emperor's decisions became the final word in its councils. The rise of the papacy succeeded in gathering the Church under its control until in 606 A.D. the Emperor Phocas decreed Pope Boniface III to be head of all the churches of Christendom. It has been stated by some writers that at this period the spirituality of the Church had practically disappeared. The woman had fled into the wilderness, to reappear in the fulness of time.

Chapter Twenty-Two - Emerging from Obscurity

And I will bring the blind by a way that they knew not; I will lead them in paths that they have not known: I will make darkness light before them, and crooked things straight. These things will I do unto them, and not forsake them. — Isa. 42: 16.

Hear the word of the Lord, O ye nations, and declare it in the isles afar off, and say, He that scattered Israel will gather him, and keep him, as a shepherd doth his flock.

For the Lord hath redeemed Jacob, and ransomed him from the hand of him that was stronger than he. — Jer. 31: 10, 11.

THE footsteps of both literal and spiritual Israel had now faded into almost total obscurity, and human consciousness entered the period of moral and spiritual eclipse known as the Dark Ages. Ecclesiasticism held Europe under its paralyzing influence, until men lost the conscious liberty to think for themselves, and civilization itself lapsed into a state of semi-barbarism. The spirit of the Master's teachings no longer vitalized the Church, purity practically ceased to be a virtue, and society, unrestrained and unrebuked, wallowed in the most abject materialism.

It was indeed the serpent's hour. The seed of the woman had apparently been uprooted and destroyed. Israel, a wanderer among the Gentiles, an exile from the Promised Land, had passed so completely out of the thought of the world as to be forgotten almost in name. The Jew was a despised outcast, the prey of all who cared to rob or persecute him. Christianity, as Jesus had practised it, no longer represented by the Church, and no longer sought for its divine power, had passed into a spiritual oblivion from which scarcely a gleam of its divinity reached mankind. It was the verification of the Master's statement, "If the light that is in thee be darkness, how great is that darkness!" The voice of the spiritual Christ had become inarticulate, while material sense was enthroned as lord over all. Sitting in the seat of authority at the council tables of church and state, receiving the homage and obedience of all classes, with nothing disputing its sway over the thoughts of men, what more could the carnal mind ask for?

To one superficially viewing the situation at that period, the serpent appeared to have completely triumphed. The grasp of evil upon the consciousness of Christendom was so universal and unqualified that if the carnal mind could be conceived of as a living entity, exercising intelligence and power independently of the thoughts of mortals, there would seem small prospect that mankind could ever regain their freedom. Goodness and spirituality were no longer demanded, and the regenerative purpose of Christianity was set aside or forgotten, a state of things which continued with little variation or respite for centuries. Had the light of revelation gone out in the darkness? and had evil succeeded in founding an enduring kingdom upon the ruins of righteousness? Had the Scriptures failed, and the work of the woman been swept away?

By no means. Not one jot or tittle of the law of God's supremacy had failed, nor had the work of the Christ been reversed in the minutest particular. Evil had not succeeded in quenching the smallest spark of divinity that had gleamed even for a moment across the perception of humanity. The figure one could as easily be eliminated from mathematical reckoning as that good could be lost from the sum of reality. Human consciousness was simply sounding the depths of the suggestion that evil is as real as good, and was passing through a sense of the obscuration of good which the acceptance of that suggestion entailed. The experience of the Dark Ages was having as much effect upon the fact of God's presence in the universe as an eclipse has upon the sun. Looking from the earth, the solar beams seem obscured, and shadow takes the place of sunshine; but looking from the sun, there would be no loss of light apparent, nothing would be touched or interfered with, and the shining would go on without interruption. Presently the shadow passes and everything is seen as before. The shadow appeared for the time to have triumphed over the sun, but it did not; and if an eclipse lasted for a thousand years, it would still have no effect upon the sun.

The Hebrew prophets had foreseen this spiritual eclipse, this deepening of the shadow cast upon human consciousness by its belief in the serpent's lie, but their knowledge of spiritual astronomy had assured them with mathematical certainty of the reappearing of the light. From the mount of revelation they were given a glimpse of the other side of the shadow, and were not disturbed over the eventual outcome. The would-be watchers of the spiritual heavens of today must look from the same point of observation, for it is obvious that the truth of things cannot be seen from any other direction. Since it is not possible to see even material things correctly in the dark, one cannot hope to judge rightly of spiritual things from the outward appearance, since materiality in all its phases is the obscuration, not the revelation, of spiritual truth.

From its earliest use, the word Israel signified dominion over evil, not subjection to it. If Israel had signified the legitimacy of accepting evil, she would have represented the seed of the serpent, not the seed of the woman. Israel was the acknowledgment of but one God, and therefore but one power and intelligence, not two. This perception, when she was obedient to it, was her vital breath, her foundation, her defense, as it afterwards became, in a greater degree, of Christianity. Apart from the correctness or the incorrectness of their differing concepts of Deity, the fundamental distinction between the religion of Israel and the religions of paganism, was that the latter were based upon plurality and the former upon oneness. The unity of God, enunciated by Moses in the First Commandment, and accepted in Israel from Abraham down, made no provision and admitted of no place for a second deity, a second power, or a second reality.

Although the light of spiritual Israel had been apparently put out by the national apostasy, it remained one with its divine source, and only awaited the passing of the shadow to shine forth more brightly than before, otherwise the eclipse would have been followed by extinction. It was this indestructibility of good which made its human obscuration necessarily transient. It is because the sun continues to shine that the mists and clouds eventually disperse. It is because God remains what He is, the infinitude of being, that evil's claim to be something and someone falsifies itself, and disappears. Their recognition of these facts helped the prophets to foresee the final collapse of evil, as the great deception or delusion of the ages, and the triumph of good as supreme in human consciousness.

Ijn the solar universe, when the totality of an eclipse is reached, it begins to move off, for the irresistible law governing the movements of the planets gives it no opportunity to become permanent. In like manner, when the Dark Ages had reached their greatest obscurity, they began, at first almost imperceptibly, to lighten. The ascendancy which evil had apparently gained during this period was simply the prestige which a deception acquires in being accounted true. The history of evil in the world, so far as it can be said to have a history, has never amounted to more than this.

In the twelfth chapter of Revelation the woman is represented as "clothed with the sun," and from that center of illumination, as everyone knows, no eclipse could be visible. In this passage St. John symbolizes the viewpoint of the highest spiritual thought of the latter days, that is to say, the viewpoint of Israel. The religion of the early Hebrew patriarchs grew out of their apprehension of the one God, but it neither included nor made mention of an evil god or power which they should fear, or which could have a place in God's universe. No capable teacher of mathematics would instruct his students to attach any truth or value to the errors that might appear in their work, for those who abide by the rules of that science know there is no provision in it for mistakes. For example, there is no opportunity for two and two to result in any other sum than four, and the supposition that the resulting sum is anything else, though it might be believed by a million persons and be persistently defended by them, would not represent anything at all except a delusion. It is certain that no right-minded student of mathematics would expect to overcome his errors by believing them to be true, but by learning more of the truth about numbers.

The spiritual thinkers of this age, enlightened by the truths of Christianity, should not lend as willing ears to the arguments of the serpent as did mortals six thousand years ago. We should have reached the point where we know enough to avoid the past follies and mistakes of our race, instead of repeating them. If we have carefully followed the footsteps of spiritual Israel, we have seen that they have ever been turned towards a better understanding of God, and must therefore have involved a diminishing acknowledgment of aught beside Him; that is, the progress of Israel must consistently mean more of good and less of evil in human consciousness. If this were not being realized, the development of what Israel represented in the world would lead humanity further and further from God until their sense of good would finally be lost. But the former position being true, it necessarily follows that, as men understand God better, evil will proportionately decrease until nothing remains to obscure God from human vision. It is towards that consummation that the prophecies point, and the query naturally arises, since the Scriptures reveal God as the same in all ages, the same today as yesterday, and as He will be tomorrow and forever, whether it is not as much of a mistake now to believe in a mixture of good and evil as it was at any time in the past, or as it will be at any time in the kingdom of heaven?

The religion which prevailed in Europe during the medieval ages was a compound of sensualism and mysticism, or the beliefs of paganism disguised in Christian terms, and bore no resemblance to Christ's Christianity. It rested upon the doctrine that evil is as real as good, and that it is, therefore, as truly a part of man's existence, a position which is precisely what the serpent has insisted upon from the beginning, and which it is cunningly working to infuse into the thought of Christendom today. Judging by its doctrines and its fruits, the religion which flourished during that period was the religion of the carnal mind, not the divine afflatus of the Church of Christ.

The necessity of resisting and overcoming evil, which had been so insistently taught by Jesus and his apostles, was reduced almost to the vanishing point. Iniquity, openly and unashamed, invaded the precincts of the Church, and was condoned and trafficked in for worldly gain. Spiritually barren, it impoverished all and enriched none. That the Dark Ages experienced the utter and complete paganization of the Church can readily be seen by a detailed comparison of its dogmas and practices with those of the nations which carried the houses of Israel and Judah into captivity. No longer animated by the spirit of Christ, medieval Christianity degenerated into a sensual, image-worshipping, mystery-enshrouded system whose only counterpart can be found in the religions of Egypt, Babylon, and Assyria.

About the twelfth century, when the intolerance and corruption of the Church had reached their climax, the priest-ridden and well-nigh bankrupt consciousness of Europe began to turn against its oppressor. Protests against the papal system arose and spread rapidly, but the gathering revolt did not develop into any effective or lasting expression until, in the fourteenth century, Wycliff succeeded in translating the Bible into English. The reading of the Scriptures had not been allowed in any but the Latin language, and their possession by the laity was forbidden. This had made the Bible a closed book to the great mass of the people. An open Bible would naturally expose the failure of the Church to live up to its requirements, unmask her hypocrisies and deceptions, and lift the superstition and fear which formed the bulwark of her power. It would mean the freedom of the people to think for themselves, always the greatest foe of despotism and intolerance. It would mean dispelling the mystery with which paganism had surrounded its claims and its inner activities. Hence the bitter opposition to the translation of the Word

155

of God into any language which the common people could understand. It was simply the struggle of the carnal mind to maintain its authority over the moral and spiritual liberty of men.

When it is learned that the religion of Rome was practically identical with the pagan cults of Babylon and Assyria, that is of the countries which had taken Israel captive, it will be seen why the liberation of the Hebrew Scriptures was so unscrupulously opposed. It was the old-time conflict of paganism with the God of Israel transferred to Occidental Europe, — "old foes with new faces." The underlying incentive of the Gentile conquest lay deeper than the desire for national dominion; it was the enmity of the carnal mind to the spiritual ideals of Israel; and the same incentive, alike in nature if not in form, lay back of Rome's attempt to hold God's revelation captive in a pagan language, and to deny access to it even under that condition. Failing to hold Israel physically captive, her old enemies had followed her into her western home in the endeavor to prevent her moral and spiritual restoration through Christianity.

All efforts to stay the freedom of the Bible failed. Its translation was completed by Wycliff and his friends, and was widely read. Other translations soon followed, and with the introduction of printing, the Scriptures became extensively circulated. Israel had truly begun to emerge from her captivity, not only as a nation, but as a spiritual movement, as the light-bearer to humanity. A mightier force was now at work against the enemies of Israel than all the armies of the world, since nothing is feared by the powers of darkness but the coming of light.

It is certain that nothing so surely threatens the hold of evil upon human thought as the Bible, read and understood. The advent of Christianity when its teachings should be understood and practised meant the extinction of evil, hence the persistent effort to subvert the new teaching. We have seen the seduction of the early Church until she laid herself unresistingly in the arms of the world. Disguised in the mantle of ecclesiasticism, the carnal mind covered Christendom with moral darkness, and by its ban upon the Bible succeeded in holding it in that darkness for centuries. But it has ever proved to be as vain to fight against God as for darkness to attack the light.

The freedom of the Bible, won through long and stern conflict, without doubt marked the beginning of Israel's return from her captivity, and from this time on the footsteps of both national and spiritual Israel will be seen to follow the higher understanding of the Scriptures, and the practical application of their teachings to human needs. It might be noted here that the Bible in its present form did not exist at the time of Israel's defeat and deportation. The collection of her sacred writings did not properly begin until after the return of the Jews from Babylon, and it was several centuries before the canon of the Old Testament was completed, and to this the Church later added the writings comprising the New Testament, also of Israelitish origin. Thus during her wanderings in exile, though lost to view as a nation, God was preserving the record of her spiritual development, and, through His revealed

Word, was preparing the way for her restoration.

The footsteps of Israel, returning to the recognition of her own identity and destiny by way of the Scriptures, present one of the most logical and satisfying proofs of prophetic fulfilment in modem history; satisfying, that is, to those who recognize the evidences of God's guiding hand in her history. The progressive revelation of the nature and being of God which came to her patriarchs and prophets, and which were subsequently recorded in her sacred literature, could not be separated from the race through whose consciousness they came. It was this relation to God, as the avenue through which He was becoming known to mankind, that gave Israel her distinctive place among other races, and that will constitute her greatness and her glory when she returns to her appointed place in the latter days. This being true, the way of her return would necessarily lie through the Scriptures, that is, through the perception and understanding of the truth about God which had been committed to her in the beginning. It is perfectly logical, therefore, that lost Israel would first begin to find herself spiritually, and that she could find herself thus only as she recognized and obeyed the covenants God had made with her fathers. As this should be accomplished, as she returned to the position which had been required of her in the days of the patriarchs and prophets, and which the Messiah amplified and confirmed, no combination of earthly powers could prevent her literal restoration, both to her own consciousness and that of the world.

As the conflict for the freedom of the Scriptures was being fought out, and as the natural offspring of that conflict, the great charter of civil liberty was obtained at Runnymede, and became the basis of civil rights in all Anglo-Saxon countries. Despotic monarchy in England never recovered from this blow, and the fight continued from that vantage ground until the Anglo-Saxon nations enjoy the freest and most democratic government in the world. Following this came the translation of the Bible at the command of King James I, a work which was done so well that, despite its defects, it still remains the standard version throughout Protestant Christendom. Whatever personal motives may have moved the king in this undertaking, its accomplishment Is an outstanding landmark in the restoring of Israel, and was as surely providential as any event in the history of that race.

The moving "upon the face of the waters" which had been taking place in England soon made itself felt throughout all Europe. The resistance to the domination of Rome, which had been steadily growing among the thinking classes, found its outlet in the crisis precipitated by Luther. The pent-up feelings of those who had been chafing under papal despotism were unloosed, and the freedom of the Bible was soon followed by the victory for freedom of conscience. The pall of superstitious fear which had lain so heavily upon men's minds was steadily lifting. The Dark Ages were passing like a long nightmare, and eyes began to open to the first gray of dawn, for a day was breaking whose sun would never again set upon Israel and her people. The prophets gave no hint of a third captivity, and we may well believe that the new order which was being wrought out in such conflict and sacrifice heralded the reappearing of the Christ, whose kingdom is to be "an everlasting kingdom."

But with all these momentous steps forward, it is not to be assumed that the return of Israel has yet been entirely accomplished. The quickening process is being resisted at every step by the Pharaoh of materialism, just as disinclined as of old to "let Israel go." National exile was but the first and simplest phase of her captivity. Her real captor was the carnal mind, which had succeeded in loosing her from her fidelity to her covenants, and so bound her to the service of the carnal senses that she lost the spiritual freedom which had been her greatest legacy. The return of Israel, therefore, means immeasurably more than the resumption of national existence, more than the freedom of conscience, more than the liberty to study the Bible: it means the will and the freedom to render full allegiance to God.

In the first covenant after the escape from Egypt, Moses announced God's promise to be the Physician of His people if they kept faith with Him. The freedom to keep this covenant has not yet been won. The carnal mind is yet in outward control of the health of Israel, and is holding her in a despotism more absolute and tyrannical than any which has preceded it. The practice of material medicine originated in pagan priestcraft, not in divine revelation, and pertains most unquestionably to the times of the Gentiles; for nowhere in the sacred records of Israel, either in the Old or New Testament, did it ever replace God's covenant of healing. The declaration, "For I the Lord am thy physician," remained operative throughout all God's dealings with Israel, and is as inseparable from her fidelity to God today as it was when it was first uttered. Until the yoke of materialism in medicine as well as in religion is broken from off the neck of Israel, she cannot be said to have truly awakened to her identity or to her destiny as the chosen of God.

Chapter Twenty-Three - The Hebrew Scriptures

He sheweth His word unto Jacob, His statutes and His judgments, unto Israel.
He hath not dealt so with any nation: and as for His judgments, they have not known them. — Ps, 147 19, 20.
Prove all things; hold fast that which is good. — I Thess, 5: 21.

THE best known but probably least understood book in the world's literature is that collection of Hebrew sacred writings which we call the Bible. Other races, it is true, have their sacred writings, but except for the student they possess little general interest outside of their own people, although these same races were powerful nations when Israel was forgotten in exile. The reason for this inequality of interest and status, dating back through the days of legend and tradition to the earliest Hebrew conception of Deity, furnishes one of the most valuable chapters in the history of religion.

What, then, gives the sacred records and literature of Israel their eminently distinguished place in the world today? What turns the thoughts of the civilized world towards this Book with such unfeigned reverence, admiration, and hope? Why do not men turn with the same feeling towards the sacred writings of other peoples? and wherefore the translation of the Bible into all known languages, and its distribution to all parts of the earth, in preference, for example, to the sacred books of the Persians, Hindus, or Chinese? What constitutes the impelling attraction which holds the thought of so many millions to this product of a people whose very existence has long been called into question?

It is evident that the answer must be found in something which is not common to the sacred books of other races. It is not to be found, for instance, in the story that man was created from the dust of the ground, for this fable may be found in the legends and literature of other nations, and is taught, moreover, with unquestioning enthusiasm by schools of thought which claim no connection with religion or theology. Neither can the answer be found in the later history of this material creation, for one can carefully examine the pages of Scripture which are concerned with the man of flesh, which record his sins and shortcomings, his weaknesses and mortality, and discover therein no vestige of reason for the supremacy which the Bible holds and maintains in the world's literature, and in human interest and valuation. Men find neither inspiration nor spiritual nourishment in the Biblical records of human depravity, or of the idolatries, misfortunes, and failures of Israel, for they already know too much of evil to find any consolation or attraction in the errors and misdoings of the ancients, or in any doctrine which offers no higher origin for man than mindless dust.

The secret of the Bible's position centers in the evidence which it contains of the actual presence of God with men, in contradistinction to the mythical nature of pagan deities. This evidence is not common to the sacred books of the so-called Gentile nations, a fact which places the Bible in a class by itself, and gives it a prestige which can only be endangered by the failure to continue this evidence. The Bible gives no representation of Deity which men may picture to the eye or embody in a form, but to them who are ready to walk in it, it presents the way by which men may literally demonstrate the divine aid with as much certainty as anything which enters into their human knowledge. Whether they take advantage of this privilege or not, men feel that this Book presents the only remedy for the evil in their lives, and this remedy is an understanding of the God whose living divinity breathes through its pages, ever waiting to uplift and redeem humanity.

The strength of the Bible undoubtedly lies in this element of proof. It is not a comparatively difficult thing to theorize about the unseen Being whom we call God, and to build up a religion upon these theories, but it is quite another question to furnish the evidence that these theories are true. If the history of the Israelites afforded no verification of the great things declared of their God, if they had had no tangible ground for their faith, nothing humanly appreciable to lay hold of, Jehovah would have been to them as mythological as the gods of their pagan neighbors.

The patriarchs of Israel had not the opportunities or the privileges of this generation. There was no Bible from which to draw their inspiration, and to learn of God; for these men were among the earliest makers of the Bible, and were opening the path for coming ages into what the apostle called "the mystery of godliness." Their senses were so clearly cognizant of the Divine presence that they knew whereof they spoke, and it was around their testimony, and the accumulation of evidence which followed, that the Scriptures began to grow up. They were not dealing with myths but with definite and pronounced facts. The foundation they were preparing for the superstructure to be afterwards built upon it was solid and enduring, so much so that the God known by Abraham, Isaac, and Jacob remained unrivaled in Israel, and is the God of the Anglo-Saxon race today.

The Bible thus grew out of the spiritual memorials of Israel, and not out of baseless traditions or the childish imaginings of an untutored people. There were men in those days who walked with God so closely that they heard and obeyed His voice, and the impression which their exalted experiences left upon the thought of humanity has never been erased. The rise of Israel as a separate people broadened the opportunity for testing the foundation of their faith, and on numerous occasions the whole nation were witnesses of God's power in their behalf. It was out of such substantial and practical testimony that the Bible came forth, and the same type of experiences accompanied its development up to the writing of the last book, and must naturally accompany its proper course and understanding to the end of time.

The fact that the Israelites were monotheists was not of itself conclusive proof that they had any knowledge of the true God, since it is as possible for one deity as for many to be the outgrowth of mythology, hence the necessity for verification under actual test, and it was on this ground that the God of Israel was found to be literally "above all gods." This explains the frequent use of the term "living God" in contradistinction to the lifeless deities of other nations, and the Scriptures made this distinction solely because the living presence of the God of Israel had been humanly realized in the history of this people until it had become established as an undeniable fact. The other nations naturally believed their gods to be also alive, but, since they had no evidence of any response to their appeals, their belief went little or no further than superstitious credulity.

The inspiration of those who in different ages were making the Bible possible was not derived from human intercourse or human events, but from individual communion with God; and it is evident that before the Bible can be understood in its highest meaning, and in the full significance of its mission in the earth, something of that same inspiration and communion will be needed. We shall have to rise to the same spiritual vision of man as the son of God if we would see the beauty and the majesty of the divine idea which underlies the Scriptures, for it is perfectly certain that this vision cannot be gained while we regard God's likeness as a worm of the earth, and His universe as doomed to ultimate destruction. We can find neither inspiration nor spiritual vision in this material conception, nor can the immortal nature of God's creation be discerned from that standpoint. So long as men make material sense their basis of reason and perception, it is plain that they will miss the spiritual sense of the Scriptures, and without this spiritual sense they can exert no divine influence over mankind.

The self-evident nature of these conclusions indicates what has veiled to a large extent the spiritual meaning and message of the Bible, and that is, the materialism of human belief, which affirms man to be of the earth earthy, and to have a consciousness separate from God. We cannot hope to understand the Scriptural revelation of God if we try to decipher it materially, for the sufficient reason that spiritual things, as St. Paul said, must be spiritually discerned. The Bible has not become the center of the world's religious thought and desire because of its material records, but because it holds the way of escape from the flesh and its evils, not through a process of death, but through the regeneration of consciousness. To the literal human sense Israel was but a group of mortals, whereas in the true sense Israel signified the coming of the divine idea to human perception; hence the real Israelites were those who, under the inspiration of this true idea, recognized themselves to be spiritually the children of God.

A material interpretation of the Bible naturally serves to perpetuate the false view of God and man which the serpent has suggested to mortals from the beginning of their history. No one could reasonably expect to discover the truth about God and man in material sense, because it is this sense alone which supports the experience of sin and death; and yet the truth about God and man is what the Scriptures are designed to reveal, and is what Jesus declared would make men free. It is obvious that one cannot see both Truth and error from the same standpoint, since opposite views are seen from opposite directions and necessarily lead to opposite destinations. One must, therefore, decide whether he will seek a knowledge of the facts of being from a spiritual or a material source, for it is certain that he cannot receive this knowledge from both. From the nature and purpose of its teaching it is readily apparent that the Bible must be interpreted spiritually to get its redemptive import, for its material aspect relates only to those things which are to pass away, and which therefore possess only a passing interest.

An indiscriminately literal reading of the Biblical text has given rise to the belief that God actually spoke the human words which are ascribed to Him, and that the allegories, parables, and metaphors recorded there are accounts of historical events; the result of such a reading has been, not only to deprive the abounding symbolism of the Scriptures of much of its meaning and value, but to impart a manlike view of Deity which virtually identifies the finite with the infinite, and mingles the divine and the human as resting on a common earthly plane.

In the simplicity of thought which was characteristic of primitive peoples, the Israelites regarded their spiritual impressions, their intuitive apprehension of divine things, as messages from God; they were His voice speaking to them, as indeed they were in so far as they were true to the divine nature; but they also regarded as coming from God what were clearly their own personal feelings in respect to the ordinary events of their existence, or to the neighboring nations, or to the results of their own and others' wrongdoing; and to their sense these were also the voice of God speaking to them in anger or repentance, defining their punishment, or inciting them to vengeance against their enemies. In this way God is often made to appear, from the literal text, in a character entirely at variance with the better view of Him which came with progress and enlightenment.

It is plain, therefore, that one needs to be guided by the spirit more than by the letter of the text in interpreting the teachings of Scripture. This is especially necessary in the earlier portions of the Bible, which were pieced together out of a mass of legends, traditions, and ancient records, with occasional lapses, repetition, and misarrangement in the narrative, and which, with the rest of the Old Testament, and to a lesser extent of the New, were subject to the errors and interpolations of copyists. Thus the verbal rendering frequently presents a view of God that is little better than the deities of the pagans, in that it pictures Him as sharing the weaknesses of mortals, whereas the spirit of the entire Scriptures declares God to be above all human error and frailty.

However widely human opinions may differ respecting the extent of Scriptural inspiration, one thing is absolutely certain, and that is that God did not reveal Himself as possessing antagonistic qualities, or as being less than the "altogether lovely." It is literally impossible for the divinity which fills all space and time and being to be anything or to do anything contradictory to His own nature, or that would deny the infinity of His goodness; nor could He inspire statements or acts which would make Him appear false to His own perfection. The perfect Creator could not forswear Himself by bringing forth that which His very perfection condemns. It should be seen as self-evident that Biblical teaching is not true simply because it is found between the covers of the Bible, but because it can justify itself as truth in its power to bring goodness into the lives of men.

In justice to the God of Israel, we must interpret the Scriptures only in consonance with the best and highest things which have been therein said of Him, and not in attempted conformity with the cruder concepts of Deity which may be found there, and which were afterwards superseded by Jesus' ideal of the perfect Father. An interpretation of Scripture as ascribing a dual consciousness to Deity, that is, as being cognizant of the presence of evil as well as of good, is manifestly incapable of inspiring mankind with the hope of ever attaining a state of being wherein is no sense of evil, and to help mankind towards that heavenly consciousness is surely the purpose of the Bible. The trail of the serpent is plainly visible in this attempt to debase the nature of Deity, and to inject this depraved concept into the thoughts of men in the name of truth.

Human thought has made some progress from the concept of God as tempting man with the opportunity to know evil, for nothing of that nature is to be found in Jesus' teachings, and we must read the Scriptures in the light of his teachings if we would know God as he did. The Bible is a progressive revelation of God and His relation to man, and to be just to it, or to understand it aright, we must keep pace with that progress and read it in the light of its nearest approach to perfection. The color which peculiarities of race and the customs of the age impart to its narratives or to its diction is purely human, and bears no relation to the message which the language is intended to convey. It is not the letter, but the spirit behind the words, finding its response in exalted human thought and action, which blesses mankind. The essential value and importance of the Scriptures lie in the spiritual truth which they unfold, a process which human language alone is unable to accomplish; hence the absolute necessity to get the inner meaning of the text, and to free it from the encumbering folds of the letter, if one would breathe the divine atmosphere which ever accompanies God's word.

There is nothing in the human mind from which the spiritual truth of being could be evolved, hence it was necessary that this truth reach mankind through revelation. The point of least density in human consciousness, and therefore the point through which the light could begin to penetrate, was first designated in the Scriptures as "the woman," and later as Israel; and Israel has remained the channel through which God's revelations have come. It was because she alone furnished the opportunity that made Israel the medium of the Messiah's advent, and it is to her spiritual restoration, or to the perception in this age of man's sonship with the Father, that we must naturally look for the reappearing of the Christ to human consciousness.

Chapter Twenty-Four - Israel's Restoration in Prophecy

And He shall set up an ensign for the nations, and shall assemble the outcasts of Israel, and gather together the dispersed of Judah from the four corners of the earth. — Isa. 11: 12.

At that time will I bring you again, even in the time that I gather you: for I will make you a name and a praise among all people of the earth, when I turn back your captivity before your eyes, saith the Lord. — Zeph. 3:20.

Yet the number of the children of Israel shall be as the sand of the sea, which can not be measured nor numbered; and it shall come to pass, that in the place where it was said unto them, ye are not My people, there it shall be said unto them, Ye are the sons of the living God. — Hosea 1: 10.

IT is now about twenty-five centuries since the people of Israel were taken captive into Assyria and passed out of the world's notice. No modern history refers to that people as an existing nation, nor do we find any mention of her expected return. It has apparently been taken for granted, not only by the world generally but by the majority of Bible readers, that the Israelites are nationally extinct; and that the nation which today is most spiritually enlightened is of Gentile origin and lineage. This position would virtually close the door upon that wonderful race which for centuries held the name of God aloft amid the universal idolatry; or at best it compromises the question in assuming that the Jews, the descendants of but one of Jacob's sons, are the only living representatives of Israel, and are, therefore, to be regarded as the legitimate inheritors of the promises. From that standpoint there is no choice but to set aside a large portion of the prophetic Scriptures as false and useless, a course which would naturally bring into question the authenticity of the remainder of the Biblical records.

The assurance which came to Jacob, after his name had been changed to Israel, was that of him should come "a nation and a company of nations," a condition which was certainly not fulfilled prior to the captivity. If this does not describe the national condition of Israel today, the prophecy must either relate to still later ages, or possesses no significance.

The completeness of Israel's disappearance may be seen from the present apathy of religious teachers regarding the prophecies of the restoration. One Bible expositor, in commenting upon Jeremiah's prophecy of that event, says, "There was no return of the ten tribes that in any way corresponded to the terms of this prophecy. Our growing acquaintance with the races of the world seems likely to exclude even the possibility of any such restoration of Ephraim." The Bible dictionaries and cyclopedias practically ignore the subject altogether, a most remarkable fact in view of the large and important place which it occupies in the Scriptures. One can drop half a circle and still have the complete circle as readily as he can drop the prophecies of the restoration out of the Scriptures and still retain their full value and importance. It is the restoration of Israel in all that it implies which is to round out the full circle of human redemption, as outlined in Holy Writ To deny this fulfilment of prophecy is to attack the integrity of the Scriptures, for they are literally built about that crowning event in the conflict between the serpent and the woman. The outcome of this struggle was never in doubt once the real nature of evil was perceived, hence the tone of absolute assurance which pervades the prophecies, and their unanimity respecting the bringing back of that spiritual type of thought expressed in Abraham; not, of course, at the same stage of development at which it disappeared, but ripened and prepared for the great work of gathering the whole human race into the recognition and understanding of the one God.

Inasmuch as Jesus and his apostles accepted these prophecies in all seriousness, there is no valid reason why Christians should not today give them the same serious consideration. One difficulty in the way of rightly viewing this subject lies in the mystery with which human thought generally has surrounded the prophetic utterances, as if they were in some occult way designed to shape the fate of empires and of men. The concept too commonly entertained of the Supreme Being as an arbitrary ruler, disposing of the fortunes of mortals with a capricious hand, favoring one set of persons more than another at His own pleasure, assigning some to honor and some to dishonor irrespective of merit or demerit, does not express the nature of divinity but of humanity, and therefore beclouds the true perception of His relation to men. The notion that the God of Israel deliberately selected that race of people to bear His name, and to express His glory to the less fortunate; that He decreed in advance what their destiny should be, outlining and describing their failures, idolatry, captivity, and return; and that at the same time He decreed the fate of other nations, — this pagan notion makes it extremely difficult or even impossible to understand history and prophecy in their relation to God's government, or as interpreting the operation and influence of divine law in human affairs.

The fulfilment of the Hebrew prophecies is by no means a case of predestination, but is rather the unfolding realization of the supremacy of good upon the earth. The evils which come upon men and nations are but the reaction of going contrary to the law of good. Men find evil in their consciousness when they turn away from the service of God, but He does not put it there. The more the human mind rebels against the presence and the requirements of God, the more evil seems to be present, and ancient and modern superstition has attributed this result to God; but such a conclusion would place Deity on a level with humanity, and thus deny His divinity. The belief that certain events must occur merely because they are predicted in the Bible is pure fatalism, and fatalism can have no place in the operation of divine wisdom and intelligence. Israel is not destined to return to her place and mission in the world simply because of the prophecies relating to that event but because the knowledge she had gained of God made it impossible to hold her forever bound in the meshes of evil. Neither did Jesus rise from the grave for the sole purpose of fulfilling prophecy, but because, as Peter declared to the Jews, "it was not possible that he should be holden of it." In like manner, and for the same reason, Israel, with her glimpse of the one almighty God, could not be held forever in bondage to the carnal mind, for what she had seen and known of Him could not experience oblivion.

It is certain that no one can love and worship the God of Israel and think of that people as an extinct race; or with any real faith in His promises can he think of Israel as never again to be known as a people and a nation. The carnal mind quite naturally argues against what it does not wish to have true, and so we find, as early as the time of Jeremiah, the suggestion being given out that Israel's unity and nationhood had passed beyond recall. "Moreover the word of the Lord came to Jeremiah, saying, Considerest thou not what this people have spoken, saying. The two families which the Lord hath chosen, He hath even cast them off? Thus they have despised My people, that they should be no more a nation before them. Thus saith the Lord; If My covenant be not with day and night, and if I have not appointed the ordinances of heaven and earth; then will I cast away the seed of Jacob, and David My servant, so that I will not take any of his seed to be rulers over the seed of Abraham, Isaac, and Jacob: for I will cause their captivity to return, and have mercy upon them." (Jer. 33: 24-26.)

If it were true, as Christendom generally seems to assume, that the night which fell upon Israel was not to be followed by a morning, it would mean that the evils which led her captive were greater and more enduring than the good which she had learned of God. Such a conclusion should be regarded as unthinkable. Israel ranked highest spiritually among the nations because in her was expressed the highest understanding of God. For this people to adhere to what had been revealed to them, and to be faithful and progressive in their allegiance to the divine demands, would mean the final overthrow and extinction of evil, hence the persistent effort of the carnal mind to betray Israel through the lusts of the flesh. But while this effort temporarily succeeded, and Israel was cast down from her exalted position, the resultant discipline could not, in the very nature of things, become permanent, for it is not in all the vain imaginings of evil to hold a spiritually enlightened sense in bondage forever.

On the other hand, however, it is evident that Israel would not be restored simply for the purpose of again giving nationhood to the Israelites, for her existence as a nation, or the exercise of her national functions, is of little moment unless she has something more than other nations wherewith to bless the world. The purpose of the restoration is to redeem humanity, not merely to exalt one nation above another; and for humanity to be redeemed from their materialism, it is essential that the spiritual sense of man and his relation to God be restored to the chief place in human thought. It was the spirituality she possessed which made Israel, in the true meaning of the word, the beloved of the Lord, and it will be her spirituality, not her material power or greatness, that will bring her into her own again. In the vision of the prophets, the restoration of Israel was but another expression of the final establishment of the kingdom of the Christ; not the reappearance of a personal king, but the human perception and demonstration of divine truth. Only in this way could Isaiah's description of restored Israel be realized: "And the Gentiles shall see thy righteousness, and all kings thy glory: and thou shalt be called by a new name, which the mouth of the Lord shall name. Thou shalt also be a crown of glory in the hand of the Lord, and a royal diadem in the hand of thy God...And they shall call them, The holy people. The redeemed of the Lord." (Isa. 62:2, 3, 12.)

Next to their description of the Messiah's advent, nothing evidenced the inspiration of the Hebrew prophets more than their vision of returning Israel. The human mind, at its highest point, had yet glimpsed but a small fraction of what lay behind that word. The real "Israel of God" takes us back to the first chapter of Genesis, where it is recorded that man was made in the Divine likeness, and was given dominion over all the earth. The prophecies of the restoration indicate the place and status of national Israel when she should come to herself, and realize the utter futility of the serpent's delusions to hold the true idea captive. Abraham's perception of God as One carried him so far beyond the thought of his age that it became the nucleus of a new nation and a new order of thinking. It was literally impossible for this light of revelation to be put out, or for this better concept of Deity to see corruption in exile. Its return or restoration, as the predominating idea, was as inevitable as the return of spring, or the dawn of another day. This would not be merely that Jehovah should keep His promises, as they were conceived and recorded by the prophets, but because good is immortal and indestructible.

That there is an exactness in God's dealings with men may be read between the lines of the Scriptural records, an exactness which reveals Deity as infinitely transcending the feeble human concept of Him which a superficial reading might seem to indicate. It is certain that no one can discover the truth about Israel unless he has the true idea of God as his point of observation; and it is equally certain that no one, who has the true idea of God, can think of Him as a man, and as actually possessing human qualities and thoughts. We should remember that the Biblical writers had to convey their spiritual impressions of the great unseen Deity through the forms of speech which pertained to a purely human sense of being. The mistake has been in literalizing the figurative descriptions of these writers, and thus assuming that Deity possesses a human form, instead of seeking the higher meaning which these metaphors and illustrations were plainly intended to express.

The capriciousness and partiality which the Israelites came to attach to Jehovah, and which may still be found in some modern types of religion, do not harmonize with the revelation which Moses received in Horeb, or with the First Commandment which was enunciated at Sinai. The eternal IAAI can have no affinity with the fickle moods of mortals, and the nature of divinity must be infinitely removed from human follies and frailties. It was inevitable and natural that those who knew most of God should soonest suffer from wrongdoing; and not perceiving that this was the working out of an exact rule, it was deemed the vengeance or wrath of the Almighty. Also, when they forsook their evil ways and obeyed God, and they experienced better conditions, they credited this in like manner to the favor of the Lord; whereas the rise and fall of their fortunes simply reflected the rise and fall of their own mental and moral state. This was clearly expressed in the saying of the apostle, "Whatsoever a man soweth, that shall he also reap. For he that soweth to his flesh shall of the flesh reap corruption; but he that soweth to the Spirit shall of the Spirit reap life everlasting." This does not put God afar off, nor make Him a cold abstraction, nor does it take Him out of the Scriptures as all that He is; but, on the contrary, it gives to God the infinite glory and goodness which inseparably belong to Him, and leaves with mortals the responsibility of their own thoughts and acts.

The fact should be borne in mind that, throughout all her backslidings and repentance, the God of Israel remained unchanged, never less than Himself, never less than divine, and never withholding from men the good which they were willing and ready to receive from Him. When the Israelites looked to God for their help, and obeyed His voice, they enjoyed peace and prosperity; but when they turned from Him and obeyed the suggestions of evil, it was their punishment to gather the fruit of their own misdoings. Their attitude towards good or evil, towards the God of Abraham or the gods of the carnal mind, was not a thing of chance, nor the result of some compelling influence independent of their own mentality. It simply expressed their state of consciousness. Therefore the restoration, when it comes, will not be a special act of God, as we ordinarily understand that term, but the result of a mental process which has been going on through generations, a gradual awakening from the stupor of their servitude to error. It is written of the prodigal that when he "came to himself" in the far country where his disobedience had carried him, he began to think of his father, and arose and returned to him. Likewise when the prodigal nation of Israel should come to herself in the lands of her exile, and recognize the delusion of the idolatry into which she had fallen, there would naturally come the desire to return to the Father; and this quickening desire, gathering volume and momentum with the disillusionment, would accomplish her restoration, both in her own spiritual consciousness of God's fatherhood, and of her allotted place in the family of nations.

The salvation of men or of nations is worked out in no other way. The writer of the book of Job clearly points out that mortals can neither give God anything nor take anything from Him on account of their righteousness or their iniquity, whereas what they are and what they do mean everything to themselves. The moral defections of the Israelites did not and could not diminish in the smallest degree the omnipresence and goodness of God; they only succeeded in darkening their sense of His presence, and in filling their thoughts with His unlikeness. It was in their own human consciousness that something evil appeared to be happening, since nothing they could think or do could fill the consciousness of God with something foreign to His own nature. Their mental consent to have another god than good, to let God be less than all to them, was the place of their exile, the "far country" of the prodigal; and the only way back lay through the reversal of that mental process, namely, the unbelieving of their beliefs in something beside God. Very obviously all this knowing and unknowing of evil, this making of mistakes and afterwards correcting them, was transpiring in their imperfect human sense of things, and had no possible place in the kingdom of God, wherein nothing contrary to His government could be known.

The reader may object to this analysis of the situation, but the demand today is to be true to the highest idea of God which we find in the Scriptures, not to the lowest. There have surely been some progress and enlightenment in the understanding of divine things since the beginning of human history. If we subtract from the narratives of the Biblical writers and from the work of the transcribers their superstitious belief that all things came to them from God, the evil as well as the good, and the impression which came down from primitive times that Deity was like unto men, we shall get a glimpse of what the inspired writers were striving to convey through the crude and sometimes barbarous notions of their age. The best things they conceived and spake of God were necessarily nearest to the truth, and it is evident we must continue towards the perfect ideal along the line of the highest revelation, until we reach the conviction that what men call Deity stands for that absolute boundlessness of good in which there is no place for evil. If we accept the anthropomorphism of the Biblical writers as purely symbolical rather than literal, we shall see that the idea of God's perfection lay back of every inspired message delivered to Israel.

It was this very perfection and infinitude of her God which made the ultimate restoration of Israel a certainty. The revelation of what God is reached human consciousness through that nation, and although she turned her back upon it for a period, the delusions of the carnal mind could not blot this revelation entirely from her mental life. Looking from their spiritual viewpoint, the prophets foresaw Israel's return to God, in all its wonderful import to mankind. In that day the power of God is to be so gloriously manifest in her that all nations will flow to Israel to learn of Him. The material signs of identification will necessarily be overshadowed by the spiritual, for Israel will not return as a seeker after earthly dominion, but as the messenger of God's covenant and the witness of His truth.

The visions of the prophets have been eloquently pointing to these things for more than two thousand years, and the invincible truth which underlies the inspired Word will make these visions come true. They are coming true now. The suggestions of doubt regarding their fulfilment are prompted by that materialistic element in human thought which is not open to spiritual truth. The fact that the Christ appeared in the order foreseen by the prophets should be ample assurance that what remains of their prophetic messages may also be verified. The return of Israel in its completeness, however, need not be looked for as the event of a day, but as the progressive reappearing to human consciousness of the truth about God. It means the recovery of man's spiritual dominion over evil, the maturing of the perception which came to Jacob at Peniel, and this attainment will be reached only as the carnal mind is resisted and subdued.

It can easily be seen that the restoration of Israel is the natural converging point of all that relates to human salvation, therefore all nations should be vitally interested in it. To overcome evil is the one necessity of the human race, and all peoples are grappling with it in some form and in some degree. Every honest effort to exalt goodness above iniquity is a struggle with the serpent, and belongs to the line of the woman, no matter in what nationality

169

it occurs. God is no respecter of nations, for with Him it is not a question of blood or of race, but of righteousness. Israel was acceptable to God to the extent that God was acceptable to her. The choice always rests on the human side. They who choose to serve God are numbered among His chosen people, while they who reject Him thereby reject their divine sonship, no matter what may be their race or creed.

Why, then, do we speak of the return of Israel more than the return of other nations? Simply because there was that in her racial mentality which was least responsive to the serpent's influence, and which would, therefore, soonest rebel against its impositions. The captivity into which Israel fell, represented the common consciousness of mankind. The Assyrian, Persian, and other Gentile peoples were held in the same captivity, but to them it expressed their native sense of things, hence they were not cognizant of its bondage; in other words, they had had no experience of something higher, which they had forsaken and to which they might return in repentance. Israel, on the other hand, had behind her a long record of better things, of wonderful experiences of deliverance and protection in times of national danger, of blessings poured out upon them from the Divine source, and the truth that these things had been, would naturally work out a desire to return, long before the more darkened Gentile consciousness reached the spiritual status of even exiled Israel. The prodigal son, even in his "riotous living," had that still within him which would arouse him to himself before those to whom such conditions were as their native element. The captivity of the human sense would, therefore, end first with Israel, because she possessed that which would not let her rest satisfied in it. Simeon spoke of Jesus as "a light to lighten the Gentiles" as well as "the glory of thy people Israel"; this describes Israel's place in prophecy, and her mission when she emerges from the captivity of materialism, and that is to light the way out for the rest of humanity.

The restoration of Israel will mean the renewal of the conflict with evil, not in the blind and hopeless manner in which it has been desultorily carried on, but with eyes open to its deceptive nature and its modes of operation. Israel had possessed, in some measure, the one weapon that avails in this warfare, and that was the truth of the one God, without a knowledge of which mankind have been struggling helplessly in the grasp of the serpent. When Israel returns it will necessarily be as possessing this truth, not in any merely academic sense, but as a working knowledge, and with satisfying proofs thereof, otherwise she will not have returned at all; for if things are to continue as before, the restoration would be a misnomer. It should be plain that Israel can become paramount among the nations only as the truth about God becomes paramount in her national and religious life; and this truth, let us not forget, is the exact reverse of the argument which has been accepted and preached as gospel truth to the dire cost of mortals, and an argument which is still too commonly received without question in Christendom, namely, that it is not wrong or unchristian to believe in power, life, intelligence, reality, besides God. The reverse of that argument was stated as the First Commandment, which is an unequivocal declaration of the allness of God, and Israel will be more or less under Gentile dominion until she recognizes this truth as the foundation of all right thought, and takes her stand upon it loyally and fearlessly.

This was clearly the expectation of the prophets in their forecast of latter day events. What else would Israel be restored for if it were not to establish the supremacy of her God in the eyes of all the world, which means that God will be sanctified in Israel before all the heathen. The prophets beheld the restoration as bringing in the new heavens and new earth "wherein dwelleth righteousness," wherein is no evil, no place for it, and no belief in it. This is undoubtedly the goal before Israel today, and in the coming days, and she cannot rest until it is reached.

Chapter Twenty-Five - At the Threshold of Fulfilment

And when these things begin to come to pass, then look up, and lift up your heads; for your redemption draweth nigh. — Luke 21: 28.

Son of man, behold, they of the house of Israel say, The vision that he seeth is for many days to come, and he prophesieth of the times that are far off.

Therefore say unto them. Thus saith the Lord God; There shall none of My words be prolonged any more, but the word which I have spoken shall be done, saith the Lord God. — Ezek. 12: 27, 28.

For the vision is yet for an appointed time, but at the end it shall speak and not lie: though it tarry, wait for it; because it will surely come, it will not tarry. — Hab. 2: 3.

And he said unto me, These sayings are faithful and true: and the Lord God of the holy prophets sent His angel to shew unto His servants the things which must shortly be done. — Rev. 22: 6.

THE Dark Ages, according to general reckoning, began at about the bisection of the "times of the Gentiles," and interpreting these times as measuring the period which was to follow the loss of Israel, and during which the dominion of the carnal mind over the thought of Israel and of Christendom was to run its course, it is evident that their completion or fulfilment is close at hand. Coming on to the nineteenth and twentieth centuries, the signs unmistakably point to the loosening of the serpent's grasp. It is obvious that a deception could not forever succeed in deluding its victims, because of the disturbing fact that the truth exists and must sometime become known; and the disturbing truth concerning Israel's captivity is, that God's creation is ever free from evil, and can never become contaminated or captivated by it. It has been the instinctive effort of the evil in human consciousness to prevent this truth from becoming known, for in the human ignorance of it is evil's only opportunity of success: hence the intense opposition of the carnal mind to the development of Israel, for the reason that in Israel the truth of man's spiritual being as the image of God was beginning to come to light. For the same reason every Godward impulse that has struggled for freedom and activity has found the serpent waiting to devour it; but notwithstanding the long submergence in materialism of the human side of Israel and of Christianity, the time is without doubt rapidly approaching when the offspring of the woman, referred to by St. John, will literally "rule all nations." The dial of human destiny points to the passing of the material conception of life which has held humanity in an ever deepening hopelessness, and is indicating the hour when men will seek to learn all things spiritually.

The nations are peering anxiously across the threshold of the morrow with serious misgivings as to what may await them there. The process of overturning spoken of by Ezekiel has plainly begun and must continue until all that obstructs human deliverance from evil is put out of the way. Many false beliefs about God which for centuries obscured the Father from human view, and filled the thoughts of men with doubt and fear, are passing away, while false notions about government, law, and human rights are losing their stability and power. Human thought is at last beginning to awaken to the omnipotence of goodness, justice, and love, and the tyrants of hatred and injustice, are being correspondingly dispossessed of their position and influence. These are undoubtedly the overturnings spoken of by the prophet, and are taking place as a direct result of a better understanding of God. The fulfilment of Scriptural prophecy is synonymous with the restoring of God's rule among men, and this necessarily involves the upsetting of whatever assumes to dispute His reign. "Until He come whose right it is," and until "every eye shall see Him," the prophetic Word will not have its entire fulfillment, and in the meantime this divine overturning must go on and on and on.

During the last half century there has been a decided awakening of interest in the significance of the Scriptural statements relating to the latter days, in the belief that that period is close at hand. The center of this interest, in its more human aspect, is the predicted restoration of Israel, with which is closely associated, in its more religious sense, the expected reappearing of the Christ. That we are at the threshold of a mighty spiritual awakening, such as might well usher in the "day of the Lord," is accepted by many, and that this awakening will be accompanied by the unusual events which the Scriptures intimate may not unreasonably be looked for. Great spiritual revolutions do not arise in human consciousness without making their influence manifest in outward phenomena. Coming events are casting their shadows before, and one need not be himself a prophet to read the signs which are beginning to appear both in heaven and earth, that is, both spiritually and materially.

The coming again of Israel into the world's attention, not as a somewhat obscure people in a small country in Asia, but as the foremost race of our time, is a subject of compelling interest, whether or not one is inclined to dispute its probability. The belief that Israel, if she returns at all, will be sufficiently few in number to inhabit her former home in Palestine, is not sustained by the Scriptures. While she was, undoubtedly, to recover the possession of her ancestral lands, and in addition, was to have dominion over the immense territory promised to Abraham, God was to lead her in her exile to a new home from which she was not to be removed. While Israel at the time of her captivity was a comparatively insignificant people, as we regard nations today, and while she was banished from her home in the deepest disgrace and humiliation, there have been twenty-five centuries of opportunity to reform and to develop, and the Scriptures inform us that she would do both.

Therefore no student of the prophetic Scriptures need look for Israel to return at the same point, morally. physically, or spiritually, at which she went away, else her twenty-five centuries of discipline would have been in vain. That this discipline was to be a mental experience, embracing the thought of the nation, is evident from the fact that neither the persons who were taken captive, nor their descendants for many generations, according to the terms of the prophecies, would return to their own land. The restoration could not possibly mean the personal return of the Israelites who were taken captive, but was plainly used in a twofold sense as (1) the bringing back of Israel to her place in the world as a nation, but not necessarily in the same locality, and (2) her return spiritually as the people of the covenants. The first of these would involve a general awakening to the facts of her racial and national identity, and the second, her return to that close relationship with God which Jacob realized at Peniel, and of which Moses gave evidence all the way from Horeb to Pisgah. It was certainly something more than the presence in Palestine of the northern tribes which was lost to Israel, and that something can only be defined and understood in spiritual terms. The subject of the restoration, therefore, must be approached from its spiritual side, because it cannot be satisfactorily or intelligently understood from any other. It is true, of course, that Israel had a human aspect or application, else that movement would have been without means or opportunity to benefit mankind, although, in the last analysis, there could be but one real Israel. What is called national Israel, or the human side, was the organization, so to speak, through which the spiritual revelation or idea, the real Israel, could have an avenue of activity, and by means of which all mankind might eventually be reached and redeemed. But when the nation, the organization, ceased to express the true idea, it became useless for its original purpose, and having no spiritual defense of its own became the natural prey of the carnal mind. We have seen how the same condition arose in the early Christian Church. When it ceased to exalt the spiritual ideal of Christianity, as exemplified in Christ Jesus, and to perform the works which he expected of his followers, it lost its usefulness as an organization, and became the prey of worldly prosperity and spiritual bankruptcy.

It has ever been that the perception of an idea has preceded its human instrument. It could not be otherwise. The spirit must precede the expression of the letter and give it life, else it has none. The human mind would reverse

173

this order and find life in body or organization, therefore it seeks to preserve the latter as of chief importance, a course which has repeatedly resulted in disaster. No cause can survive by making the spiritual subservient to the material. The safety and success of Israel or of Christianity were not contingent upon the details and externals of organization, but upon fidelity to the spiritual ideal, and upon subordination of the human to the divine. The breaking up of the human instrument, as in the case of national Israel, did not imply the destruction of the spiritual idea, and when the thought of Israel should again be prepared to perceive and exalt it, the means for its human activity would also be revived.

It is thus apparent that the restoration of Israel was not rendered necessary because of the captivity of the persons who comprised the nation at that time, but because something was lost sight of that was indispensable to human welfare and salvation, and without which not only the Israelites but the whole human race would continue in captivity. For the same reason the return of the Christ was not made necessary simply because the personal Jesus disappeared from human sight, but because of the failure of the Church to fulfil the mission which he entrusted to it. What is needed in either case is not the return of person but of the true idea, the recovery or restoration of that spiritual discernment of God's presence and oneness, the loss of which had sent the Israelites into exile, and in the Christian era permitted the Church of Christ to become little more than an empty name.

In the visions of the prophets the reappearance of Israel and of the Christ appear to coincide in point of time, and the evident conclusion is that they cannot be regarded as distinct or independent spiritual events or processes, except for the fact that the former involves the restoration of national identity to the exiled people of Israel, while the latter relates only to the spiritual illumination which the restored understanding of the spirit and power of Christ will bring to men. It will be remembered that the loss of spiritual Israel wrought the disunity and disappearance of a national consciousness, whereas the defection of the early Church did not entail the loss of human organization, but only of its inspiration and power. The rehabilitation of national Israel does not, however, imply that she will then become a nation for the first time since her exile, for the Scriptures indicate that at the time of her restoration she will possess a larger national existence than before, but without the knowledge of her ancestral lineage or racial identity. It will be her own recognition of who and what she is, and the same recognition on the part of other nations, that will constitute Israel's national restoration. This will not necessarily involve any change in her national name, but she will acknowledge herself as the Israel of God's covenants, and as inheritor of the promises, duties, and responsibilities which pertain to the descendants of Jacob. This means vastly more than the simplicity of its telling might seem to indicate. It will be no small thing for a nation to find herself identified beyond reasonable question as the people whom, according to the Scriptures, God had chosen as an instrument to express His glory, to bear His name to the nations, and to be His messenger and representative in the earth. No worldly honor, dominion, or prosperity could begin to compare with the greatness of that discovery, and the wonderful opportunities and sacred burdens that will accompany it. Let no one treat this matter as inconsequential or of light moment, for it fills a large place in the Scriptures, and will constitute the greatest event in the history of nations.

The God of Israel, let it be added, is not a mythical personage, or a fictitious character in the religious literature of a nation, nor is He the central subject or object of primitive superstition, — He is the creator and governor of the universe, beside whom there is no other, whose actual existence and power were proved again and again in the history of the Hebrew race. Let that nation or race which comes nearest to the description of Israel, as she is to be in the latter days, neither scoff nor doubt, but prepare herself to answer to the call. Scepticism does not alter facts, nor will it prevent that from being wrought out which has the impulsion of truth behind it.

That the Christ is the expression in its fulness of the spiritual ideal of Israel would be more readily seen were it not that Christendom generally has been taught to think of the former as a man, rather than as the name which signified his Messianic mission or ministry. There was but one man given the name of Israel, as there was but one man given the name of Christ, but no one now thinks of Israel as a man. The restoration or reappearing of Israel is never spoken of, by either Christians or Jews, as the return of the person of Jacob. The word Israel was used in a distinctive sense, and signified something which had existence before the birth of Jacob, and which was too great to be measured by any human personality or to be compressed within the limits of solar time. The same must be true also in respect to Christ, which, the Scripture says, was "without beginning of years or end of days," a description which could not be applied to any man born of woman.

Israel was the designation of that spiritual movement which had been going on in the consciousness of the Hebrew people, preparing the way for that perfect revelation of God which came through Jesus, and which was demonstrated in its completeness by him. Because he was the avenue of the Messianic truth, he was given the title of Christ, as Jacob before him had been given the title of Israel. If Christ was intended to be the personal name of the son of Mary, the angel would not have instructed Joseph to give him the common name of Jesus. The belief that the Christ was identical with the flesh and blood of the human Jesus, which gained currency among the early Christians, eventuated in the dogma that he is to return to earth as a physical personality. This settled conviction was due, in part, to a misapprehension of the prophecies relating to the Second Advent, or, perhaps more correctly, to a misapprehension of the conditions which would make a second coming necessary, and in part to a deified conception of the personal Jesus. This deification of the great Teacher, in the place of obedience to his teachings, gave rise to the assumption that Christ left the earth at his ascension, notwithstanding the assurance, "Lo, I am with you alway."

It will be remembered that Jesus almost invariably spoke of God as the Father, and, like a true Israelite, he never intimated that there was more than one God. The First Commandment gives the keynote of "the alone God," but this keynote is lost when we attempt the impossible, namely, to increase the number of the infinite. "In that day," said the prophet Zechariah, "shall there be one Lord, and his name one," and this oneness of divinity runs throughout the entire Scriptural revelation, and is summed up by St. John in the Apocalypse as "the Alpha and Omega," or the all-inclusive One. Let us hold fast to this infinite One and All, for no other God pertains to Israel, and in the day of the restoration His name shall be *One.*

The student who has carefully followed the development of the spiritual idea of God, as first brought forth in Israel, and as presented in the writings of her prophets and poets, will see that in the Messiah the fulness of this idea was to appear. On various occasions Jesus plainly and conclusively differentiated between himself and the Father. It is clearly the work of the carnal mind that a covering of mystery has been permitted to conceal from human understanding the true relation between Jesus and the Father, lest mortals should see that they also might reach that same relationship by attaining the same Mind, and striving to do the same works, even as the Master had enjoined. The controversies over the personality of Jesus and the Godhead which beset the early Church, and which only resulted in confusing the thoughts of Christians through succeeding centuries, did not contribute to the strength or usefulness of Christianity. It was not within the province of the Church fathers to dogmatize about the nature or person of Deity, but to obey the First Commandment, and to follow the Christ in their lives. "Why call ye me Lord, Lord," said Jesus, "and do not the things which I say?" Had these Church leaders, and their successors, devoted their attention to repeating the works of the Master, and to obeying the spirit and letter of his teachings, instead of contending over their different interpretations, and of reading into the gospels and epistles their own personal views, and forcing these views into church creeds, the mission of our Saviour might have been continued, and the falling away and subsequent apostasy of the Church avoided. The deplorable consequences of injecting uninspired opinions and pagan doctrines into the teachings of the Christian Church should arouse us to the danger of repeating their mistakes or of adopting their undemonstrable and unlivable dogmas.

Jesus taught no confusing or mystical doctrines, for the simple but sufficient reason that his teachings could be lived by his followers, and whatever may be proved in practice is not open to argument or contention. The mistake of the early Church lay in entering into disputes over theories which were extraneous to Jesus' teachings, instead of steadfastly obeying these teachings, a course which would have blessed humanity abundantly, and established the Church upon an impregnable foundation. Probably no field is more prolific of conflicting theories and opinions than that of religion, notwithstanding the fact that Jesus presented a simple and practical course of living by means of which all may work out their salvation from evil.

The assumption that Jesus would return in the latter days as a corporeal personality doubtless arose from the passage in Acts which reads, "this same Jesus, which is taken up from you into heaven, shall so come in like manner as ye have seen him go into heaven." And in what manner did they see him go? Not as one who had taught them to revere the material concept of man, the man of dust, but as one who was laying it down, not only for himself but for their sakes and for the world. He was leaving them as the conqueror over death, the corruption of the grave, and over the sense of matter itself. He had been working up to this accomplishment from the beginning of his career. He had been bringing matter into subjection, changing water into wine, walking on the waves, raising the dead, passing through closed doors, making the diseased whole, etc., and now his pure spiritual consciousness was rising above the material sense altogether, so that he became invisible to the physical sense of his disciples. In the fulness of time, when the human understanding should have become prepared for it, he would be seen to return in the same manner, that is as having risen above all materiality, not as being still in possession of the flesh.

Jesus never taught that the Christ, the truth about God, would leave the world in the spiritual or real sense; it was only the human material concept of the Messiah that it was "expedient" should be taken away, in order that the Comforter, the spiritual sense of the Christ, might become known. Jesus recognized the tendency, even in his own day, to exalt his human personality, and the danger attaching to such a course. We read that after feeding the five thousand with the five loaves, he went away alone lest the people should forcibly "make him a king." He taught very plainly that he had not come to be worshipped, but to serve and to save. If it was not right for the Jews to worship his personality in that day, it must be equally wrong for Christians to do this today.

Jesus' statement that "the kingdom of God cometh not with observation," or to the outward appearance, but is "within you," within a man's cognizance of divine things, should indicate that when the Christ comes again, it will be to the individual spiritual consciousness, and not as a material form. The prediction that "every eye shall see him" would be impossible of fulfilment, with the present limitation of human sight, for a personal descent could be visible to only a portion of the earth's inhabitants. Deity, being omnipresent, could not be more present than He now is, except that the materiality of human consciousness hides this divinity from view, so that what is plainly needed is not more material but more spiritual vision. Even were Jesus to appear again in a physical form, it would not lessen one iota of the demand for human regeneration, for an individual is made better only as he forsakes evil and obeys the law of good. It is perfectly certain that unless the kingdom of God is welcomed into the hearts of men, no personal appearing can establish it upon the earth.

Paul apparently recognized this when he said, "Although we have known Christ after the flesh, yet now henceforth know we him no more." The apostle understood God to be Spirit, but popular belief would reverse his statement to the Athenians, and say, "In matter we live and move and have our being." To conceive of God, or of God's idea, as inhabiting flesh and blood, is to contradict the Scriptural statement, that the flesh and Spirit are contrary the one to the other, and similar passages. If it be true that man lives in God, man must live in Spirit and spiritually, not materially; and Christ, his Saviour from the flesh, would necessarily appear to his understanding in the spiritual sense, since "spiritual things," we are taught, are "spiritually discerned." It is for this spiritual appearing, this transforming perception of divinity, that we should not only be waiting and watching for, but preparing.

But what has all this to do with Israel? Everything; for all that pertains to the true idea of Israel is bound up with the truth which declares God, and is therefore inseparable from the Christ, whether in the first century or the twentieth. It has been plainly seen that Israel must realize her restoration through an understanding of the Scriptures, that is through a knowledge of the Christ, or divine Truth, to which the Scriptures point and which they reveal from Genesis to Revelation. In other words, Israel must return from her exile through the practice of Christianity, because there is no other possible way.

Israelite and Christian are terms which differ in degree but not in quality or character, and in their true essence are identical. Jesus said to Nathaniel, "Behold an Israelite indeed"; and this Israelite saw in Jesus the "Son of God" and the "King of Israel." The Messiah said of the great Hebrew patriarch, "Abraham rejoiced to see my day, and he saw it, and was glad," by which he evidently meant that what Abraham had glimpsed of the truth about God was, in its degree, the same that Jesus presented. Abraham saw the day of Christianity as the goal towards which his seed were to journey. It was Jacob's perception of the same truth which was given the designation of Israel, a name which was to mark his descendants, in something more than racial difference, from the other peoples of the earth. The seed of Jacob were called the children of Israel, or the Israelites, whether they were individually true to the ideal of Israel or not; in the same way that members of the Anglo-Saxon race are known as Christians, whether or not they individually conform to the teachings of Christ.

The consummation of the journey of Israel during six thousand years will not be the occurrence of a day or of a year, but of a period. This prophetical fulfilment is undoubtedly taking place, but of the time of its completion "knoweth no man." That the Christ, in a higher meaning than ever before, is knocking at the door of human consciousness cannot be questioned, but how great or how prolonged may be the ordeal required in finally establishing God's rule among men, the Scriptures do not reveal.

Chapter Twenty-Six - Anglo-Israel: The Second Witness

I will ordain a place for My people Israel, and will plant them, and they shall dwell in their place, and shall be moved no more. — I Chron. 17: 9.

He shall cause them that come of Jacob to take root; Israel shall blossom and bud, and fill the face of the world with fruit.

For thou shalt break forth on the right hand and on the left; and thy seed shall inherit the Gentiles, and make the desolate cities to be inhabited.

And their seed shall be known among the Gentiles, and their offspring among the people: all that see them shall acknowledge them, that they are the seed which the Lord hath blessed.

And the Gentiles shall see thy righteousness, and all kings thy glory: and thou shalt be called by a new name, which the mouth of the Lord shall name. — Isa. 27: 6; 54: 3; 61: 9; 62: 2.

THE Scriptures are so definite and outspoken on the subject of Israel's restoration as a nation, that there is no ground for the claim that that restoration will be fulfilled in its spiritual meaning only. In the prophecies the spiritual and national phases of Israel's return are parallel, and it is not implied that either of these will supplant the other or render its existence and functions unnecessary. The importance of spiritual Israel cannot be overestimated; but literal Israel, the Israel that the eyes can look upon, must also have its place "while the earth remaineth." If, then, we are to accept the statements of Holy Writ, we must be ready to acknowledge that the house of Joseph, the representative tribe of Israel, has not been literally obliterated any more than has the house of Judah, and must be as capable of being disclosed to the world, and will be so disclosed when the time comes for the veil to be drawn aside.

The Mosaic law required a second witness for the substantiation of evidence, and it is this second or confirmatory witness with which the present chapter is mainly concerned. We are not taught that the restoration of Israel would be one-sided, and it is a reflection upon the verity of the Scriptures to describe it thus. The literal side of a church is its organization and membership, without which it would have no present means or avenue for its identity and activity. It is not otherwise with Israel, which we may look upon as the great spiritual church of the early ages, the spiritual center out of which the progress and enlightenment of the race have come. A New Testament writer speaks of the church as the body of Christ, and when the church returns to her first vision of the great Physician and Redeemer, it will not mean the loss of that body, but its restoration to life and power. In like manner we should not expect Israel to return from her captivity without a body or without an outward medium of expression but rather that that body will be restored to its proper place and purpose. Let us assume that these things are too obvi-

179

ously true for argument, for it is certain that until human thought is wholly regenerated, spiritual truth will require human channels through which to become humanly operative and tangible.

The specious argument, that Israel's national recovery is of no consequence because the world has all that it needs in Christianity, not only belittles the place which the Scriptures assign to that people, but ignores two very pertinent facts: (1) that Christianity itself, as presented in creeds and doctrines, must return from its captivity to materialism and unbelief before it can do the things which Jesus said would redeem the world from its errors; (2) that the exclusion of the second witness would rob humanity of the complete verification of the Scriptures and of the validity of God's covenants therein recorded.

To summarize the situation in a few words: the spiritual perception of truth which came through "the woman" found the least resistance among the Israelites, who were the outcome through Jacob of the selective process which had been going on for upwards of twenty centuries. The descendants of Jacob, who were nationally known as Israel, were to be a witness in the world to the one God, and an instrument for making His power known to men. This nation later fell into idolatry, worshipping other gods, as Christians are doing today under different names, and was carried captive out of her own land to endure a long period of exile, during which she was to become unknown to herself and unknown to the world as the Israel of former days. In the latter days, according to the Scriptures, this exiled race is to be brought forth from her long concealment and resume her place in the family of nations.

As the end of the times of the Gentiles drew near, an interest began to be felt in the possible existence and whereabouts of Israel, and efforts were made to locate her among some of the more insignificant nations and in the most unlikely places. The prevalent but deplorable lack of information respecting the status of Israel at the time of her restoration may be judged by a statement in one of the encyclopedias, to the effect that one nation answers to the specified conditions about as well as another. This condition is due in large part to the silence and indifference which the churches generally have maintained towards this subject. The only official reference on the part of any of the Christian denominations, implying that Israel is to be restored, which has come to the attention of the writer, is found in the Church Manual of The First Church of Christ, Scientist, in Boston, which is The Mother Church of the Christian Science denomination throughout the world. In a "Historical Sketch," briefly relating the history of the organization, it reads: "Mrs. Eddy was appointed on the committee to draft the Tenets of the Mother Church — the chief corner-stone whereof is, that Christian Science, as taught and demonstrated by our Master, casts out error, heals the sick, and restores the lost Israel: for 'the stone which the builders rejected, the same is become the head of the corner.'"

The claim that the Anglo-Saxon or English-speaking race is modern Israel is something more than an argument or a sentimental fancy. It is presented with a mass of detailed evidence, in a literature of its own, which covers every aspect of national identification, and which is too convincing to the thoughtful and unprejudiced reader to be reasonably contradicted. While much of the picture remains to be filled in, the general outline and perspective are clear and true. The description of Israel when she shall emerge from her past obscurity, which is furnished by the Hebrew prophets, corresponds to no other race or nationality. A careful survey of the races and peoples of the world today leaves no possible competitor in the field. The marks of identification which are given in the Scriptures are evident alone in the Anglo-Saxon people, a fact which remains unaffected by idle controversy or sceptical indifference.

The opening sentence of Green's *History of the English People* reads, "For the fatherland of the English race we must look far away from England itself," and then the historian proceeds to locate it in northern Europe; but he does not go back beyond the fifth century. Had he gone a little further in his exploration he would have found the fatherland of the English race in Palestine. Briefly stated, as may be learned from various sources, when the Israelites broke from their Assyrian captivity, at a time when their captors were engaged in war, they made their way along the southern shore of the Caspian Sea, and gradually on into central and northern Europe, where Green found them in the fifth century as Angles, Jutes, Saxons, etc. All this ground has been gone over carefully again and again, and in view of the fact that, according to the Scriptures, the Israelites were to be neither exterminated nor absorbed by Gentile races, but were to develop in the "isles of the sea," into a mighty people, both in number and power, there is no sufficient reason for disputing the evidence, disclosed by loving and devout research, which identifies the English people with the ancient house of Israel. This, of course, does not apply to the Jews, who have remained throughout their separation and dispersion a marked race, entirely distinct from their brethren of Israel.

Contrary to the outlandish fiction which has been and still is taught in our schools, in the name of history, the inhabitants of Britain at the time of Caesar's invasion were not a race of savages and illiterate barbarians. They were the equals of their Roman invaders in learning, and their superiors in religion and morals. Britain was probably the most anciently settled of the countries of Europe, the recorded genealogy of whose kings goes back hundreds of years before the founding of Rome. It was the one country which Rome failed to conquer, with the exception of the southern portion which it was subsequently forced to relinquish. Britain was the first country to adopt Christianity nationally, a significant fact in its bearing upon the identity of Israel. The Gospel was brought to Britain direct from Palestine by Joseph of Arimathea and others within a few years of the Master's ascension, and later by St. Paul, the British royal family being among the first converts. Some idea of the extent of the Christianization of the island may be had from the fact that ten thousand British Christians perished in the Diocletian persecution. Authorities for these and other related facts are given in Rev. R. W. Morgan's *St. Paul in Britain.*

The British Isles were not unknown to the ancients, and were doubtless identical with "the isles that are afar off" mentioned in the Scriptures. The trade in tin, of which Britain was the earliest source of supply, would naturally involve some measure of development and colonization, in which the Hebrews would in all probability participate, especially the Danites, whose territory lay along the sea and who engaged in maritime commerce. It has been supposed that, long before the captivity, Ireland had been colonized by the Danites and Phoenicians, and that the prophet Jeremiah, following the captivity of Judah, journeyed with a small company to that country and remained there, a belief which is supported by strong circumstantial evidence. It is also highly probable that during the Assyrian subjugation of the northern kingdom many of the Israelites made their way to the British Isles and permanently located there. St. Paul and other early Christian missionaries were no doubt aware of the Hebrew colonization of Britain, and were attracted there on that account, for did not Jesus say that he had come to "the lost sheep of the house of Israel"?

But the strength of the Anglo-Israel cause does not lie in tracing the devious ways by which the exiles eventually found their gathering place in the "isles of the sea"; or in the fact that the genealogy of the Royal House of Britain goes back in an unbroken line, through the family of the mother of Jesus, to the first King David of Israel; nor does it lie in the thousand and one intensely interesting links of human evidence which connect the English-speaking people of the British Empire and the United States with the Israel of the Old Testament. This chain of evidence should not be wanting, but it is what this race is ready to be and to do that must furnish the final proof of her heirship of the covenants.

The discovery of lost Israel in the Anglo-Saxons does not crown that race with a halo of vainglory, rather does it invest that people with a lasting and sacred responsibility to God and to mankind. The bare proof that the Anglo-Saxons are Israelites possesses nothing more than passing interest, unless that race is ready to occupy the place and fulfil the mission which God gave to Israel. The resurrection of buried Israel to life and light is for something far greater than can be expressed-, in material terms. It is that she may be literally God's "battle-axe and weapons of war," not against other peoples, but against the evils which oppress mankind. It is that she may be His witness, that is the demonstrator of God, to all the Gentile peoples of the earth; for how else could God be sanctified in Israel? Certainly not by external proofs of our racial descent from Jacob, or by the possession of predominant power and influence, or because we hold the gateways of the world, but by purifying our land of its idolatries, and by exalting God's name in righteousness and true holiness.

The return of Israel as a worshipper of false gods would naturally be anomalous. Neither will she return as the special charge of a national Jehovah, for in that limited and selfish concept were planted the seeds of her downfall, because it developed a false view of Deity as humanly partial and capricious. She will have learned that God was not the God of Israel in any exclusively proprietary sense, but only because His oneness was acknowledged there. Jesus never spoke of the Father as a national or tribal Deity; nor did he refer to Him as Jehovah. He had risen above the superstitious and stultifying beliefs of a past age, and was opening a new and brighter chapter in the revelation of man's relation to God, and the Israel of whom Jesus was King must rise to the same recognition and demonstration of the Father, if the prophets' visions of the restoration are to be realized. Is the Anglo-Saxon race ready to do this?

The importance of the second witness should be too obvious to be rashly controverted, hence the necessity that this witness shall be forthcoming at the proper time. With the disappearance of spiritual Israel this second witness was no longer needed, and passed into a state of virtual oblivion, until the return of spiritual Israel should call it forth. The "dry bones" of Ezekiel's vision, to be revived by the winds of God, represent the second witness, which shall "stand up upon their feet, an exceeding great army." These bones have been dried up so long that many of them blandly deny the necessity of coming to life again, but the quickening of the Spirit will be found irresistible, despite their sleepy protests that it makes no difference where or who the Israelites are today; and the whole house of Israel, united with wandering Judah, must again stand before the world, "an exceeding great army."

The word in the Hebrew which is translated "spirit" means wind or air, so that the breath from the four winds, which breathed upon these dry bones, may well be the restoration of spiritual Israel sending forth its quickening influence from every part of the world. Under this compelling power, Israel of the flesh, human, literal Israel, will open her eyes to the facts of her real identity, and in humility behold the verification of the Scripture, "None can stay His hand." There is no power on earth that can withhold this resurrection when the time has come. The truth of the Scriptures is surely not a matter of small importance. Since the return of literal Israel has been given such a prominent place in the prophetic Scriptures, it must be of some consequence that it shall take place. The infidel has scoffed at the Bible because lost Israel was not restored as promised, — is the believer to join in the scoff by minimizing the necessity or importance of this restoration? In various instances in the life of Jesus we read that certain things were done in fulfilment of the Scriptures — for example when he rode into Jerusalem upon an ass's colt. The disciples afterwards remembered "that these things were written of him." Why, then, should it be thought of no value that the Scriptures be fulfilled in these days also?

It may be well to remind the reader again that human nationalities embody types of human thought, and that these types are preserved although individuals and generations pass, a fact which is verified, again and again, in the pages of history. From her inception Israel expressed the highest spiritual thought among the nations of the earth, and was therefore more susceptible to spiritual discernment and the reception of divine revelation. This type or quality of thought was not to be irreparably lost in the captivity, but by its very nature was bound to revive, and to develop to an even greater degree because of the refining experiences of the exile. Beyond question the same type of thought, and in the same relative sense, is found today in the Anglo-Saxon race, and in those of other races who have mentally adopted and assimilated her ideals. This mental coincidence with the Israel of the Scriptures is the most convincing or satisfying mark of identification that can be produced, unless one ignores the metaphysical constituency of human history. The nation whose mentality is nearest to the discernment of divine truth is the nation that must correspond with the line of Israel. When it is recognized that the types of thought which inhere in races are not interchangeable, and that it is the best in any nation which survives the wear of time and the friction of adversity, it will be seen that the race which today presents the mental and spiritual qualities of the ancient people of God must be, beyond peradventure, the same race and people.

Too much attention is sometimes given, albeit with worthy motives, to external evidences in the effort to identify national Israel, for all such testimony is incidental rather than fundamental. It should be apparent that the better things which made Israel different in the early period of her history must necessarily be the determinative evidence in identifying Israel in the present day. It may be proper on occasions to emphasize the fact of Anglo-Saxon supremacy; it may be well to point to the wealth, prosperity, broad dominions, etc., of this race, since these were prophesied of Israel in the time of her restoration; but all these things are purely secondary to the identity of mind or consciousness.

When we consider the moral and religious ideals of Anglo-Saxondom, together with her almost universal acknowledgment of the God of Israel, and her devotion to the Hebrew Scriptures; and when we add to these the multiplying evidences of language, history, and prophecy, there is no reasonable ground for disputing the Israelitish origin of this race. Israel was not doomed to extinction, but on the contrary the promise in the Scriptures was that she should be presented.

In the latter days Israel was to be found as a company or federation of nations, a federation of peoples united by a common ancestry, and by common ethical and religious ideals. America is naturally included in that federation, although the union is not expressed in political terms. In the English language, law, literature, and government, the God which was declared in Horeb and in Sinai, which called Abraham out of idolatry, and which brought enslaved Israel out of Egypt, is acknowledged as the central fact in human affairs, notwithstanding that we as a race move slowly towards the more practical application of the facts of divinity.

At the same time it must be remembered that the Anglo-Saxon race is only touching the hem of her privileges and duties as the inheritor of Israel's destiny. The discovery of Israel in the British Empire and in the United States is but one link in a chain whose end is the establishment of Christ's kingdom on the earth. Another link in this chain is the union of Judah with Israel, so that they shall again have one God, and take their places in a common heritage. This has not yet been accomplished. While Israel accepted the Messiah and became Christian, Judah, or the Jews, rejected the Messiah and have remained as they were. The Jew is evidently waiting for a presentation of Christianity that he can understand; not as a set of doctrines and dogmas over which Christendom itself has quarreled for centuries, but as the redemptive truth which he can lay hold of and demonstrate, and which is infinitely greater than a human person or a church creed. Judah's wanderings and persecutions will cease when she gets this vision of the Christ, and wakens from her age-long hatred and misunderstanding of the great Nazarene.

A descendant of the Davidic dynasty, the sceptre family of Judah, sits on the throne of England. The unicorn of Israel and the lion of Judah are on the crest of her kings, and no other nation and no college of heraldry have challenged their right to have them there. No nation and no royal line can be named which would become them more, — but how came they there? The crests of ancient kings are not lying in the street to be picked up by the passer-by. Obviously they are there because they rightly belong there. These may seem small things in themselves, but they fit into the picture, and with many others point so uniformly in the same direction that there is nothing to do but to follow.

Archbishop Trench's *On the Study of Words* traces the history of the word "thrall" as descending "to us from a period when it was the custom to thrill or drill the ear of a slave in token of servitude; a custom in use among the Jews (Deut. 15:17), and retained by our Anglo-Saxon forefathers, who were wont to pierce at the church-door the ears of their bondservants." Why did the writer use the word "retained" rather than "adopted," unless "our Anglo-Saxon forefathers" were of Israelitish origin? One may *adopt* the customs of another race, but we do not *retain* customs which were not ours originally. And how would the Anglo-Saxons of the early centuries of the Christian era be likely to know of the customs of the Israelites in such matters?

An English writer, in reviewing Lord Bryce's *American Commonwealth*, said, "It needs no prophet to perceive that the race (Anglo-Saxon) is to dominate the world when time is old enough." In other words, when Gentile dominion shall have worn itself out, the spiritual ideals of Israel shall predominate, and her government hold the sovereign place. In the Scriptures this dominion was promised to Israel; then, if the identity of Anglo-Saxon-Israel be not genuine, or if it be not admitted, to what other of the world's races would this dominion more logically pass? What other people gives greater promise of blessing the families of the earth by the administration of power?

Mr. George R. Parkin, In a magazine article back in the eighties, writes, "The development of the Anglo-Saxon race...has become, within the last century, the chief factor and central feature in human history." This is a strong and startling statement, If this race is not the Israel of the Old Testament, because, In such a case. It would mean that the prophecies in Holy Writ regarding the restoration are proved false, for in the foregoing sentence the writer has described the relative position of Israel in the latter days. If the Anglo-Saxon race is of Gentile lineage, yet is occupying the place and fulfilling the destiny of Israel, the argument of the infidel is well founded, and we shall have to discredit the statements not only of a large portion of the Old Testament, but of many important passages in the New.

The recognition and acknowledgment of our racial origin and history as identical with Israel would not mean that Englishmen and Americans would henceforth call themselves Israelites or Hebrews. Shakespeare has told us that another name for a rose would not change its nature and qualities, neither would the fact that Israel is emerging from her long obscurity under a new name affect the great destiny which lies before her. The prophets indicate that she will not only bear another name but speak another language in the day of her return. While it might not seem essential from one point of view for the descendants of Jacob, other than the Jews, to be nationally or otherwise identified, the value of preserving unbroken the chain of Scriptural testimony, as Jesus took care to preserve it, need not be questioned.

It is becoming more and more apparent that the Anglo-Saxons in the British Empire and in the United States are only politically divided. They are the two branches of the main trunk of Israel, and have the same perspective in history and in prophecy. They are joined in the brotherhood of a common destiny to bear the light of divine Truth to the dark places of the earth. Subtle and insidious influences have been persistently at work to forestall this unity, and to prevent an understanding friendship between these two great peoples, because in this unity and friendship lie the safeguard of human democracy and the assurance of world progress. The keynote of the serpent's suggestions from the beginning has been division, not unity. To the human senses this evil activity began by insisting upon man's separation from his Maker, representing him as possessing a different mind, and as inhabiting a sphere outside the divine presence. The natural outcome of accepting these suggestions has been the separation of men from each other, resulting in a conflict rather than a community of interest.

Because of their common religious ideals, the unity between these nations, or rather this "company of nations," will result from spiritual progress, not political expediency; therefore it will not be severed by the selfish ambitions of politicians or by the efforts of alien enemies. This alliance of the two families of the house of Joseph, known today as Britain and America, is not only necessary to the future peace of the race, but to its ultimate evangelization.

The restoration of Israel as foretold by her prophets, and as viewed in its higher significance, will kindle "the desire of all nations" for that spiritual consciousness of life which the practice of genuine Christianity brings to men. The standard-bearers of Israel in the days of her return will be found marching together on the side of the best things which that race has stood for, that the prophecy may be fulfilled in her, "and they shall be My people."

Chapter Twenty-Seven - Israel's New Covenant

Behold, the days come, saith the Lord, when I will make a new covenant with the house of Israel and with the house of Judah:

For this is the covenant that I will make with the house of Israel ... I will put My laws into their mind, and write them in their hearts; and I will be to them a God, and they shall be to Me a people. — Heb. 8:8, 10.

I have yet many things to say unto you, but ye cannot bear them now.

But when the Comforter is come, whom I will send unto you from the Father, even the Spirit of truth, which proceedeth from the Father, he shall testify of me. — John i6: 12; 15 .26.

MORE than nineteen centuries had come and gone since Jesus preached the gospel of the new birth, and the consciousness of Christendom still remained under Gentile oppression, or the rule of materialism. The mission of Christ was to break this yoke, first in the experience of his followers, and through them of all mankind; but human thought proved to be too deeply buried in the dust to be ready for the conquest of the carnal senses, or even to recognize that Christianity demanded this conquest. How long before the dream of consciousness in matter, gorging itself with the husks of sensualism, would wear itself out in the suffering which attends it, and how soon the dawn of the spiritual facts of life would begin to appear, might well have been the question of the watchers throughout the long night of Israel's captivity.

One fact had been calling for the attention of earnest thinkers, and the call was becoming louder and more imperative, and that was that if the Christianization of the world were to be accomplished, there would have to be a return to the course mapped out by the Founder of Christianity; that is to say, Christendom would need to regain the vision of the Christ which he had presented Jesus knew that his work could not ultimate in failure My words shall not pass away," he said, but that they might for a time be forgotten in their true significance and would have to be brought again to remembrance, is implied in his promise of the Comforter. In the apostolic writings this revival of Christian faith, or Christianity's new day, is spoken of as "the day of the Lord" It is logical to conclude that the apostles would not have referred to that day in the future tense if it had been realized in their own time, or if the fulness of the truth taught by Christ Jesus were embodied in the church of that age.

It is certain that so long as the fleshly sense continues to sway the thoughts of Christendom, the day of the Lord, the day of mankind's redemption, has not fully dawned there. The conclusion is obvious, even to an unbeliever, that only as consciousness and life are becoming less material, can one truly merit the distinction of being a disciple of Christ. The Christian world has been held in the grasp of the carnal mind simply because it has not recognized that the reign of Spirit is supreme in the earth; and it was this faith in matter still prevalent in the church and the consequent loss of spiritual power, which constituted the necessity for a return to the teaching and practice of Christ Jesus.

If we have followed carefully the course of Israel towards a better understanding of God, as recorded in the Scriptures, we have seen that its ultimate goal was he attainment of a purely spiritual consciousness of life, and that the Messiah, the Deliverer to whom all Israel looked forward in hope and anticipation, came to lead humanity to that goal. Jesus taught that he came forth from the Father to do His will or, as the apostle phrased, to "destroy the works of the devil" the carnal mmd He certainly did not come to validate the demands of so-called physical sense, but he plainly taught that the way of salvation which he was blazing for mankind lay through the denial of that sense; hence the spiritual darkness which later spread over the Church because of the failure to follow him in his crucifixion of materiality, and the consequent failure to share in his spiritual resurrection.

Coming on to the middle of the nineteenth century we find the same conditions continuing as they had been. The sturdy Protestantism which had won liberty of conscience and an open Bible laid its neck unresistingly under the heel of materialism, an oppression more merciless and tyrannical than the ecclesiasticism of the Dark Ages, and more hopeless because it was believed to be divinely sanctioned. Although the Gospel of Christ Jesus was preached to men as providing their relief from sin, the door of that divine Gospel was closed upon their relief from the ills and evils of the flesh. Since it is not possible that Christ's garment could be thus divided, the natural result was that the consciousness of sin, as well as of its effects in disease and death, was not overcome. Materialism profanely sat on the throne of Spirit, and none dared to openly question its decrees. It was a time of spiritual dearth and darkness, when men were trying to subsist on the "serpent's meat," the dry dust of barren doctrines, and the Church slumbered over the tarrying of the bridegroom.

Looking forward to a new and better era of thought, when superstitious credulity should no longer dominate the domain of religion and good would rule in the hearts of men because it was understood and loved, Jeremiah was moved to write, "Behold, the days come, saith the Lord, that I will make a new covenant with the house of Israel, and with the house of Judah." And the writer of the book of Hebrews thus continues the quotation: "For this is the covenant that I will make with the house of Israel after those days, saith the Lord; I will put My laws into their mind, and write them in their hearts." In

Ferrar Fenton's translation, the word *mind* is rendered *understanding,* a rendering which takes religion out of the realm of mere belief, and lifts it to the plane, not only of intelligent apprehension, but of scientific application and proof. Jeremiah's prophecy clearly points to the time when the whole truth about God shall be revealed to the understanding, and the true spiritual relation between God and man will not only be acknowledged but practised.

In different phraseology Jesus pointed to the same new covenant in the promised coming of the Comforter which he defined impersonally as the "Spirit of truth" whose mission is to lead into all truth or to unfold to spiritual apprehension the real meaning, power and presence of the Christ. The fulfilment of Jeremiah's prophecy and of Jesus' promise are substantially identical a fact which establishes the spiritual Israel of the Old Testament and the Christianity of the New as essentially one.

Jesus was "the mediator of a better covenant," founded upon an infinitely higher ideal of Deity than the Jehovistic concept with its ordinances and sacrifices; but the age was not then ready to receive it in its fulness, as witness the lapse of the Church into pre-exilic ideals and the attempt to pour the new teachings of Christianity into pagan moulds. The anthropomorphism of primitive belief, which was ingrafted into the Hebrew conception of God, and later embodied in Christian creeds and dogmas, is not found in the teachings of the Master Even as late as the last century, if not entirely true of our own time, the theological schools of Christendom, almost without exception, were basing their teaching upon a view of Deity which did not touch the fringe of Jesus revelation of Him as the perfect Father. It may be said beyond peradventure, that the pagan description of God as the source of both good and evil, as consenting to the affliction of His own children with disease, misfortune and death and as consigning the wayward ones of earth to unending torture, pertains neither to the new covenant with Israel, nor to the Comforter which is to teach the truth to men.

Jesus did not imply that he had uttered the final word in declaring the truth about the Father. It was just before the crucifixion that he said to his disciples, "I have yet many things to say unto you, but ye cannot bear them now...These things have I spoken unto you in proverbs: but the time cometh, when I shall no more speak unto you in proverbs, but I shall show you plainly of the Father." In these and other sayings Jesus left the way open for a fuller revelation of the truth than the world was then ready to receive. Many centuries have passed since the Master's words were spoken, and it is not too soon to think of their fulfilment if we are to expect the restoration of spiritual power to the Christian Church, and the return of the woman from the wilderness. The expectations of men are not turning prematurely towards the coming of that perfect revelation of truth which is to bring them freedom from error, nor is it too soon to look about us for some sign of the promised bruising of the serpent's head.

Six thousand years from "the woman" in the metaphorical story of Eden, to "the woman" pictured in the symbolism of the Apocalypse, would seem a far cry, but the distance is one of spiritual development rather than of time. In reality they are identical. Her great destiny may be traced in prophetic outline in every step of spiritual progress, both in the Scriptural records and in subsequent history, and in the fulness of time, however distant that consummation may now appear, her seed, the recognition of spiritual truth, will fill the earth.

While it is evident that "the woman" is not in any literal sense a person, but is named as a type of spirituality, she has not been without a personal representative in the world's great epochs. She has ever stood for that higher quality of thought through which the spiritual facts of being have found recognition. It was woman who ushered the human conception or incarnation of the Christ into the world in the infant Jesus, and we must look to woman to usher in, or to give expression to, that fuller statement of the truth about God to which the Scriptures consistently point, and of which they are themselves a prophecy.

The year 1866 was a memorable date among students of the prophetic Scriptures, because it was reckoned as ending the "time, times, and half a time" of the woman's sojourn in the wilderness (Rev. 12: 14). Also, according to one computator, it was believed to date the beginning of the Lord's return to earth, as the restoration of living faith in Christ is sometimes termed. In that year, in a small town in New England, a woman, believed to be on her death-bed according to the verdict of her physician, was wrestling with the scepticism of an age that denied healing virtue to Christianity. It had long been taught that Christ was not to be regarded, in any practical way, as the "Great Physician" of men, so that it could be said of the Church also, but with less excuse, that "He came unto his own, and his own received him not."

But the woman did not yield to this materialistic unbelief. Physical means being of no avail she turned to God, and while reading of the healing by Jesus of the palsied man, the eternal presence and power of the same Truth which brought him deliverance dawned upon her consciousness. She was immediately made whole. In that moment of illumination and discovery she saw the healing Christ. She had verified the Scriptural statement, "unto them that look for him shall he appear the second time without sin unto salvation."

To this spiritual discovery Mrs. Eddy gave the name, "Christian Science," a name which naturally implies an intelligent and demonstrable knowledge of the Messianic Truth, and which points to the consummation of the New Covenant with Israel. A few years later, finding her message unwelcome to the religious teaching of the time, she organized a church, or denominational movement to provide the means for making this message and its practical benefits more widely known, and the increase of this movement throughout the world has been a modern wonder. But, while Mrs. Eddy found this course expedient, not only for the promulgation but for the protection of her teaching, and although its expediency may be apparent for an indefinite time, none knew better than she that a practical understanding of the divine Word is undenominational, and that Truth, because of its universal divine nature, is

190

necessarily independent of human organizations. Inasmuch as the Christ is indivisible, there must come a time in Christian history when denominational lines will be obliterated, and "there shall be one fold, and one shepherd."

But why was this message of Christian healing accompanied by its proof, unwelcome to the religious thought of her time? Evidently for the same reason that it was unwelcome to the religious thought of the Jews in the first century. Jesus' teachings were a rebuke to the dead formalism of the Judaic religion, and the carnal mind crucified him to silence his spiritual appeal. The call of Christian Science for a return to the works of the Master was a rebuke to the barrenness of doctrinal Christianity, while its uncompromisingly spiritual attitude threatened the peace of the materialist. It had been easier to drift with the current of materiality than to stem the stream, although the great Teacher had solemnly declared that unless a man denied himself — the man of dust — and bore his cross after him, he could not be his disciple; in other words, he could not be a true Christian. It was this demand for denial, which Christian Science insisted upon so relentlessly, that once more brought forth the cry which had resounded in the judgment-hall of Pilate; for when has materialism felt at peace in the presence of the Christ?

Mrs. Eddy stood before the world as the lone pioneer of a monotheism so absolute that few were ready to accept it, yet withal so comprehensive that only evil and its concomitants were excluded from it. In this new exposition of Christian truth, the First Commandment was taken at its full value, and God was, therefore, acknowledged to be infinite in the literal meaning of that word. In her unreserved protest against materialism and its idolatries, or the endowment of matter with the prerogatives which belong to Deity alone, Mrs. Eddy was establishing an order of Protestantism such as the world had not yet known. In general terms it simply meant the refusal to admit that life, intelligence, substance, or reality are to be found in God's unlikeness, or in that which does not express His glory, immortality, and goodness.

While all this was plainly in accord with the best views which the Scriptures give of Deity, and with the evident intent and purpose of Christianity, it struck too hard at the material idolatry of both Christians and unbelievers to be readily acclaimed. It has never been the nature of the carnal mind to submit tamely to rebuke, or to caress the hand threatening to destroy it; and so we find the critics of this new message taking refuge in the subterfuge that, because Christian Science denies reality to evil, it is not Christian; and because it teaches the allness of Mind, it is not scientific. This atheistic argument would condemn every effort for reform since the world began, inasmuch as human beings can reach a diviner consciousness only as they become more spiritually-minded, and good replaces evil in their thoughts.

Mrs. Eddy very sanely based her teaching upon the highest and most absolute statements in the Scriptures which define Deity and devil, instead of following the beaten track of a rigid and unprogressive theology, with its insistent belief in a finite divinity. Recognizing as he did the perfection of the Father and the Son, Jesus could not define devil in any other light than as a falsity, as a lie or liar. His analysis was justified by what he knew and was daily proving of the truth about God, and it remains the one correct and scientific definition of that element in human thought which arrays itself against God's government.

The difficulty in securing a friendly or even impartial examination of this subject is due, not only to the bias of religious education, but to the fact that most people think of Christian Science as a sect, rather than as a Science, presenting Christ's teachings as the practical guide to right thinking and right living, by means of which sickness may be healed and sin eradicated from human consciousness. The New Covenant with Israel distinctly implied the understanding of God's laws, and that their observance would be inspired by love of good ("written in the heart"), not by fear of punishment. The great Teacher summed up God's laws as supreme loyalty to God as One and All, and as love for one another. On these two divine statutes "hang all the law and the prophets." That these laws are Christian is beyond dispute; and that they are capable of being practised in accordance with the unerring rules which Jesus laid down must also be accepted; yet these divine laws and their demonstration comprehend, in their fulness, the whole of Christian Science.

Mortals' deliverance from evil cannot be called an accident, nor can it be conceived of in any sense as a lawless process. (There is a power impelling and attending the new birth that does not spring from fear, or from an indolent acquiescence in another individual's sacrifice and resurrection: and that power is the law of good, whose operation in human consciousness, as it is understood and adhered to, is unvarying and certain "It is God that worketh with you," said Paul; hence God is the Principle of human redemption, and its progressive accomplishment must be correctly designated as scientific; that is, it is being wrought out on the basis of Divine truth and law.

That there is a Science of Christianity, or Christian Science, should be unquestioned by all who understand the significance of these two words, and their wonderful message to humanity when united. If we believe there is a science dealing with material things, how much more should we believe in the relation of science to spiritual things; for the former at their best are ephemeral, while the latter are eternal. But science in these opposite aspects is no more identical than the mortal sense of man is identical with the immortal. The Science of Christianity stands alone, since it alone can interpret the truth of divine things and define its rules, by means of which men may reach the understanding of their relation to the Father, and of the Father's relation to His offspring, and may apply that understanding to the solution of all human problems.

Thus it should be readily seen that Christian Science is not a sect, or a philosophy peculiar to a class, but the unfolding to human understanding of the law of divinity. In its simplest statement it is the practical overcoming of evil with good, but with nothing else. It is plain that in the knowledge and application of God's law there is no class or sectarian discrimination, for in the presence of His impartial demands all human beings stand upon the same footing of necessity, and must ultimately walk the same road in meeting them. However widely sects and denominations may differ in their religious views, when it comes to the question of actually ridding consciousness of evil, they have no possible alternative but to put into practice the truth of man's divine sonship, a truth which is not "hedged with forms," and is "too large for creeds."

Since Christianity rests upon the infinity of God, it is idle to deny its scientific nature and construction, for this infinitude must naturally include all law and order, and in consequence be the foundation or source of all cause and government. From that standpoint God would necessarily be divine Principle, as Mrs. Eddy very properly defines Him; not as a cold or meaningless abstraction, but as the omnipresence of divine Love, expressing intelligence and perfection throughout the universe. It is obvious that it was this Christian Science, or the Science of Christ's teachings, which lay back of Jesus' remarkable works; but the Father was none the less the Father because the Son could thus prove His love and goodness with the unerring certainty of law.

It is true that Christian Science differs from other systems of religion in its method, but not in its purpose. and this difference arises from the different conclusion which it draws from the Scriptural promise of God's infinitude. Christian Science very naturally and logically concludes that, if God is All-in-all, there can be nothing real unlike Him, and it attacks the evil in human consciousness upon that basis. But before questioning this position, it should be considered that every church which acknowledges the omnipotence, omniscience, and omnipresence of God must take the same position, or be untrue to its affirmations. It is not wise to maintain an attitude of vacillation, or to evade the responsibility of decision by quibbling over terms and definitions, since every system of religion, irrespective of creed and dogma, must stand or fall on this fundamental point.

The First Commandment requires an unequivocal adherence to the infinity of God, else it is without force or value; and it is the truth declared in this command that Israel was to teach and to prove to the Gentiles. Is not the time to come when all men shall be taught "plainly of the Father"? And when that time comes, shall it not be taught equally as plainly, without sophistry or reservation, that He creates or makes manifest all that is true, and that there is, consequently, nothing true unlike Him? Until it is thus seen that divinity embraces the whole of being, the import and purpose of true religion is not fully perceived, and the experience of seeing God "face to face" remains to be realized.

The uniform design of all the Christian religions is to overcome evil, and if Christianity is to be successful there must come a time when evil has been entirely overcome, and there is no longer a witness to its existence. When that point is reached will God be more than He now is? Will He exercise greater power, or fill a larger space? Can it be reasonably supposed that the overcoming of evil by mankind is adding aught to the sum of God's being, increasing His omnipotence, or making His presence more universal? Is it not apparent that whatever change is being effected in this process is in the human consciousness only, that is, human beings are coming to see things differently. Men naturally see more of good as evil is successfully resisted, until the time shall come when good is seen to be supreme and fills all their thoughts: but God will then be the same as He was yesterday, and as He is today.

Let it be supposed, on the contrary, that Christianity fails, and that evil succeeds in blotting good out of consciousness; what would there be left? Would men and women continue to exist, and to express activity, sustained by evil alone? Would there be happiness and love and immortality without God? Would the sun still shine, and flowers bloom, and trees bring forth fruit? Would there be consciousness anywhere? If, then, God is essential to the life and reality of things, it necessarily follows that nothing apart from Him can actually exist, nor can anything be literally present anywhere which does not derive its being from Him. These things being true, as they unquestionably are, in what sense can Christian Science be at fault in holding fast to God as the sole reality? If we accept the apostle's statement that "all things were made by Him," it is certainly anomalous to believe in a creation of which God is not the author, or that there can be real things, real power and intelligence, which have no relation to divinity at all.

It cannot be said that Christian Science came without reason or necessity, for, if the consciousness of Christendom was to be saved from spiritual inanity and starvation, it was imperative that the church awaken to Christ's demands, and bring forth the fruits of her discipleship. The crying need of the world was for a more practical interpretation of Christianity than had been presented during the last fifteen centuries, for the simple reason that none of the various branches of the Christian religion had succeeded in repeating the works of its Founder, as he had enjoined, nor had even made any consistent or sustained effort in that direction. Which school of doctrinal theology points to the teachings of Christ Jesus as containing the remedy for all human ills, or as providing the solution of the many problems now facing mankind? Can it be said that Christianity, as Jesus practised it, has been imparting its blessings and its redemption to men here on the earth, in the way that he plainly intimated?

It has been said that the recent world war did not result from the failure of Christianity, but from the failure to practise it. At what door must we lay this failure? Not the lack of preaching, or of churches, or of Bibles, or of creeds. Then what has been lacking in all this religious teaching and preaching, that there has been so little serious effort to make Christianity the vital power in human affairs which it was designed to be? What has been given to the world in the name of Christ, that the Christian world is still effusively crying, "Lord, Lord," but are not doing the things which he said?

The coming of the Comforter is, very obviously, not the advent of a person, but would seem to refer to that unveiling to human understanding of the spiritual truth of being, which opens the door of freedom from materialism

194

and its evils. Standing before a world of hostile critics, making her lone but immensely significant protest against the reality of matter, Mrs. Eddy easily became the leader of the human crusade against materialism, and precipitated the final stages of the conflict between the flesh and Spirit. It is evident that no permanent help or comfort can come to mortals from any material source. The captivity of Israel, the captivity of the higher thought of humanity to the seductiveness of physical sense, can end only through regaining the spiritual idea of God and man. Hence the momentous act of "the woman" in the present age, in challenging the long-standing claims of matter and evil on the basis of the allness of Mind and the sovereignty of God.

The movement which arose in the last century under the name of Christian Science is a movement towards primitive Christianity, and the restoration of its original standard and requirements. It has been predicted by some of its critics that in the course of the twentieth century all the Protestant churches will adopt and practise Christian Science; and no fair-minded person, thoughtfully reading the writings of the Founder of this movement, and observing their influence upon those who consistently follow her teachings, could deplore the possible fulfilment of that prediction. The religion which is most spiritual, and which most closely approximates the example of Jesus, must be nearest the ideal of Christianity, and will survive the opposition of its foes and the mistakes of its friends.

Although Mrs. Eddy, like every true reformer, did not find her views at first welcomed by the world, she lived to see much of that attitude reversed, and her cause rapidly spreading throughout the World. The new light had dawned, and the leaven of a woman's higher perception of Truth was safely laid away in human consciousness, in the place God had prepared for it, until the whole should be leavened. At the passing of this notable woman, after devoting more than half a century to the work to which she had been called, she was honored almost universally by the very press which, in earlier years had attempted to discredit her; and some of the churches which had refused to acknowledge any truth in her teachings, are now beginning to recognize the value and far-reaching influence of her work.

In a sermon delivered in 1893, Rev. Joseph Wild, D. D., author of *The Lost Ten Tribes,* said: "I believe there will come a female who will rule and lead, and her son will be the chief ruler and leader among the nations of the earth, and he will be accepted by God, and he will be accepted by the nations, and she will be accepted as his adviser and director, and they will be of the family of David for a special mission unto the world." Just what this well-known expositor of the prophetic Scriptures had in mind is not disclosed, but the quotation is given as evidence that the woman's place and mission in the final stages of human redemption were beginning to be recognized.

Commenting upon the occasion of Mrs. Eddy's centenary, a prominent secular newspaper said: "That Mrs. Eddy was an American, born of a long line of Puritan ancestors, and whose genealogy is that of the Anglo-Saxon founders of this country, is, in the minds of many thoughtful people, but another concrete evidence of the vast spiritual destiny of America. To those not unmindful that genealogy has a place in the affairs of the world, it will be of interest to note that Mary Baker Eddy's lineage goes back to those Scotch forbears who were mightily associated with the affairs of their times, for a direct ancestor was a daughter of a king of Scotland, and thus her line is connected with the present royal house of Great Britain, which, as has recently been shown by many authorities, goes straight back in history through Scotland and Ireland to David, King of Israel."

Mrs. Eddy was a woman of wide sympathies, and was broadly interested in the great questions of the day, among which was what is known as the Anglo-Israel cause, whose position and evidence not only elicited her interest but won her conviction. In some of the earlier volumes of the *Christian Science Sentinel,* one of the periodicals of the Christian Science movement, and which for several years was under her personal supervision, are to be found a number of quotations from the writings of Lieutenant C. A. L. Totten, one-time Professor of Military Science at Yale University, and a recognized authority upon the subject of Anglo-Israel.

In a letter to Rev. W. M. H. Milner, M.A., F. R. G. S., in 1902, as recently quoted in the press, she said in part, "Your work. *The Royal House of Britain an Enduring Dynasty,* is indeed masterful: one of the most remarkable Biblical researches in that direction ever accomplished. Its data and the logic of its events sustain its authenticity, and its grandeur sparkles in the words, 'King Jesus.'" From a poem entitled, "The United States to Great Britain," contributed by Mrs. Eddy to the *Boston Herald* during the Spanish-American War of 1908, the following significant verses are taken:

"List, brother! angels whisper
   To Judah's sceptred race, —
Thou of the self -same spirit,
   Allied by nations' grace,

"Wouldst cheer the hosts of Heaven;
   For Anglo-Israel, lo!
Is marching under orders;
   His hand averts the blow.'

"Brave Britain, blest America!
   Unite your battle plan;
Victorious, all who live it, —
   The love for God and man."

Perhaps the particular feature of Christian Science which has attracted the widest public notice is the importance which it attaches to the healing function of Christianity, not only in the day of its establishment by Jesus, but so long as the need of healing shall endure. Although its insistence upon this function was at first resented by most of the so-called orthodox churches, there is now an organized movement in a number of these same churches to reinstate healing as an element of the Christian ministry.

It is a matter of simple record, as before pointed out in these pages, that the healing of disease by spiritual means was not uncommon in Israel prior to the captivity, and that this practice was carried into the New Testament dispensation in abundant measure. In the time of Elisha it was sufficiently prominent to attract the attention of outside nations; and there must be other Naamans among the Gentiles of today who will have cause to say, "Now I know there is no God in all the earth, but in Israel." The Scriptural description of the restoration of Israel makes it absolutely certain that none of her former functions and privileges will be omitted.

The covenant, in which God was committed to the maintenance of the health of His people so long as they obeyed His commandments, has not lost its importance, or its place in human welfare. The repetition of this covenant in various forms, and the absence in the Scriptures of any intimation that human agencies might sometime be substituted for God, proclaim the renewal of His relation to Israel as One "who healeth all thy diseases, who redeemeth thy life from destruction." The attempt in the present day to evade the terms of this covenant, or to treat it as outgrown, means either that human inventions are believed to be more potent than the God of Israel, or that health is believed to be attainable independently of Him, that is, without regard to the law of righteousness. It is useless to preach the identity of the Anglo-Saxons with God's covenant people, and at the same time ignore or deny the very covenants which Israel represents and by which she must continue to be bound.

In Micah 5:2, 3, we read, "But thou, Bethlehem Ephratah, though thou be little among the thousands of Judah, yet out of thee shall he come forth unto me that is to be ruler in Israel; whose goings forth have been from of old, from everlasting. Therefore will he give them up, until the time that she which travaileth hath brought forth; then the remnant of his brethren shall return unto the children of Israel." Between these two verses, Dr. Scofield places the period between the first and second advents of the Christ. "The remnant of his (Jesus') brethren" are the Jews, and these have not yet returned to the children of Israel, so that the latter part of this prophecy plainly relates to the time of the restoration, and involves the coming through a woman of that which is to reunite the houses of Israel and Judah; and that is the impersonal appearing of the Messiah, the recognition in this age of the healing and redemptive Truth which was humanly manifested in Christ Jesus, or the coming of the divine Comforter. It is a well-known fact, of particular interest in this connection, that many Jews have accepted the teachings of Christian Science, and now call themselves Christians.

The ideal of a demonstrable Christianity to which Mrs. Eddy gave the name "Christian Science" may well be defined as Israel's new covenant of understanding. Those who object to receiving anything progressive in religion from a woman should call to mind that, according to the first Scriptural prophecy, mankind's final deliverance from the serpent was to be effected through woman. The dawn of the Christian era came through woman, and her child opened the door into the kingdom of heaven, thus becoming the wayshower for humanity, and the central figure in its human history. And in this age also, as implied in the prophecy of Micah, the restoring truth, which is to bring back Israel and Christendom from the captivity of materialism, is to be born of woman, or to come to light through her. Shall we not, then, welcome this Heavenly guest, and humbly verify the Scripture, "As many as received him, to them gave he power to become the sons of God."

The writer gratefully acknowledges his indebtedness to Mrs. Eddy's writings for their illumination of the Scriptures, without which he feels he would not have discerned the inner meaning, purpose, and destiny of Israel, not only in relation to Biblical times, but to modern history and the future of the race. In devoting one chapter to the subject of Christian Science because of its intimate relation, as the author views it, to the restoring of lost Israel, he has refrained from any attempted explanation of its teachings, his purpose being to show the logic of its appearance, and its essential place in the plan of human redemption.

Chapter Twenty-Eight - Armageddon and After

And He will destroy in this mountain the face of the covering cast over all people, and the vail that is spread over all nations. — Isa. 25: 7.

For thus saith the Lord of hosts; Yet once, it is a little while, and I will shake the heavens, and the earth, and the sea, and the dry land. — Hag. 2: 6.

And this word. Yet once more, signifieth the removing of those things that are shaken, as of things that are made, that those things which cannot be shaken may remain. — Heb. 12: 27.

The creature itself also shall be delivered from the bondage of corruption into the glorious liberty of the children of God. — Rom. 8: 21.

THE seeds of all human conflict have their root in the conviction that man is a material being, a creature of the dust, for from that belief proceed all the passions and appetites which link mortals with the beast. Covetousness, envy, hatred, lust, ambition, fear, have their source and support in the conception that power, wealth, success, pleasure, and all earthly glory, are to be attained and enjoyed materially; and the natural offspring of that conception, the supposition that one person, or one family, or one nation can be despoiled or oppressed to the advantage of another, has kept the race in perpetual strife. The material sense of existence makes no provision for human brotherhood, has never yet given birth to the faintest divine impulse, for self-interest is the alpha and omega of its creed.

It should be seen, therefore, that the great struggle which looms up before the world today, and which must ere long be faced and fought out, is not between nations, or between capital and labor, or between any of the conflicting questions engaging human attention, but it will be the great struggle of humanity for spiritual freedom. It will be the final chapter in that long conflict between the awakening spiritual thought of humanity and the carnal mind, and the peace of the world will be in proportion to the triumph of righteousness. Although every movement towards the lessening of warfare between nations is welcome, permanent peace will not be realized until human consciousness is spiritually transformed.

It has been quite freely admitted that the recent great war was not so much a war between races as between ideals. This fiery experience was, in reality, a call for national consecration to the charge which God has laid upon this race. Israel finds herself returning from her exile, not to a world at peace, but to a war of conquest; not the conquest of peoples, but of the errors which ever betray humanity into captivity. It is nothing less than the conquest of the carnal mind, the pantheon of the human race, to which Israel as Britain-America is committed; for the idolatry of ancient and modern times is but the exaltation of matter and material concepts in place of the one infinite Spirit and His manifestations. Israel, however, need not go back twenty-five centuries in order to renounce the gods of the Gentiles, for their altars are to be found today in every nook and corner of her land. They appear under different names, but their natures are the same, and as surely alienate the affections from the one good, which Jesus said was God. These are precisely the same delusions against which Israel was warned in the First Commandment, and which have ever beguiled humanity into the belief of an evil consciousness.

Although appearing today under a different national name, with different environments, customs, and conditions, Israel is still, in the quality of her thoughts and in her relation to God's covenants, the Israel of a long past yesterday. She finds the same weaknesses to be overcome, the same demands attaching to her position, and the same destiny awaiting her. Moreover, the Philistines, Assyrians, and others of her ancient enemies, are also existing today under different names, but their types and characteristics are the same, and they bear the same relation to their ancient foe, and feel much the same unthinking antipathy. But the world is beginning to discover the folly of fighting out its disagreements or its antipathies on bloody battlefields, since these have never healed the disagreements or made friends out of enemies. Israel will not commemorate her restoration by reviving or perpetuating old feuds. Christ Jesus taught a more successful way of conquering an enemy than by war; and that new day is at hand when better ideals instead of bigger guns will figure largest in a nation's armament, and will exercise infinitely more power than gunpowder or poison gas.

The peace of the world is not contingent upon a League of Nations, or upon international conferences, or upon reduction of material armaments, although these are footsteps in the right direction, but upon the perception and acceptance by the nations of the Christian ideal. The nations must learn to disarm mentally as well as materially. They must be willing to scrap their hatreds and their jealousies and their selfishness along with their battleships and guns; and to this end they will need to learn what the new Israel, or the Israel of the new day, should be able to teach them; and that is the truth about God, or demonstrable Christianity. It is for this purpose that Israel is returning from her captivity, and it is this near approach of a better recognition of God and of His demands which is disturbing the "powers of darkness." The false confidence of Gentile ascendancy is broken. What the apostle called "the powers of this world" are now fighting a defensive campaign, but which for that reason is all the fiercer. The carnal mind's dream of world dominion is fast fading, and in its place is looming up the outer darkness into which its own evil nature is forcing it, and the bottomless pit of its final self-extinction.

The magnitude and world-wide nature of the recent war naturally attracted the attention of Bible readers to the subject of Armageddon, the great final gathering of the nations against Israel described in Ezekiel xxxviii and xxxix, and in Revelation xix. This general upheaval without doubt marked the beginning of the final phases of that conflict between the flesh and Spirit which has been going on in human consciousness ever since the necessity of overcoming the serpent of materiality was first recognized. At this date, after four years of military peace, the nations find themselves still being tossed about in the economic after-swell of that storm, tired of war but too distrustful of each other to beat their swords into plowshares. Governmental despotism and national warfare have had their inevitable counterparts in industrial or economic despotism, injustice, and class enmity, which are the outcome of the same brute selfishness, and are equally successful in sowing the seeds of disaster. The danger of the human extreme, in one form or another, stalks menacingly across the horizon of civilization. No one can foresee clearly the nature of the ordeal through which humanity may have to pass in the refining and purifying process spoken of in the Scriptures. That this will come in some form to individuals and nations is plainly stamped in the impartial offhand for perfection, for whatever is unlike God cannot "abide the day of His coming," or "stand when He appeareth." The truth of man's divine origin is as a "consuming fire," which sooner or later will "try every man's work of what sort it is."

The Hebrew prophets were not alarmists, but they painted one side of their picture of latter-day developments with a strikingly forbidding aspect, and their example was followed by the prophets of the New Testament, including our Lord himself; but that was only the side of the picture which appears to the sinning human sense. The "winds of God" seem as storm and tempest to the carnal mind, but they "thoroughly purge His floor," and although they blow away the chaff, the wheat is gathered unharmed "into His garner." Jesus did not point to the dark side of the picture as a cause for anxiety, but quite the reverse. "When these begin to come to pass," he said, "then look up, and lift up your heads; for your redemption draweth nigh."

The closing act of Armageddon, in its relation to nations in conflict, apparently is yet to come. Metaphysically considered, it is the struggle of the human mind to be free from its materiality, and this conflict will necessarily have to go on and on until the goal is gained and the New Jerusalem appears. But the interim may be a long one, for neither individuals nor nations are transformed from evil to good overnight. When the English-speaking peoples fully awaken to the fact that they are God's instruments to save the nations, and to make His name known to all people, they will constitute in themselves a League of Nations which will guarantee the righteous adjustment of all international difficulties or disagreements.

We have undoubtedly come to the most important stage of the human journey, when old things are preparing to pass away, and history and prophecy mingle their testimony of the approach of the new day. The six days in which human thought has wrestled with a material view of life and creation are drawing to a close, and beyond the smoke of Armageddon the spiritual apprehension of all things, which is making its appeal heard in every department of right human activity, will become the paramount factor in human experience, and the new idea of heaven and earth, "wherein dwelleth righteousness," will appear to mortals. If this were not to be the case, if the mistakes of past ages were not to be recognized and treated as mistakes, they would perpetuate their delusions, and human consciousness would still remain in the darkness of its errors. Whether they think of it or not, the feet of the nations have entered the path which is leading them to that day which "shall burn as an oven," but a day also in which "the Sun of righteousness" shall "arise with healing in his wings." Let Israel gird herself for the days lying just ahead of her, not with material armaments and human diplomacy, but by casting out of her borders the things that defile and pollute her people.

Armageddon is something more than a battle between humans beings. It represents the opposition of the carnal mind to the rising tide of spirituality in Israel. The serpent is used in the Scripture as a symbol of material sense, for by no stretch of imagination can it be thought of as a symbol of spiritual sense; while the woman, all the way through, has ever stood for the supremacy of spiritual law. The enmity between the woman and the serpent has ever been characterized in this way. "The world of time and sense" has offered its sacrifices upon the altars of materialism, and even Christendom herself has passed her sons and daughters through the fire of those sacrifices, as if the things which are earthy had the precedence over the things which are heavenly, and as if material codes were decrees of the Almighty which it were impious to challenge or disobey. And matter has surely ruled mankind with a tyrannical hand, giving in return for their allegiance only a fitful and fleeting sense of pleasure, with an almost continuous consciousness of fear, and an experience of disease, misfortune, suffering, infirmity, and certainty of death, such as only the mentality of demons could be conceived of as devising and administering. Held under the spell of its deceitful sense, mortals have exalted this "accursed thing "to the very seat of divine power, and have thus made it "the abomination of desolation" for all the ages.

The stirring of spiritual awakening in the woman sent out the first protest against this serpentine delusion, and Israel was the logical offspring of her spiritual seed; but Israel, with all her wonderful experiences of God-bestowed dominion, afterwards lost sight of her inheritance in a night of materialism. The Christian Church, with an even richer history of the proofs of divine power over so-called material law, went into captivity for the same thing as her predecessor, and in so doing spread a covering of spiritual darkness over her people. And now, in this third stage of the human struggle for salvation and freedom, the Spirit of God is again brooding over the darkness of the world's error, and the Science of Christianity, or Christian Science, appears, and challenges the Goliath of matter.

This sudden appearance of woman, striking boldly at' the very head of the serpent, aroused its latent antagonism until even many professing Christians entered the lists as unwitting champions of materialism. The decisive and final conflict towards which the ages have been moving has been joined, and its various phases will be fought out until the emancipation of mankind from the deception that life is material and mortal, has been accomplished. Jesus alluded to the tremendous disturbances which this mental conflict would produce on the surface of human consciousness. Ezekiel and Daniel described their visions of the same events in graphic and picturesque figures, but they left us in no uncertainty as to the spiritual outcome. In the Apocalypse St. John confirmed all these descriptions, so that we need not hesitate in looking for the literal and complete dethronement of the false gods of this world. The testimony of prophets and apostles point to the period upon which we are now entering, not because it is to continue the material conceptions of past ages, but, on the contrary, because it will bear witness to the absolute supremacy of Spirit.

When Mrs. Eddy declared for the infinitude of Mind, and the consequent unreality of matter as being substantial, living, or intelligent, there was a storm of protests from both thinkers and non-thinkers; but since that time there has been, especially of late years, a steady trend on the part of physicists towards her position; and it is plainly only a question of time when they will stand on the same platform with Christian Science and acknowledge, with all reverence, not, as some are doing, that matter is but another name for force, but that Mind is infinite and divine. When that time comes the world will not have gone backward but forward, and science will have glorified its name far beyond its present doubtful accomplishments in the line of physical experimentation.

If it was ever true that life and intelligence have their source in matter, it is true still, and must so continue; but what, then, of the "mind which was in Christ Jesus," which Christians are enjoined to have? If this Christ-mind is not materially derived, then all material-mindedness stands condemned as false to God, and as unrelated to the man whom He created. Matter cannot rationally be conceived of as godlike, either in itself or in its effects, since it is materialism which holds the race in bondage to passions and appetites, and which, instead of dispensing life, consigns mortals to disease and death. How can mankind believe it possible to achieve the freedom of the sons of God while yielding to its debasing lusts and limitations? They cannot. What is called matter stands revealed in human experience as the merciless tyrant of the race, whose service has not enriched its devotees with even a molecule of tenderness and love. Shall we, then, argue in its behalf, defend its usurped rights, and thereby prolong human fear and suffering? or shall we as true Israelites and true Christians stand for man's right to be governed by Mind alone?

It should be apparent, therefore, if Armageddon is to mark the final overthrow of Gentile power, that it must have a broader meaning than a battleground between nations, for in the latter case the outcome would simply leave one nation or combination of nations as the victor. It must also mean more than a conflict between material forces, for that would simply result in establishing one expression of physical force as stronger than another. It will not be a conflict between different forms of error, for that would simply mean the triumph of the greatest error, and leave mankind worse than before. Neither will it be a conflict between different expressions of truth, for Truth is one and indivisible and there can be no conflict between its manifestations. Armageddon, so far as it relates to the salvation, that is to say the regeneration of mankind, will be, and is, the decisive struggle in human consciousness between what the apostle calls the carnal mind, and the Mind which was in Christ Jesus; or between the divine or spiritual sense of things, and the temporal, sinning sense of mortals.

Whatever hostile lining up of the nations may yet occur, and however sanguinary such a struggle may prove to be, it can only prefigure the mental conflict between the ideals of Israel and the ideals of paganism, that is, between the spirituality typified by the woman and the sensuality typified by the serpent. Is Christendom ready to fight on the side of spirituality? or is it still in the valley of decision, temporizing over the fallacies of materialism, and unheeding the spiritual Christ knocking at the door?

The restoration of Israel means the bringing back of the spiritual sense of being, the lost Israel which Jesus came to save, and which Christian Science is here to restore; it cannot by any form of human sophistry be construed as meaning the opposite. Materialism is the foundation and bulwark of Gentiledom, whereas the God of Israel is infinite, divine Spirit, and she acknowledges none beside Him. If this position were reversed, then the Gentiles, not the Israelites, would have been known as the people of God. Israel was not taken captive by a spiritually-minded people, but by idolaters whose gods were the apotheosis of sensual human concepts. Did the "times of the Gentiles" refer to the dominion of matter, or to the reign of Spirit? Does the ending of these times mean that matter is to be enthroned or dethroned as the basis of human life, activity, happiness, and intelligence? Will Israel take part in Armageddon as the avowed champion of materiality, or as the exponent of spirituality? The right answers to these and other related questions cannot be left out of a consistent discussion of this subject, nor can any useful end be served in evading or ignoring them.

It is undeniable that the course of Israel was set towards the attainment of a spiritual and godlike sense or consciousness. This being so, her restoration would imply a necessary increase of spirituality from the time of her captivity, and a corresponding decrease of materiality; otherwise the restoration would be of little consequence to herself or to the world. The course of Israel can lie along no other road than the overcoming of the fleshly nature, else humanity would be quite as well conditioned under Gentile dominion. The achievement of her aims cannot stop short of that universal knowing of the Lord which is a feature of her new covenant, and when God is universally known in His true nature, all that is unlike Him will be universally unknown.

These are not idle statements; they indicate the goal towards which the practice of Christianity must necessarily take us, and they define the real battle-issues of Armageddon, in which the Christian Church must fight out its freedom from pagan and worldly influences, and stand uncompromisingly for the supremacy of Spirit and spiritual law. The decisive conflict with materialism has been postponed until this age because Christendom joined hands with the world instead of overcoming it; and Christians are still being taught to accept the authority of so-called material laws as final. When mortals come under the doom of disease or disability, they are still taught that there is no power in Christianity to prevent the sentence from being carried out.

This attitude, in a period of supposedly Christian enlightenment and progress, does not indicate that Israel is awake, but that she is still asleep to her inheritance and her privileges. Such unprotesting submission to materialism would not resurrect Israel in a million years, but could only serve to bury her that much deeper in the dust. The assumption, that material authority or law transcends the spiritual, finds no support in the records of Israel, in the teachings of the prophets, or in the testimony of Jesus and his apostles; it is a fungus growth which the Church has acquired from her fellowship with the world, and which will have to be burned out of her in "the day of His coming." The Injunction to "come out from the world and be separate" has not been reversed; but neither has it been obeyed. The apostle, very obviously, is not alluding to the spiritual world, and must mean that consciousness of materiality in which the human sense is engulfed, and from which it is the mission of Christianity to bring deliverance.

Matter is the medium of the carnal mind, not of the Mind which was in Christ Jesus, and has never been a factor but a hindrance in the moral uplifting of men. It has never contributed to the emancipation of mankind from the lusts of the flesh, therefore it is not the door by which men may enter into the kingdom of heaven.

The work of dethroning this tyrant from the seat of authority it has so long usurped will have to be undertaken before the new earth can appear, and will constitute a greater Armageddon than any battle in which the nations of the world could engage. How long before the end of this struggle will be reached "knoweth no man." It is the mental process, described in Jesus' well-known parable, of separating the wheat from the tares, between what is and what is not of God. In designating the tares as the "children of the wicked one," he clearly did not mean persons, but the offspring of the one wicked deception that life and reality exist apart from God; and these tares or errors are to be burned or destroyed at the full appearing of Truth. That human consciousness is now entering this period of mental separation wherein the old things are passing away and all things are becoming new, there is no doubt. In the consummation of this process, as the apostle intimates, "the elements shall melt with fervent heat, the earth also and the works that are therein shall be burned up" — not in the heat of material fire but of divine revelation. That which expresses no divine quality can have no place in God's kingdom, and must belong to the "things that offend," to be consumed in the full realization of the allness of God.

It is time that Christians cease thinking of Armageddon as a coming maelstrom of blood and fire into which the nations are to be drawn, but rather as designating the period of human triumph over the flesh, or the material sense of creation, through the attainment of the spiritual ideals of Christianity. While it is true that the pathway of Israel, or spiritually awakening humanity, on the way to the Holy City, lies through Armageddon, that battle is with the serpent, not with men; and it will be for the possession of the New Jerusalem of spiritual dominion, and not the Jerusalem of worldly power and authority.

Giving an exclusively literal interpretation to the metaphors of the prophecies, or looking only at their material aspect, will not disclose the glory of latter-day events wherein God is to be understood as dwelling with men, but covers that period of joyous realization with the sombre anticipation of woe and disaster. The Christians of these troubled days should not forget Jesus' injunction to "look up," or away from the evidences of the carnal mind's commotion, and get the vision of the spiritual Christ again appearing to men.

The heavenward progress of the race need not be accompanied by warfare and bloodshed, and the reign of righteousness in the earth will not be advanced by preaching the doctrine of impending evil. Human thought has improved since the days when the Hebrew prophets uttered their direful predictions; and while we know they had in view the deliverance of God's people Israel, we have reached the point where we can at least begin to impersonalize evil and its oppressions, and to look forward to the redemption of all men, without respect to race or nationality.

The Comforter has appeared to direct mankind towards the heights of holiness and away from the strife and the passion of material thinking and living. Whatever may yet come to the surface in the course of evil's resistance to the forward movement of humanity, we can well leave to the morrow, and devote all we have to the tasks which are ours today. We may know that the will of the Father will yet be done on earth as it is in heaven, and we can ever turn to that wonderful prayer and prophecy with unfaltering desire and expectation.

Chapter Twenty-Nine - The First and Second Commandments of Israel

Because he hath set his love upon Me, therefore will I deliver him. - Ps. 91: 14.

By this shall all men know that ye are my disciples, if ye have love one to another. - John 13: 35.

THE freedom of humanity from the oppression of evil is an experience to be worked out in individual consciousness, and necessarily includes the recognition and fulfilment of the demands of God. The Scriptures state these demands in terms which place them wholly outside of all denominational creeds, theological dogmas, or philosophical theories, and in language so plain that "wayfaring men," however simple, need not err therein. In both the Old and the New Testaments, the Divine commandments are epitomized in a few sentences, and may be summarized in a single phrase, as love for God and man.

The all-inclusive nature of divinity forbids an acquaintance with, the illusion of anything else, and this fact was perceived and stated by the inspired teachers in Israel. The law which inheres in the truth of God's allness was so clearly enunciated in the First Commandment, that it has remained the standard expression of His demands upon men, and includes in its simple finality everything pertaining to human salvation. It covers the whole ground, not only of man's relation to God, but of men's relation to each other. It sums up the necessities of right thinking and living and is, consequently, the foundation of all true religion. The force of this commandment is not binding upon men because it is stated in the Scriptures, but because the universality of good leaves no room for another god. Its application is not contingent upon the evil suggestion, that God permits men to know something beside Him, but in the truth that something beside the infinite is impossible. It were certainly no sin to acknowledge other gods if other gods there were, nor to acknowledge another creator if there were in reality another creator producing persons and things independently of God.

The allness of Deity, which is implied in the First Commandment and in subsequent Scriptural revelation, does not, however, assign man and the universe to a region of nebulous nothingness, but places them in the divine consciousness where they rightly belong. Obviously an infinite Creator could fashion the universe only out of what is in Himself, so that we cannot regard creation as something set apart from Deity, but as the expression of His own thoughts. The son cannot be lost from the Father's presence, because His presence is universal, and in relation to which there is no outside sphere in which another creator and creation could exist. What, then, are we to say of that which assumes to contradict the First Commandment, and to assert a presence, power, intelligence, cause and effect which do not belong to God or come forth from Him? What other consistent attitude can one take than to treat it as that which has, in reality, neither substance nor existence?

It should be plain that God's view of things does not coincide with the conclusions of materialism, and that it is only the material view which sees man as having lost his unity with his Maker, and to be moving in an orbit of sin and death. The law in Israel was, that God created man in His own likeness, and this law was never superseded. It was in the sophistry of the serpent, whom Jesus pronounced a liar, that this divine order was reversed, and man appeared as God's unlikeness; but the First Commandment does not recognize the serpent. It does not acknowledge a loss of unity or agreement between creator and creation, nor does it imply that there is a creation and government going on outside of infinity; but it does signify and involve the absolute nonexistence of any cause or effect apart from God.

According to the Scriptures, it was the great purpose and design of Israel to make good known, not to make evil known; it was to honor and obey God as supreme, not to acknowledge and bow down to other gods; it was to make the Gentiles acquainted with the God of Israel as the only God in all the earth, as the only power and intelligence, — it was not to teach these nations, or their own children, that evil was possessed of the same attributes which belong to Deity. It is time for Israel to awaken to her duty as God's witness in the earth, and to cease giving her testimony on the side of evil, because she cannot reasonably hope to inspire the Gentile nations with respect for her great First Commandment while she continues to dishonor it. Nor can she consistently teach this commandment to the heathen while in her own domain the belief of something beside God is endowed with such tremendous power.

Abraham, it will be remembered, left his father's house and kindred that he might have the freedom to worship and obey the one God, and the people of the earth were to be blessed in his obedience. It later devolved upon Israel to destroy idolatry with the truth that there is but one God; and her troubles came upon her when she failed to carry out that trust, and bowed down to the false gods of the carnal mind precisely as the Gentile nations were doing. Is it not true that she is doing this today? Is not the array of evils, which fling out their challenge to the First Commandment, still acknowledged in Anglo-Saxon lands? Is it not true that everything which denies the presence and power of God is given a place there? And is not the formation of man from the dust of the ground still accepted in modern Israel as the true modus of God's creation, although her own prophets rejected it?

We have reached the time when the scientific or exact meaning of the oneness of Deity should be recognized and applied, inasmuch as human salvation cannot be worked out on any other foundation, or by any other rule. No amount of emotional zeal for the personality of our great Master, nor of fervent professions of faith in his tragic self-sacrifice on the cross, will absolve any one from the requirements of this commandment; for Jesus said he came not to destroy but to fulfil the law. He came to "destroy the works of the devil," that is, the idolatry of evil. No more imperative demand exists in Anglo-Saxon-Israel today, than to apprehend the inner meaning of that greater commandment which she outwardly acknowledges, and the absolute necessity of complying with its terms, not perfunctorily or academically, but in deed and in truth. For of what avail is the effort to establish the identity of Israel in the present day, if she is to go on with the worship of her false gods? Or of what advantage will it be for the Anglo-Saxon race to know herself and be known as the present house of Israel, if the original purpose of Israel is not to become her paramount purpose also?

The conditions of Israel's covenants are embodied in the First Commandment, and it must needs be obeyed in both the letter and the spirit before her part of these covenants can be satisfied and her debt cancelled. It is very evident that this command is not satisfied by an intellectual affirmation of belief in but one Deity, for the actual recognition of this divine oneness necessarily calls for the disavowal of aught else. For example, the acknowledgment that evil is power and intelligence is directly contrary to the clear meaning of the First Commandment, for a belief in other powers or minds than God is the very essence of idolatry, and cannot be made to appear as anything else.

The law of the one God was, without exception, to have the precedence in Israel, and is inseparably bound up with everything pertaining to that people, and with every aspect of her position and destiny. Her natural selection as God's instrument in the earth could be for one purpose only, and that was, that through her everything unlike God in human consciousness was to be cast down and destroyed, a process which would necessarily have to take place first in herself. Until this is done, she can do little towards casting evil out of other nations. The Master's metaphor of the mote and the beam is particularly applicable to Israel as the exponent of the one God, and the sooner she realizes this, and the sooner she ceases to endow the carnal mind with the attributes which rightly belong to Deity alone, the sooner she will be fitted for her appointed task.

If the conditions of this commandment are to be interpreted as purely relative, we shall have to look forward to a universe perpetually divided between good and evil, and therefore perpetually at strife; but this is not the outlook furnished by the Scriptures. It was given to Israel to establish and uphold the truth of God's supremacy, not simply as one among many lesser deities or powers, but as one alone. Let it be repeated again because of its importance, that it is the serpent of evil suggestion, not divine Truth, that has always argued for the reality of a power beside God, and that is still continuing that argument; but the place of Israel has never been on the side of the serpent. The very fact of her existence is a challenge to the carnal mind, and the Scriptures imply that her work will not be completed until all "enmity against God" has been destroyed.

Jesus interpreted the First Commandment to mean such an undivided love for God as to leave no possible rival in the affections and thoughts of men. He did not intimate, however, that they would lose anything in putting all evil out of their consciousness; but on the contrary, that the sacrifice of a false view of life, and of its relationships, pleasures, and possessions, would bring an abundant realization of the true idea of all that human sense holds dear. The logical inference is, that if one gives up his whole consciousness to good, he will find there is nothing else to truly have, hence that there is nothing to lose. To love God with all the mind would be equivalent to denying the existence of any other mind than good, since one could not love God with an evil mind. It follows, therefore, that evil-mindedness, expressing itself in the various forms of selfishness and vice, defines the false god which all mankind must renounce before God can reign supreme in their lives, and the kingdom of Satan be overthrown.

Jesus' analysis of "the great commandment of all" should leave no one in doubt as to its requirements. It makes no provision for a nominal, halfway obedience, or for any concession to the argument that there is something apart from divinity that men may know and love. Jesus placed the relation between God and man in such a light as to leave no opportunity for evasion or misunderstanding. Men are either doing these things or they are not doing them. There is no subterfuge by which one can honestly deceive himself that he is obeying the First Commandment, while he is willingly sharing his thoughts with evil. It is little wonder that Israel of old fell down in her observance of this commandment, when we of Israel today, with our superior advantages, with all the lessons of past experience, and with the higher teaching of Christianity, are so ready to withhold part of our consciousness from God.

Immediately following his paraphrase of the First Commandment, Jesus said, "And the second is like, namely this, Thou shalt love thy neighbour as thyself. There is none other commandment greater than these." In thus linking these commandments as practically one, Jesus made it plain that man as well as his Maker is to be found and acknowledged in the First Commandment. While Christians generally profess an adherence to this command so far as it relates to God, there is not the same readiness to accept its obviously implied injunction regarding man. It is not consistent, neither is it just to God, to acknowledge Him as the only power and creator, and then declare His creation to be evil and imperfect. Although human sense claims to see the evidence of evil and imperfection, a supreme loyalty to God should prompt the correction of that sense, instead of accepting its testimony without question or protest.

If Christians agree that there is but one God — and they professedly do — and that there is, therefore, but one power and creator, they should in all consistency agree that there is but one type of man as His offspring. The very obvious corollary of the First Commandment is, Thou shalt have no other man than My image and likeness; for if God has continued the same from the beginning — and the Scriptures imply that He has — if His power and infinitude have continued the same, then the truth regarding man must have continued the same. The true God and the true man must of necessity be the only God and man there are at any time. If it were true, as the carnal m.ind would suggest, that God bestowed upon His own image the faculty to know evil and the power to obey it, then the First Commandment has been superfluous; for, according to that assumption, good and evil would proceed from the same source and be essentially one.

The general human belief in a type of man which is not the likeness of God necessarily implies a corresponding belief in a creator unlike Him to have fashioned man thus, a belief which at once involves the believer in idolatry. According to the inspired record, man was brought into being to express God, hence it naturally follows that all that is really true about a man is what he expresses of good. One cannot take an opposite position and at the same time honor the infinity of God. It is divinely and humanly impossible to identify omnipotence with Deity, and at the same time identify His creation as under the dominion of evil. The point that is too easily forgotten is, that according to the Eden allegory it was the serpent which first suggested man's separation from divinity, and which still works in the thoughts of men to perpetuate it.

At the close of his last supper with his disciples, Jesus said, "A new commandment I give unto you, That ye love one another." He had centered the observance of the commandments into that one word, the sweetest in human language, which, in its highest and purest significance, the apostle named as synonymous with Deity. St. Paul summed up the whole situation in other words when he said, "Love is the fulfilling of the law"; while St. John made the issue still more emphatic in his analytical question, "He that loveth not his brother whom he hath seen, how can he love God whom he hath not seen?"

It stands without argument that a little more love would bring consciousness nearer heaven in every home, business, society, or nation where it is given the opportunity. All that opposes this divine giving is the selfish human will determined to sacrifice all other interests for its own, but nothing can compensate an individual or a nation for success or advancement achieved on that basis. However stubbornly human sense may struggle against this heavenly impulse, it must eventually reach the point where love will be recognized as the only bond among men, and nation will no longer lift up sword against nation.

The realization of human brotherhood has remained the great unsolved problem of the ages, and will continue unsolved until mankind learn the lesson of love, and cease returning wrong for wrong and hate for hate. The utterly heathenish concept of Deity, as approving the ancient custom of exacting an eye for an eye and a tooth for a tooth, which naturally inculcated the belief that it was justifiable to hate one's enemies, expressed the antithesis of the God of Israel. This was the doctrine of the carnal mind which, as Jesus taught, "was a murderer from the beginning." Hatred between nations and peoples is not removed by conquests or by treaties, but by the divine spirit; for the former simply bank the smouldering fires of jealousy and distrust, while love would put them out. It is evident that nothing is more urgently needed at the nation's conference tables, in their legislatures, clubs, homes, industries, and associations, than less resentment, passion, and greed, and more kindness, generosity, and love. Once this divine plant begins to take root and to grow in the hearts of men, and the nations begin to gather its heavenly fruit, the coming of the kingdom will be drawing nigh, but not until then.

Jesus' new commandment makes loving a law, and law declares itself as a necessity, not as a choice. Since "all the law is fulfilled in one word," namely, love for one's neighbor, as the Scripture states, then love is the only remedy for lawlessness in all its forms, and there remains no other foundation for right government. This law of divinity is perpetual in its demand, and admits of no exceptions. There are no crossroads into the kingdom of heaven, and it is the kingdom of heaven that each individual and each nation are striving to enter, whether they would define their aims in these terms or not. What all mankind are seeking for is happiness, however differently they may spell the word, but that search cannot be permanently successful except as consciousness becomes identified with goodness and love. The tragic records of history disclose the bitter failure of mortals to find satisfaction through any of the avenues of the carnal mind. Were it otherwise, were it possible to enter the Heavenly City by any other road than the attainment of the mind that was in Christ Jesus, the commandments reaffirmed by him would cease to be a law to men, and his teachings become as idle words.

The new commandment of Jesus has this feature in common with the old, that it is wholly outside the realm of doctrinal differences and limitations. It belongs to one church or creed no more than to another, but without it, no church or creed possesses any real power or vitality. It is the new commandment of Christianity, and must be the watchword of Israel when she reappears; hence its close relation to this whole subject, for it is plain that one cannot rule with God, or be conscious of sonship with Him, without love. Israel, be it not forgotten, is not a sentimental name for a race supposed to be historically dead; in its highest spiritual sense it represents that living reality of God's fatherhood which belongs to every age, and which pertains to one people more than to another only as that people possesses and expresses more of its meaning and power. Israel, therefore, can develop into the fulness of fruition only as she is nourished by that love which discerns the godlike in man as embodying the only truth of creation.

The awakening and return of Israel through the Scriptures, which has already been referred to, means her awakening to the revelation of God as Love, and of His law as love; not as meaning the expression of human emotion, but as possessing the consciousness which "thinketh no evil." The love which "worketh no ill" to one's neighbor is surely the most practical feature of all ethics and religion, but it does not stop at that negative point of accomplishment, for it finds its powder in the performance of good deeds. This must of necessity be the activity which is to prevail in Israel in the time of her restoration, since without it she would have no means by which to become God's witness among the nations. Without it, she could not show the Gentiles the nature of the God of Israel, whereas with it she will divinely impel them to acknowledge and worship Him. This neighborly love, this charity which "suffereth long and is kind" to enemies and friends alike, which forgives wrongs and cherishes no revenge, is the only weapon which will make her mighty in the earth.

We learn from the records that the people of Israel shared the general weaknesses of mortals. They loved their friends and hated their enemies after the fashion of the day, believing that that was the right thing to do. Although they acknowledged but one Deity, they did not fully perceive that that one must be infinite in order to be supreme. They had not seen the other side of the First Commandment in its inclusion of man, and it remained for the Messiah to announce the law of loving, even to the extent of including one's enemies, as correlated to the great commandment of Israel. Jesus taught that it was as binding upon men to love one another as it was for them to love God. This was an entirely new doctrine, in the light in which he presented it, and after almost two thousand years it is not yet universally accepted and practised, even in Christendom. As the great Teacher pointed out, with his usual incisiveness, it is no virtue to love one's friends, or to do good to them who do good to us; but to love them that hate us, and to do good to them that despitefully use us, is the demand which is waiting to be satisfied before it can truly be said that we are disciples of the Lord.

It particularly rests with the people of Israel, the people who are learning the reality of divine things, to light the beacon fires of love upon her high hills, that the nations may catch the vision of a people willing to live and to prosper only in their consciousness of good. How long it may be before that day dawns is not so important as that Israel shall now begin to see and acknowledge that her destiny lies in the direction which God had pointed out to Abraham, "Walk before Me, and be thou perfect."

Chapter Thirty - "A Light to Lighten the Gentiles"

The Lord hath made bare His holy arm in the eyes of all the nations; and all the ends of the earth shall see the salvation of our God. — Isa. 52: 10.

In every nation he that feareth Him, and worketh righteousness, is accepted with Him. — Acts 10:35.

That was the true Light, which lighteth every man that Cometh into the world. — John 1: 9.

IN early Biblical times, when the descendants of Jacob had become a nation by themselves, the God of Israel was little known or acknowledged outside of her own borders, and this contributed to the conception and development of a sense of exclusiveness in their relation to Deity; but there is nothing in the Scriptures, when read in the light of the whole, to indicate that the function of Israel as "a peculiar treasure" unto the Lord was a selfish one, or that the Israelites were to continue the sole people of His pasture. Their better knowledge of God undoubtedly set them apart from the pagan nations, but that very knowledge was itself an inexorable and continuous command to take it to all the earth.

Israel's relation to the rest of mankind was plainly set forth in the covenant with Abraham, but was apparently lost sight of by the majority of the Israelites, until the belief that they, out of all the inhabitants of the earth, were to be the people of God became firmly grounded in the national consciousness, and was practically a part of the national religion. That they should entertain this view of their position is not surprising when one considers the unusual circumstances which attended the birth of this nation, together with the extremely impressionable nature of all primitive people. The nations about them with whom they came in contact were quite as fixed in their racial prejudices, and quite as strongly imbued with their own religious peculiarities, and these differences served to separate them mentally from the Israelites. It is this fact of mental separation, the product of unlike concepts of Deity, which has constituted and maintained the barriers between the nations, and particularly between Israel and the Gentile peoples.

The coming of Christianity changed the whole face of the human problem, for in its teachings, and in the possibilities which it includes for all men, the lines between races and peoples were erased. When Jesus said, "Call no man your father upon the earth," he not only rebuked the claims of human parentage but of racial distinctions, and his words prophetically point to the time when all national differences will be obliterated. His statement that he was sent to "the lost sheep of the house of Israel" did not imply that his mission ended there; but on the contrary, that these lost sheep were to be brought back for the purpose of filling their destined place as God's light-bearers to the Gentiles.

Nations, like individual mortals, have been moulded by influences which date back to the earliest beginnings of humanity, when a sense of evil was supposed to have entered the nature and consciousness of man, and the race was cradled in the belief, of the naturalness of animal propensities, and in the freedom to obey them. Although believed to have sprung from a common ancestor, differences in individual temperament, qualities, and inclinations arose from the outset, afterwards widening and extending into family and national distinctions. The conditions peculiar to each of these divided groups, implanted in their offspring and confirmed in the education of successive generations, perpetuated the distinctive customs, manners, and appearance of the various branches of the human family, and they still continue to differentiate the races of the earth.

In the face of these deep-rooted dissimilarities and antagonisms, the task of working out the expression of a common human brotherhood would seem stupendous; yet only as this is being accomplished is the world-family coming nearer together in any permanent or redemptive sense. The leaven which is to permeate and spiritually homogenize this mixed human multitude is the truth embodied in Christianity, embracing as it does the universal fatherhood of God and the universal kinship of man in His likeness. Jesus' mission, it is very clear, was not to preserve the standing antipathies between the nations, but to bring all mankind into the one fold of Christian brotherhood. He made no attempt to accomplish this through a belief in the physical creation of man, but upon the ground of the new birth, or the recognition of man's spiritual origin, wherein and whereof God is the sole Mind or intelligence.

The theory, generally believed and acted upon, that there are "as many minds as men," came forth from the carnal mind, and is but another edition of its original lie that man was endowed with a consciousness independent of his Creator. This is the doctrine of the old birth, not of the new; of the "old man," not the "new man"; and it fathers and fosters all the dissensions and discords which have turned the earth into a battle ground. It is plain that the harmonizing influence which is to bring mankind into accord cannot emanate from such a source or exploit such a doctrine.

The light which was to shine forth from Israel upon the nations was not a personality; it was the truth of being demonstrated, the truth which antedated Abraham, which was present when "the morning stars sang together," and whose human appearing was welcomed by the Judean shepherds, a truth which is waiting at every man's door to bring him freedom from the oppressor. This light, which was radiant in the life and ministry of Jesus, is called the Christ, the truth of man's divinity as the Son of God, which alone can illumine the darkness of the world's materialism, and light the way to the "City of God."

Although this truth and its embodiment came to human recognition in the consciousness of the Hebrew people, it was not for the exaltation of that people above other nations, but that they should tread humbly in the footsteps of their King. The crowning glory of Israel, as made manifest in the advent of the Messiah, was in lighting the dark places of the earth; it was not to treat the outside nations as inferiors, or as unworthy of Jehovah's care, but to know that her Lord was the Lord of all men. The narrow view that would set Israel, in the sense of racial superiority, apart from the rest of the world, was lost sight of in the broad application of the truths of Christianity, and there is no ground today upon which to revive it. Thus while Israel would seem to present an exclusively peculiar and self-contained type of national consciousness, upon closer approach her doors are seen to stand wide open, not only that the stranger may enter and find a new home, but that her messengers may go out to all people with the good tidings committed to her. The prophecies of the restoration, it is true, include the resumption of her nationhood, but they do not point to the revival of that overweening belief of personal preeminence to which the early Hebrews so fondly clung.

The relations between the various divisions of the human family have greatly changed since Israel went into captivity. With improved means and methods of transportation and communication the nations of the world have come closer together, — in their associations if not in their ideals; and when Israel again recognizes herself as a nation it will be with a vastly different sense of her relation to other peoples. Her many centuries of exile among other races have served largely to obliterate her old-time prejudices, although the Jew, on the other hand, living much in his thought of the past, feeling the sting of Gentile persecution, and untouched by the liberalizing influence of Christianity, has retained a large measure of his contempt for all races but his own.

Although national jealousies and conflicting ambitions, unless tempered by the Christian spirit, are easily irritated into war, the freer intercourse of the advancing centuries has brought the peoples of the earth into a larger feeling of fellowship and interest, and it only waits the leavening power of a live Christianity to break down the wall of partition between them. This end, of course, is not something to be reached in the space of a few years, but we can welcome a beginning in that direction, and with more intelligent expectations can contemplate the world situation in a tolerant attitude, and prepare for that spiritual unity of consciousness which must sometime be realized before heaven and earth can universally become one.

While it is true that Great Britain through her colonies, and the United States, do not, under pardonable exceptions, close their gates to the people of other lands, the unity of the human race will not be accomplished through the absorption of one nation by another. The Anglo-Saxon race cannot become the melting-pot for all humanity, for even if a fusion of the world's races were physically possible, it would not uplift human consciousness or blend its discordant elements. The amalgamation of unlike qualities is neither practicable nor desirable, for that which is unholy will be unholy still, and that which is filthy will be filthy still, and the presence of these defiling and destructive states would make unity and peace impossible. Such things do not spring from blood, but from unrighteous thinking, hence there is no way through the mixture of races, no naturalizing process by which mortals may become one in mind and heart. Therefore the cause of human brotherhood will not be radically (advanced by simply opening the front door to the alien and the stranger, but by lighting their way to better things. The hand which Israel holds out to the Gentiles must have a torch in it to illumine the path to God's kingdom, if it is not to be a case of the blind attempting to lead the blind.

But Israel can hold that torch aloft only as the spiritual ideal of being is lifted up in her. While the world and the flesh absorb the thought of Anglo-Saxondom, what has she wherewith to light the way of the nations to the God of Israel? How can she reflect to them the light which glows in the face of Christ if she permits the presence of materialism to hide that light from herself?

There is no doubt that the disclosure of Israel's identity in the Anglo-Saxon race will prove a louder call to that nation than she has ever heard to forsake the mammon of worldliness and to become God's missionary in the earth in a larger meaning and in a more practical form than she has yet realized.

The reader will have learned to bear with the repetition of certain truths as he recognizes their essential application to the various phases of this great question. The restoration of national Israel, in fulfilment of the Scriptures, can be for one purpose only, — also in fulfilment of the Scriptures, — and that is the Christianization of mankind. There is no other end in which the Scriptures are concerned, or towards which they point. Therefore it is not at all a question of power or wealth or numbers, as the world reckons these things, except as they are being devoted to that one paramount task of this age. It were surely better that nothing be said about the restoration of Israel if that event is simply to promote the prominence of one race, or to class that race as being superior in the sight of God, or as possessing a privileged place in His design.

Unless evil is to gain the mastery over good and materialism smother the divine impulses of spirituality, the conclusion is unescapable that the people of all the nations will sometime have to recognize themselves as children of God; and that awakening knowledge will have to reach them from the people whose consciousness reflects the most divinity; and that people will be the Israel of today. If Anglo-Saxons answer best to that description, it is no cause for vainglory, or for any assumption of self-importance, but for humility and prayer that they may be loyal to their trust. A good beginning has been made in distributing the Word of God among practically all the tribes and races of the earth, but is this being followed up with the proofs of the power of that Word? Will the letter of the Scriptures, however widely scattered and fervently preached, accomplish the quickening work of the Spirit? If the signs of Moses are not being taken to those in bondage to the carnal mind, why are they not?

The task of bringing mankind into spiritual agreement faces Anglo-Saxons today, and it is plain to even the wayfaring man that this cannot be brought about by any human expedient, political treaty, or war of conquest. If the disparities of education, environment, opportunity, and so forth, could be equalized, the members of the less privileged races would be found the equals of the more favored of mankind; but for most of them these disparities are not yet equalized, hence the call for the helping hand and the reflected light that the less privileged among humankind may find their way to a better experience and a larger life, and thus bring that new earth nearer wherein are only right things.

The differences of thought, temperament, ideals, and aims which now exist among the races are not intrinsic but incidental, and will disappear as men arrive at the same conception of Deity. The light which reveals God as the only Creator, reveals also the way by which all men may come into oneness of thought, love the same things, feel the same impulse of goodness, and travel together up the hill of the Lord. In this light, and no other, men may come to see one another as God's image, and acknowledge no other law and feel no other bond than love. This is not the vision of a dreamer; it presents the logical outcome of the practice of Christ's teachings, and will come into human experience when humanity is ready to have it there.

Let no member of a so-called Gentile race feel that the stigma of inferiority has been stamped upon his people, or that the door into the spiritual heritage of Israel is closed upon him. The pathway to a knowledge of the true God, not in the narrow sense of a national Jehovah, but as the Father whom Jesus revealed to men, is open to every human being. In the words of Isaiah, "The Gentiles shall come to thy light, and kings to the brightness of thy rising," and in that bright light of Truth there will be "neither Greek nor Jew, circumcision nor uncircumcision. Barbarian, Scythian, bond nor free: but Christ is all, and in all." (Col. 3: 11.)

Chapter Thirty-One - Paradise Regained, or the Dream Dispelled

Awake, awake; put on thy strength, O Zion: put on thy beautiful garments, O Jerusalem, the holy city: for henceforth there shall no more come into thee the uncircumcised and the unclean.

Shake thyself from the dust; arise, and sit down, O Jerusalem: loose thyself from the bands of thy neck, O captive daughter of Zion. — Isa. 52: 1, 2.

And that, knowing the time, that now it is high time to awake out of sleep. — Rom. 13:11.

WE have now traversed in review that long journey, if stated in terms of time, which started from the gates of Eden towards the realm of spiritual being. We have seen how the woman's protest against the sophistry of evil suggestion took root in human consciousness, and brought forth the movement known as Israel, a movement which in time was destined to fill the earth with a knowledge of the truth. In retrospect we have walked with the early Hebrew patriarchs, watched the rise of Israel and its development into a nation, and have followed the remarkable course of that nation during the fifteen centuries between Abraham and the captivity. We have stood with Moses in Horeb where he received such a revelation of the being of God that he was enabled to bring the Israelites out of Egypt, take them safely through the Red Sea, and to feed and clothe them during their forty years' sojourn in the wilderness. We have observed with reverent awe the many wonderful things which were done by Moses and the prophets, in the name and by their knowledge of the God of Israel, not as spectacular marvels but as proofs of divine power. We have noted how, in later years, the mesmerism of surrounding idolatry, or the worship of matter in the place of Spirit, enticed national Israel from allegiance to her God, and led to her long banishment among the Gentiles, an exile in the course of which she lost her national unity and identity. Coming to our own day we have observed the unmistakable signs of Israel's return from that exile, both literally and spiritually, and have witnessed her entrance into the earliest phases of Armageddon; but from this point on, one's consideration of this subject must be largely prospective and introspective.

The present period without doubt marks the early dawning of the "day of the Lord," or that seventh day of holiness which completes the record of creation, in which the goodness and perfection of God and of His work is to be recognized. It is the so-called millennial age in which mankind will learn to rest from their labors with matter, and will turn to Mind as the source of man's existence and activity. In the brighter light of divine revelation which has come to this period, men will rise to the perception of heavenly things, and no longer content with the false teaching that man is of the earth earthy, will recognize their spiritual sonship with God.

Whatever of progress has been achieved by our race is due to the fact that men have not been satisfied to remain in ignorance of better things, and this wholesome discontent with un-ideal methods and conditions has wrought a vast betterment in human affairs. The existence of perfection makes improvement not only possible but imperative, a rule which applies also to moral and spiritual things. Religion cannot remain forever unprogressive. It is undeniable that the truth about God and man exists and is available, and because of this there is that in the hearts of men which will not let them rest satisfied until they perceive and possess it. Although the inertia of animality may seem for a time to resist the demands of man's inherent divinity, its latent power or attraction will eventually make itself felt, until it becomes humanly irresistible. Human salvation from evil is more than a privilege, it is a necessity; and the impelling force of this necessity is expressing itself with increasing earnestness and insistence through every avenue of enlightened thought.

The only changes in human belief which can be genuinely classified as progressive are those which conduce to a better acquaintance with God; but whatever leaves the thoughts of men as firmly in the grasp of matter as before, or impresses its demands more deeply upon them, clearly is not progress. It is their sense of materiality, and not spiritual law that binds mortals to the experience of sin and death, and their freedom or deliverance from such experience cannot be obtained from a material source. Thus it becomes unavoidable that men must become spiritually-minded in order to reach immortality, which means that material-mindedness and mortality are synonymous. Why, then, is the teaching still current in Christendom, that God's image and likeness, the original man, was created from dust, inasmuch as this teaching has been the great bulwark of materialism, in investing its decrees with the sanction of divine law? To make progress spiritually while fettered to this doctrine is not possible; yet to grow more spiritual and less material is what Christianity distinctly calls for.

The regaining of paradise, the end which all men hope for, is not something to be experienced suddenly, either here or hereafter. It is the transformation of human consciousness, in which a material sense of life is given up for the spiritual, a transformation which will be objectified to that consciousness in the new heaven and earth. It is the putting off of the "old man," and the putting on of the new or perfect man as constituting the only reality of God's creation. St Paul thus wrote to the Ephesians concerning this process: "For you have learnt with regard to your former way of living that you must cast off your old nature, which yielding to deluding passions, grows corrupt; that the very spirit of your minds must be constantly renewed; and that you must clothe yourselves in that new nature which was created to resemble God, with the righteousness and holiness springing from the Truth" (Twentieth Century Translation). This regenerative practice plainly involves the laying off, or the outgrowing, of the fleshly nature entirely, not in a moment of material dying, but in progressive, spiritual living.

In the foregoing passage, and in the phrase immediately following, "Since, therefore, you have cast off what is false," the apostle confirms the position taken by Christ Jesus, and in this age by Christian Science: namely, that the evil in human nature is delusive and untrue, and that it must be denied, put aside — call it what you will — in order that the true man, the only man whom God creates and acknowledges, may come to light. Jesus never taught any other mode of salvation or regeneration than this. The apostle, it is true, said, "Believe on the Lord Jesus Christ, and thou shalt be saved," and Christians have thereby been encouraged to found their hope of salvation upon the popular meaning of the word belief; but the Master gave the meaning of this saving faith in no unequivocal terms when he said, "He that believeth on me, the works that I do shall he do also." It should be too apparent for argument that one cannot enter the Holy City and take his old self, or the man of dust, along with him; and that admission covers, in practically all its details, the whole ground of the unreality of whatever is not of God. Somewhere along the line of our journey we must be willing to learn the truth about these things, and to understand the significance of Jesus' saying, "If any man will come after me, let him deny himself."

The footsteps of Israel, as they emerge from her exile among the Gentiles, are turned towards the Holy City, the New Jerusalem; they are not turned towards her former errors. They are not set towards the old Jerusalem of worldly pride and dominion, of ecclesiastical bigotry and formalism, but towards the consciousness of her new inheritance in the Messiah. Israel was to be the pathfinder for the nations to "the mountain of the Lord's house," and in days to come, if she is true to her trust, we shall find all of them gathered there. All this means, of course, that the coming back of Israel, in the spiritual sense, will be such a revival of the Messianic teaching and practice as to be denominated the second appearing of the Christ, not as a human being, but as the redemptive or regenerative Truth revealed to mankind by Jesus of Nazareth.

It is logically undeniable that these days of prophetic fulfilment are to witness the reappearance of the Christianity which its Founder identified with healing the sick and casting out evil. It is certain that the absence of healing power from the doctrinal Christianity which has been presented to the world leaves a tremendous gap between it and the example of Jesus, and this gap must be bridged over before it can be truly said that the Christ has returned among men. Indifference or unbelief respecting this Christian requirement proves neither one's superiority to it nor exemption from it, but only how great is the necessity of being aroused to the true situation. The wide acceptance of material means and methods as a substitute for divine power does not prove that God is not the best healer, or that these substitutes are consonant with Christ's Christianity; it only proves in what a strong grasp the carnal mind is still holding the thoughts of Christians.

This is a much broader question than the mere restoration of physical health. It is an integral part of human salvation from evil, and for that reason permanent healing cannot be effected materially. One phase of the carnal mind cannot correct another. The primary purpose of Christian healing is not merely to restore the enjoyment of sensuous comfort, or to prolong a physical sense of life, but to prove, in a degree, that God is the life of man, and to lift individual thought that much higher. "The fruit of the Spirit," said the apostle, "is love, joy, peace, long-suffering, gentleness, goodness, faith, meekness, temperance." These are the pharmacopoeia of Christianity, the health-giving and health-restoring qualities pertaining to true manhood; while their carnal opposites are the source and condition of weakness and disease, and these no material agency can remedy. Jesus never taught that there were two Saviours for men, nor did he authorize his followers to divide the function of Christianity between matter and Spirit. When the Christ appears the second time it will not be to exonerate the neglect to obey his commands, but to resurrect the dead faith of Christendom, and again to seek and to save "that which was lost."

The covenant with Israel was, "I will take sickness away from the midst of thee," and the condition on the part of Israel was, "Ye shall serve the Lord your God." Is Israel today serving the Lord her God? If not, why not? What "strange gods" are being worshipped in her? The lamentable fact that sickness still flourishes throughout Christendom, and that, too, under the very shadow of her churches, proves that something is wrong, either with the prevailing exposition of religion, or with the practice which grows out of it, for the God of Israel has ever proved to be a covenant-keeping God. It is evident that the appeal for help to other so-called powers is not serving God according to the terms of the First Commandment; therefore this covenant has remained inoperative except in its negative application. One of the foremost signs of returning Israel will be her recognition of this covenant; and unless there is some definite and sincere attempt on the part of this people to seek the divine way out of sickness and kindred evils, we had better not talk overmuch of what is being accomplished in the way of Israel's restoration; for, as has been said in these pages over and over again, if the spiritual restoration is lacking, the mere literal or external return would mean absolutely nothing, so far as blessing the nations of the world is concerned.

The Scriptures consistently point to the time when the human material sense of things will be replaced by the spiritual, and then will come what is called the end of the world, — not the end of anything which God has created, but the end of mortals' mistaken beliefs about creation. It is plain that we cannot take the things of the material world into paradise, for everything which the eyes see and the hands handle is perishable and impermanent. The things which make up the world of human sense, bounded by time and embraced in matter, short-lived in beauty and born only to decay, express the ephemeral nature of dreams; and the plain inference is that mortals must waken from this phantasmagoria of sensuous living and dying and open their eyes spiritually to the things which are eternal.

The "first resurrection," spoken of by St. John the Revelator as belonging to the period of the Second Advent, is, without doubt, the awakening of human sense from the belief that life is material and mortal, to the perception that man is spiritual and immortal. Speaking prophetically of the same period and the same event Daniel said, "And many of them that sleep in the dust of the earth shall awake." Human sense or consciousness has buried itself in its belief of animated dust, and is waiting for the quickening voice of the Christ to break its delusion. Those who look for a literal resurrection of material bodies from the earth fail to grasp the abounding use of metaphors and symbols in the Scriptures. When Paul wrote to the Ephesians, "Awake thou that sleepest, and arise from the dead," he was not implying that they were literally asleep or literally dead; but to the extent that mortals accept matter as the source and fact of life, they are dead to the spiritual sense of life as God.

In his proof that life is not in the material body, and that the grave could not lay its corrupting hand upon the Son of God, Christ Jesus has been called "the first-fruits of them that slept"; but this phrase very clearly does not refer to those who had passed away in death, for Lazarus and others had been raised from the dead, in that sense, before Jesus' resurrection. The apostle was evidently referring to the human sense of life as material, for the Master was the first to prove that sense to be absolutely false. The first resurrection, therefore, is the human emergence from the conception of life as in and of matter, described in Genesis as the "deep sleep" which came upon Adam, to the perception that Spirit is the life of all that exists.

"Afterward they that are Christ's at his coming," — what coming? Not a vision of flesh and blood, surely, for what could such a vision do towards arousing men to the consciousness of spiritual life? The first coming of the Christ to human sense was as a fleshly babe; but the second coming, — "unto them that look for him," — which is to lift those who get this vision to the spiritual apprehension of being, must necessarily transcend all physical sense. "He is not here, but is risen," the angel said to Mary at the sepulchre, and we in this day must also cease looking for Christ in the flesh if we would see the Lord.

"The hour cometh and now is," said Jesus, "when the dead shall hear the voice of the Son of God, and they that hear shall live." And again, "Ye will not come unto me that ye might have life." It is apparent that he was not here speaking to dead men, nor concerning men's dead bodies, but of the materially deadened consciousness of mortals. "To be carnally minded is death," said the apostle; in other words, the concept of life as existing in matter is mortality's self. The sense of man as animated dust is the "first Adam," in which, as Paul pointed out, "all die," or all are dead; but in Christ, the "last Adam," the image of God, "shall all be made alive." These passages clearly illustrate the figurative meaning of the word "dead" in its relation to the first resurrection.

This awakening of human thought to the perception that man is the spiritual image and likeness of God, and not a sinful mortal, is the central feature of the return of the Christ, and the vital element in the millennial period. Without it there could be no genuine advance towards the Heavenly City, the New Jerusalem of restored Israel, for without it things would naturally continue as they were. That this spiritual quickening of thought has begun in the coming of Christian Science, and is making its influence widely felt, cannot be reasonably questioned. Its effects are being made manifest in various departments of thought where material conservatism had long held control. They may be seen in the improvement taking place in denominational creeds, in the increasing conviction that the churches must return to the healing works enjoined by Christ Jesus, and in the growing desire, felt among all classes, for a more practical adaptation of Christianity to daily living, so that it may become the power in human life it was plainly designed to be.

From age to age mankind have been wearily seeking the way to lost paradise, and the means of reopening its gates, but the serpent has held them in the wilderness by perpetuating the belief that material existence is the waking reality of life. The human sleepers in the dust of the earth, held in the spell of the deceitful senses, have looked for happiness in every direction except the one way of spiritual awakening. The hope held out to mortals, that they may eventually die their way into paradise, has been the sop of materialism in religion, and the most pathetic of the deceptions foisted upon the race in the name of Christianity. A careful study of the inspired Word, and especially the teachings of Christ Jesus, plainly show that men must *live* their way into heaven. Neither reason nor revelation points to any other possible way.

It should be obvious to every one that death cannot open the door for mortals into spiritual and immortal consciousness, since death is itself but a phase of materiality, and is the natural outcome of believing that life exists separate from its divine source. Inasmuch as God is omnipresent. He can be no nearer to a mortal after he stops breathing than he was before. Men are no further from heaven now than their own thoughts put them, and until they lessen and overcome that distance by purer thinking and by the actual possession and practice of goodness, they will not reach the consciousness of perfect and immortal being. Death is a denial of life, a contradiction of immortality, not the pathway to it; and God, in whom alone man can truly live, does not make his heavenly security conditional upon death.

Jesus did not teach that men must die to enter the kingdom of heaven, but that they must be "born again," which is an entirely contrary proposition. Mortals begin their earthly education with an erroneous concept of life as beginning with dust instead of with God; and from that wrong starting-point everything has been learned wrongly, man being represented all the way through as the exact opposite of God's image and likeness. Hence the absolute necessity of reversing this false teaching and of getting the true and spiritual starting-point whence to learn the divine facts of being.

Jesus' uncompromising statement regarding the new birth is the strongest arraignment of the material concept of life or of man's creation from dust that has ever been uttered; and not until this new birth, this transformation of human thought to a spiritual basis, has truly begun in one's experience, does he get a glimpse of the new heaven and earth of Spirit. St. John's wonderful vision of the Holy City, the "new Jerusalem coming down from God out of heaven," is evidently not something to be seen after death, but relates to the spiritual awakening to be sometime realized on earth, when the beliefs of materiality have been put out of consciousness, and nothing is left that "worketh or maketh a lie."

It is self-evident that a dream is not dispelled by tarrying contentedly among its delusions, nor by peering credulously into its shadows, but by opening one's eyes to reality. The night-dreams of mortals yield sooner or later to the waking phenomena and disappear as illusions. If there were no facts of the day to return to, the night-dream would be the individual's normal experience and would permanently continue. Likewise, if there were no waking spiritual reality, the events of so-called material existence would necessarily be the truth of being, and there would be no hope or opportunity of escape from its evils; but Jesus demonstrated the actuality of spiritual life, and thereby proved the dread shadows of material sense to be as the fallacies of dreams. In his final evidence of man's deathless being, Jesus became the hope of the race, and the Wayshower for mortals out of all error, including even the "last enemy."

When one awakens from a dream he knows that it was unreal. We do not play the parts or perform the grotesque acts depicted there. No one erects the houses or builds the ships or plants the flowers or paves the streets which appear to mortals in dreams. The people we meet there have no ancestry, no past or future, no power to harm or to bless. The misfortunes we. encounter, the pains we endure, the ills we suffer from, fade into nothingness when our eyes open. All this is quickly realized when we awaken, although we are unaware of it while the dream is on, for the simple reason that we identify ourselves with the dream and see ourselves as taking part in its delusions. In our normal human consciousness we never question the illusive character and texture of dreams, no matter how vividly real they have appeared to us. We not only know that there was nothing there to frighten or to give pleasure, but that there was actually nothing taking place there at all.

What, then, is there for mankind to do but to awaken to the facts of God's day, in which there is no night for the dreaming of dreams? In that day of spiritual awakening we shall find the "unseen things" which God hath prepared for them that love Him." When the feet of returning Israel cress the threshold of the Heavenly City, when the eyes of her people open to the consciousness of things as they are and "see realities face to face," the vision of the prophets will be realized, as described by St. John in these glowing words: "Behold, the tabernacle of God is with men, and he shall dwell with them, and they shall be his people, and God himself shall be with them, and be their God. And God shall wipe away all tears from their eyes; and there shall be no more death, neither sorrow, nor crying, neither shall there be any more pain; for the former things are passed away."